MULTICULTUR.

James A. l

MW00806684

Education for Liberal Democracy: Using Classroom Discussion to Build Knowledge and Voice
WALTER C. PARKER

Critical Race Theory and Its Critics: Implications for Research and Teaching
FRANCESCA LÓPEZ & CHRISTINE E. SLEETER

Anti-Blackness at School: Creating Affirming Educational Spaces for African American Students
JOI A. SPENCER & KERRI ULLUCCI

Sustaining Disabled Youth: Centering Disability in Asset Pedagogies
FEDERICO R. WAITOLLER & KATHLEEN A. KING THORIUS, EDS.

The Civil Rights Road to Deeper Learning: Five Essentials for Equity
KIA DARLING-HAMMOND & LINDA DARLING-HAMMOND

Reckoning With Racism in Family–School Partnerships: Centering Black Parents' School Engagement
JENNIFER L. McCARTHY FOUBERT

Teaching Anti-Fascism: A Critical Multicultural Pedagogy for Civic Engagement
MICHAEL VAVRUS

Unsettling Settler-Colonial Education: The Transformational Indigenous Praxis Model
CORNEL PEWEWARDY, ANNA LEES, & ROBIN ZAPE-TAH-HOL-AH MINTHORN, EDS.

Culturally and Socially Responsible Assessment: Theory, Research, and Practice
CATHERINE S. TAYLOR, WITH SUSAN B. NOLEN

LGBTQ Youth and Education: Policies and Practices, 2nd Ed.
CRIS MAYO

Transforming Multicultural Education Policy and Practice: Expanding Educational Opportunity
JAMES A. BANKS, ED.

Critical Race Theory in Education: A Scholar's Journey
GLORIA LADSON-BILLINGS

Civic Education in the Age of Mass Migration: Implications for Theory and Practice
ANGELA M. BANKS

Creating a Home in Schools: Sustaining Identities for Black, Indigenous, and Teachers of Color
FRANCISCO RIOS & A LONGORIA

Generation Mixed Goes to School: Radically Listening to Multiracial Kids
RALINA L. JOSEPH & ALLISON BRISCOE-SMITH

Race, Culture, and Politics in Education: A Global Journey from South Africa
KOGILA MOODLEY

Indian Education for All: Decolonizing Indigenous Education in Public Schools
JOHN P. HOPKINS

Racial Microaggressions: Using Critical Race Theory to Respond to Everyday Racism
DANIEL G. SOLÓRZANO & LINDSAY PÉREZ HUBER

City Schools and the American Dream 2: The Enduring Promise of Public Education
PEDRO A. NOGUERA & ESA SYEED

Measuring Race: Why Disaggregating Data Matters for Addressing Educational Inequality
ROBERT T. TERANISHI, BACH MAI DOLLY NGUYEN, CYNTHIA MARIBEL ALCANTAR, & EDWARD R. CURAMMENG

Campus Uprisings: How Student Activists and Collegiate Leaders Resist Racism and Create Hope
TY-RON M. O. DOUGLAS, KMT G. SHOCKLEY, & IVORY TOLDSON

Transformative Ethnic Studies in Schools: Curriculum, Pedagogy, and Research
CHRISTINE E. SLEETER & MIGUEL ZAVALA

Why Race and Culture Matter in Schools: Closing the Achievement Gap in America's Classrooms, 2nd Ed.
TYRONE C. HOWARD

Just Schools: Building Equitable Collaborations with Families and Communities
ANN M. ISHIMARU

Immigrant-Origin Students in Community College: Navigating Risk and Reward in Higher Education
CAROLA SUÁREZ-OROZCO & OLIVIA OSEI-TWUMASI, EDS.

"We Dare Say Love": Supporting Achievement in the Educational Life of Black Boys
NA'ILAH SUAD NASIR, JARVIS R. GIVENS, & CHRISTOPHER P. CHATMON, EDS.

Teaching What Really Happened: How to Avoid the Tyranny of Textbooks and Get Students Excited About Doing History, 2nd Ed.
JAMES W. LOEWEN

Culturally Responsive Teaching: Theory, Research, and Practice, 3rd Ed.
GENEVA GAY

Music, Education, and Diversity: Bridging Cultures and Communities
PATRICIA SHEHAN CAMPBELL

For a complete list of series titles, please visit www.tcpress.com

(continued)

Multicultural Education Series, *continued*

Reaching and Teaching Students in Poverty, 2nd Ed.
Paul C. Gorski

Deconstructing Race
Jabari Mahiri

Is Everyone Really Equal? 2nd Ed.
Özlem Sensoy & Robin DiAngelo

Teaching for Equity in Complex Times
Jamy Stillman & Lauren Anderson

Transforming Educational Pathways for Chicana/o Students
Dolores Delgado Bernal & Enrique Alemán, Jr.

Un-Standardizing Curriculum, 2nd Ed.
Christine E. Sleeter & Judith Flores Carmona

Global Migration, Diversity, and Civic Education
James A. Banks, Marcelo Suárez-Orozco, & Miriam Ben-Peretz, Eds.

Reclaiming the Multicultural Roots of U.S. Curriculum
Wayne Au et al.

Human Rights and Schooling
Audrey Osler

We Can't Teach What We Don't Know, 3rd Ed.
Gary R. Howard

Engaging the "Race Question"
Alicia C. Dowd & Estela Mara Bensimon

Diversity and Education
Michael Vavrus

First Freire: Early Writings in Social Justice Education
Carlos Alberto Torres

Mathematics for Equity
Na'ilah Suad Nasir et al., Eds.

Race, Empire, and English Language Teaching
Suhanthie Motha

Black Male(d)
Tyrone C. Howard

Race Frameworks
Zeus Leonardo

Class Rules
Peter W. Cookson Jr.

Streetsmart Schoolsmart
Gilberto Q. Conchas & James Diego Vigil

Americans by Heart
William Pérez

Achieving Equity for Latino Students
Frances Contreras

Literacy Achievement and Diversity
Kathryn H. Au

Understanding English Language Variation in U.S. Schools
Anne H. Charity Hudley & Christine Mallinson

Latino Children Learning English
Guadalupe Valdés et al.

Asians in the Ivory Tower
Robert T. Teranishi

Our Worlds in Our Words
Mary Dilg

Diversity and Equity in Science Education
Okhee Lee & Cory A. Buxton

Forbidden Language
Patricia Gándara & Megan Hopkins, Eds.

The Light in Their Eyes, 10th Anniversary Ed.
Sonia Nieto

The Flat World and Education
Linda Darling-Hammond

Diversity and the New Teacher
Catherine Cornbleth

Educating Citizens in a Multicultural Society, 2nd Ed.
James A. Banks

Culture, Literacy, and Learning
Carol D. Lee

Facing Accountability in Education
Christine E. Sleeter, Ed.

Talkin Black Talk
H. Samy Alim & John Baugh, Eds.

Improving Access to Mathematics
Na'ilah Suad Nasir & Paul Cobb, Eds.

"To Remain an Indian"
K. Tsianina Lomawaima & Teresa L. McCarty

Education Research in the Public Interest
Gloria Ladson-Billings & William F. Tate, Eds.

Beyond the Big House
Gloria Ladson-Billings

Teaching and Learning in Two Languages
Eugene E. García

Improving Multicultural Education
Cherry A. McGee Banks

Education Programs for Improving Intergroup Relations
Walter G. Stephan & W. Paul Vogt, Eds.

Teaching Democracy
Walter C. Parker

Transforming the Multicultural Education of Teachers
Michael Vavrus

Learning to Teach for Social Justice
Linda Darling-Hammond et al., Eds.

Learning and Not Learning English
Guadalupe Valdés

The Children Are Watching
Carlos E. Cortés

Multicultural Education, Transformative Knowledge, and Action
James A. Banks, Ed.

Education for Liberal Democracy

Using Classroom Discussion to Build Knowledge and Voice

Walter C. Parker

Foreword by James A. Banks

TEACHERS COLLEGE PRESS

TEACHERS COLLEGE | COLUMBIA UNIVERSITY

NEW YORK AND LONDON

Published by Teachers College Press,® 1234 Amsterdam Avenue, New York, NY 10027

Front cover by Rebecca Lown Design. Texture by 55th / Shutterstock.

The author gratefully acknowledges these publishers for their permission to reprint the following works:

Chapter 2: Parker, W. C. (2022). Structured Academic Controversy: What it can be. In J. Lo (Ed.), *Making classroom discussions work* (pp. 73–89). Teachers College Press.

Chapter 3: Parker, W. C. (2005). Teaching against idiocy. *Phi Delta Kappan, 86*(5), 344–351.

Chapter 4: Parker, W. C. (2008, Spring/Summer). Pluto's demotion and deep conceptual learning in social studies. *Social Studies Review, 47*(2), 10–13.

Chapter 5: Parker, W. C., & Lo, J. C. (2016). Reinventing the high school government course: Rigor, simulations, and learning from text. *Democracy & Education, 24*(1), Article 6. http://democracyeducationjournal.org/home/vol24/iss1/6

Chapter 6: Parker, W. C. (2010). Listening to strangers: Classroom discussion in democratic education. *Teachers College Record, 112*(11), 2815–2832. doi:10.1177/016146811011201104

Chapter 7: Parker, W. C. (2003). Promoting justice: Two views. In W. C. Parker, *Teaching democracy: Unity and diversity in public life* (pp. 54–75). Teachers College Press.

Chapter 8: Parker, W. C. (2008). "International Education"—What's in a name? *Phi Delta Kappan, 90*(2), 196–202.

Chapter 9: Parker, W. C. (2018). Human rights education's curriculum problem. *Human Rights Education Review, 1*(1), 5–24. doi:https://doi.org/10.7577/hrer .2450

Chapter 10: Parker, W. C. (2022). Review of Angela M. Banks (2021), "Civic Education in the Age of Mass Migration: Implications for Theory and Practice." Teachers College Press. *Multicultural Perspectives, 24*(4), 241–248. doi:https:// doi.org/10.1080/15210960.2022.2131160. Copyright © 2022 by the National Association for Multicultural Education, reprinted by permission of Taylor & Francis Ltd.

Library of Congress Cataloging-in-Publication Data is available at loc.gov

ISBN 978-0-8077-6818-1 (paper)
ISBN 978-0-8077-6819-8 (hardcover)
ISBN 978-0-8077-8164-7 (ebook)

Printed on acid-free paper
Manufactured in the United States of America

Contents

Series Foreword   *James A. Banks*   ix

Preface   xv

Acknowledgments   xvii

PART I: A CENTRIST APPROACH TO CIVIC EDUCATION

1.   Introduction   3

    Liberal and Illiberal Democracy   6

    Knowledge and Voice   11

    Curriculum and Instruction   15

    An Autobiographical Note   19

    Overview of the Chapters   21

    Conclusion   23

2.   Teaching Academic Controversies   25

    Cooperative Learning and SAC   26

    The Revised Model   29

    Conclusion   39

3.   Teaching Against Idiocy   41

    Dodging Puberty   42

    Schools and Idiocy   44

    Schools Are Public Places   46

    Three Keys   47

The Social Curriculum   48

The Academic Curriculum   50

The Three Rs?   51

PART II: TOWARD DEEPER CIVIC LEARNING

4. **Concept Development**   **55**

   Teaching and Learning Concepts   56

   Classifying   57

   Some Examples   59

   Conclusion   60

5. **Reinventing the High School Government Course**   **63**

   Method and Design Principles   65

   Curriculum   73

   Discussion   76

   Conclusion   80

6. **Listening to Strangers**   **83**

   Seminar and Deliberation   85

   Listening to Strangers   89

   Political Friendship   90

   Listening to Strangers at School   92

   Practices of Listening to Strangers   93

   Conclusion   96

7. **What Is Justice?**   **99**

   Just Individuals   102

   Just Societies   110

   Cutting Through Conventional Wisdom   114

   Conclusion   117

PART III: GLOBAL CIVIC EDUCATION

8. **Educating World Citizens**   123

   National Security   124

   Marginal Voices   127

   A Solution on the Loose   130

9. **Human Rights Education's Curriculum Problem**   133

   Problem: Access to *What*?   135

   Solution: Toward an Episteme for HRE   140

   Conclusion   146

10. **The Right to Have Rights**   149

    A Curriculum Proposal   150

    Rationale   151

    The Immigrant Labor Paradox   151

    Classroom Activities   153

    Instructional Supports   156

    Conclusion   159

11. **Afterword: Cultivating Judgment**   161

    Classroom Discussion   162

    Uncoerced Decisions   165

    The Social Studies   167

    Conclusion   170

Notes   173

References   177

Index   193

About the Author   201

Series Foreword

This eloquent, engaging, and timely book by Walter C. Parker argues compellingly that the United States is experiencing a legitimacy crisis *and* an epistemic crisis. A manifestation of the legitimacy crisis is the widespread belief among the followers of past president Donald Trump that the election of 2020 was rigged and that Joe Biden did not fairly win the presidential election. Many Trump followers believe that the election was stolen, despite the mountain of empirical evidence that contradicts this belief and indicates that President Biden fairly won the election. The ascendency and popularity of Marjorie Taylor Greene (Draper, 2022), the House representative from Georgia who perpetuates QAnon conspiracy theories, and the brutal attack on Paul Pelosi, Congresswoman Nancy Pelosi's husband, on October 28, 2022 (Browning et al., 2022; Dowd, 2022; Edmondson, 2022), indicate the extent to which the nation is experiencing legitimacy and epistemic crises. The attack on the U.S. Capitol by Trump supporters on January 6, 2021 is another ominous manifestation of these crises in the United States and the serious threats to the nation's democracy (Leonhardt, 2021; The New York Times Editorial Board, 2022).

Parker, an optimist and a discerning political and curriculum theorist, believes that the school can implement teaching and curricular reforms that can help citizens attain faith in the nation's political system and other institutions and become less influenced by conspiracy theories and other spurious beliefs that are widely available on social media. These goals can be accomplished by strengthening civic education in the nation's schools with a focus on teaching *knowledge* and *voice* and *liberal democracy*. Disciplinary knowledge should be emphasized in civic education because "it is the kind of knowledge that establishes the standard of truth—the shared reality—on which our lives together depend" (p. 12, this volume). Parker uses "voice" to describe the importance of giving students opportunities to express their views and to exchange opinions and perspectives with classmates. He maintains that "liberal democracy" should be the aim of civic education in the nation's schools, a goal also articulated in *Our Common Purpose: Reinventing American Democracy for the 21st Century* (2020), developed by the Commission on the Practice of Democratic Citizenship, cochaired by Stephen Heintz, Danielle Allen, and Eric Liu., and published by the

American Academy of Arts and Sciences. Parker carefully describes how his use of "liberal democracy" differs from the ways in which the term is used in the popular media and in everyday speech. Liberal democracy "refers to the philosophy of classical liberalism. This is the philosophy of individual rights and the rule of law. Both Republicans and Democrats, generally, are 'liberal democrats' in this sense, for liberal democracy is the basis of the U.S. Constitution and the regime it created and amended" (p. 6, this volume).

The school, as Parker points out, is an ideal place for students to learn knowledge and voice because schools teach disciplinary knowledge and are populated by students from diverse racial, ethnic, cultural, linguistic, religious, and gender groups. The diversity of beliefs, perspectives, and ways of viewing the world that exist in most public schools provides a rich and prodigious context for students to develop voice, to interact, and to exchange views and opinions with students who have divergent beliefs, insights, and interpretations. This visionary and engaging book is a valuable contribution to the Multicultural Education Series because when students acquire the social science knowledge taught in schools and develop voice, they are less vulnerable to the myths and fictions about racial and ethnic groups that exist on social media and are institutionalized within society writ large.

The major purpose of the Multicultural Education Series is to provide preservice educators, practicing educators, graduate students, scholars, and policymakers with an interrelated and comprehensive set of books that summarizes and analyzes important research, theory, and practice related to the education of ethnic, racial, cultural, and linguistic groups in the United States and the education of all students about diversity. The dimensions of multicultural education, developed by Banks and described in the *Handbook of Research on Multicultural Education* (Banks, 2004), in *The Routledge International Companion to Multicultural Education* (Banks, 2009), and in the *Encyclopedia of Diversity in Education* (Banks, 2012) provide the conceptual framework for the development of the publications in the Series. The dimensions are content integration, the knowledge construction process, prejudice reduction, equity pedagogy, and an empowering institutional culture and social structure.

The books in the Multicultural Education Series provide research, theoretical, and practical knowledge about the behaviors and learning characteristics of students of color (Conchas & Vigil, 2012; Lee, 2007), language minority students (Gándara & Hopkins 2010; Valdés, 2001; Valdés et al., 2011), low-income students (Cookson, 2013; Gorski, 2018), multiracial youth (Joseph & Briscoe-Smith, 2021; Mahiri, 2017); and other minoritized population groups, such as students who speak different varieties of English (Charity Hudley & Mallinson, 2011) and LGBTQ youth (Mayo, 2022).

The problems that are described in this illuminating book about the legitimacy and epistemic crises in the United States also exist in other nations, such as Russia, China, Hungary, and Turkey. Liberal democracy is in trouble and retreat in nations around the world. Bokat-Lindell (2022), in an editorial in *The New York Times*, asks, "Is Liberal Democracy Dying?" He describes decisively how liberal democracies are in retreat in nations around the world. Bokat-Lindell writes, "Today, only 34 liberal democracies exist, down to the same number as in 1995, according to V-Dem. (The share of the world population living in liberal democracies also fell in the last decade, to 13 percent from 18 percent.)" Russia, China, Hungary, and Turkey have authoritarian leaders who have taken steps to remain in office for infinite terms, and who prohibit democratic protest and a free press. Madeleine Albright (2018) cautions in her book, *Fascism: A Warning*, that leaders such as Vladimir Putin (Russia), Xi Jinping (China), Viktor Orbán (Hungary), and Tayyip Erdoğan (Turkey) can become fascists if they are not restrained.

Democracy in nations around the world is becoming increasingly fragile as virulent nationalism and authoritarianism accelerate. Giorgia Meloni, a hard-right political leader, was elected prime minister of Italy in 2022 (Povoledo & Bubola, 2022). The Sweden Democrats, with roots in neo-Nazism, came in second in national elections in Sweden in September 2022 (Erlanger & Anderson, 2022). Sweden's parliament narrowly elected Ulf Kristersson, a conservative leader, prime minister on October 17, 2022 (News Wires, 2022). Migration and the growth of inequality are contributing to the rise in pernicious nationalism and xenophobic attitudes toward migrants in many nations. David Brooks (2022), *The New York Times* editorialist, argues that growing inequality is an important factor causing a "rising tide of global sadness," and that "civic discontent—riots, strikes, anti-government demonstrations—increased by 244 percent from 2011 to 2019."

The analyses that Parker makes in this book about the threats to democracy in the United States and the need for students to engage disciplinary knowledge and participate in discussions and exchanges in which they develop voice are as appropriate and beneficial for reenvisioning civic education in other nations as they are for the United States (Banks, 2017). Parker explicates how his work intersects with global civic education in Part III. He discusses what students should learn about the world and its peoples, human rights, and citizenship boundaries and law.

This theoretically rich, highly readable, and erudite book is also practical. In preparing this book, Parker drew from his impressive oeuvre of teaching strategies that are a product of teaching high school for 8 years and social studies methods courses at the university level for 37 years. The teaching strategies described in this book include those for teaching concepts, involving students in productive and deep discussions, teaching controversies, revising the high school government course, and human rights education. Parker was a master teacher at the University of Washington. His courses were popular and the students viewed him with high regard and affection. The teaching strategies described in this book convey the toolkit of the master pedagogue Parker is.

I am pleased to welcome this second book that Walter Parker is publishing in the Multicultural Education Series. His first book in the Series, *Teaching Democracy: Unity and Diversity in Public Life*, published in 2003, was the 13th book published in the Series, which now consists of more than 70 published books, with others in various stages of development.

I am also pleased to welcome this book to the Multicultural Education Series because Walter Parker, an internationally recognized scholar, is one of my former students at the University of Washington and has been a cherished colleague and friend for almost 4 decades. I hope this illuminating, useful, and heartfelt book will attain the wide and influential audience that it deserves in these toxic times, in which liberal democracy is fragile and severely challenged in the United States and in other nations.

—James A. Banks

REFERENCES

Albright, M. (2018). *Fascism: A warning*. HarperCollins.

Banks, J. A. (2004). Multicultural education: Historical development, dimensions, and practice. In J. A. Banks & C. A. M. Banks (Eds.), *Handbook of research on multicultural education*. (pp. 3–29). Jossey-Bass.

Banks, J. A. (Ed.). (2009). *The Routledge international companion to multicultural education*. Routledge.

Banks, J. A. (2012). Multicultural education: Dimensions of. In J. A. Banks (Ed). *Encyclopedia of diversity in education* (vol. 3, pp. 1538–1547). Sage Publications.

Banks, J. A. (Ed.). (2017). *Citizenship education and global migration: Implications for theory, research, and teaching*. American Educational Research Association.

Bokat-Lindell, S. (2022, September 28). Is liberal democracy dying? *The New York Times*. https://www.nytimes.com/2022/09/28/opinion/italy-meloni-democracy-authoritarianism.html

Brooks, D. (2022, October 27). The rising tide of global sadness. *The New York Times*. https://www.nytimes.com/2022/10/27/opinion/global-sadness-rising.html?searchResultPosition=1

Browning, K., Arango, T., Broadwater, L., & Secon, H. (2022, October 28). Pelosi's husband is gravely injured in hammer attack by an intruder. *The New York Times*.https://www.nytimes.com/2022/09/28/opinion/italy-meloni-democracy-authoritarianism.html

Charity Hudley, A. H., & Mallinson, C. (2011). *Understanding language variation in U.S. schools*. Teachers College Press.

Commission on the Practice of Democratic Citizenship. (2020). *Our common purpose: Reinventing American democracy for the 21st Century*. American Academy of Arts and Sciences.

Conchas, G. Q., & Vigil, J. D. (2012). *Streetsmart schoolsmart: Urban poverty and the education of adolescent boys*. Teachers College Press.

Cookson, P. W., Jr. (2013). *Class rules: Exposing inequality in American high schools*. Teachers College Press.

Dowd, M. (2022, October 28). The Pelosis and a haunted America. *The New York Times*. https://www.nytimes.com/2022/10/28/opinion/pelosi-nancy-paul-attack.html?smid=nytcore-ios-share&referringSource=articleShare

Draper, R. (2022, October 23). The problem of Marjorie Taylor Greene. *The New York Times Magazine*, pp. 20–25, ff. 42–44.

Edmondson, C. (2022, October 29). Pelosi attack highlights rising fears of political violence. *The New York Times*. https://www.nytimes.com/2022/10/29/us/politics/paul-pelosi-political-violence.html?searchResultPosition=1

Erlanger, S., & Anderson, C. (2022, September 15). Rise of far-right party in Sweden was both expected and shocking. *The New York Times*. https://www.nytimes.com/2022/09/15/world/europe/sweden-election-far-right.html?searchResultPosition=2

Gándara, P., & Hopkins, M. (Eds.). (2010). *Forbidden language: English language learners and restrictive language policies*. Teachers College Press.

Gorski, P. C. (2018). *Reaching and teaching students in poverty: Strategies for erasing the opportunity* gap (2nd ed.). Teachers College Press.

Joseph, R. L., & Briscoe-Smith, A. (2021). *Generation mixed goes to school: Radically listening to multiracial kids*. Teachers College Press.

Lee, C. D. (2007). *Culture, literacy, and learning: Taking bloom in the midst of the whirlwind*. Teachers College Press.

Leonhardt, D. (2021, January 19). Inside the Capitol attack. *The New York Times*. https://www.nytimes.com/2021/01/19/briefing/trump-biden-brazil-1776-report.html?searchResultPosition=1

Mahiri, J. (2017). *Deconstructing race: Multicultural education beyond the colorbind*. Teachers College Press.

Mayo, C. (2022). *LGBTQ youth and education: Policies and practices* (2nd ed.). Teachers College Press.

News Wires. (2022, October 17). Sweden's Ulf Kristersson elected PM with support from far right. https://www.france24.com/en/europe/20221017-sweden-s-ulf-kristersson-elected-pm-with-support-from-far-right

Parker, W. C. (2003). *Teaching democracy: Unity and diversity in public life*. Teachers College Press.

Povoledo, E., & Bubola, E. (2022, October 28). Italy's hard right feels vindicated by Giorgia Meloni's ascent. *The New York Times*. https://www.nytimes.com/2022/10/28/world/europe/italy-hard-right-giorgia-meloni.html?searchResultPosition=1

The New York Times Editorial Board. (2022, August 26). Donald Trump is not above the law. *The New York Times*. https://www.nytimes.com/2022/08/26/opinion/trump-documents-jan-6-prosecute.html?searchResultPosition=1

Valdés, G. (2001). *Learning and not learning English: Latino students in American schools*. Teachers College Press.

Valdés, G., Capitelli, S., & Alvarez, L. (2011). *Latino children learning English: Steps in the journey*. Teachers College Press.

Preface

When Jim Banks asked me to collect a set of my articles and essays for a new book in his *Multicultural Education Series* at Teachers College Press, I welcomed the opportunity. Having just retired from the University of Washington, I wanted to gather 10 or so chapters that would integrate my work on civic education in schools while addressing the political calamity we face in the United States today. I had the time, thanks to the convergence of retirement and the pandemic, and then a civic crisis struck the nation: The 2020 presidential election was held and, for the first time since the nation was created, the losing candidate refused to concede and then incited an attack on the Capitol and Congress. And that's not all. Millions of voters continued to support him.

Can voters be educated in a way that will support the continuation of democracy in the United States? I believe they can. The book's main title, *Education for Liberal Democracy*, summarizes this book and its aim. The subtitle reveals the featured pedagogy and curriculum goals: *Using Classroom Discussion to Build Knowledge and Voice.*

As I explain in Chapter 1, "liberal" in the title and in the book does not mean what it does in everyday speech: left-of-center or progressive. Rather, it is a formal term from the social sciences to refer to the classical liberalism that was born in the Enlightenment. This is the political philosophy of individual rights and the rule of law, of equality and freedom, that underpins and stabilizes our otherwise raucous political culture.

The book is about teaching civics at school. It has 11 chapters divided into three parts. Chapter 1, an introduction to the book, and Chapter 11, an afterword, were newly written for this collection. The nine chapters between them were published between 2003 and today. The introductory chapter explains the terms in the book's title, outlines the political crisis we face today, and shows what civic education at school can do about it. Most important, I argue that shoring up liberal democracy is the proper aim of civic education. This is a centrist or moderate aim suitable for a polarized society. Throughout the book, I provide concrete models of curriculum and instruction related to this aim. These rely on rigorous forms of classroom discussion, which bring students into dialogue with one another around the central questions of the social studies curriculum—especially in history and government—and nurture the habit of speaking and listening to people with different perspectives and opinions.

Complementary types of classroom discussion are featured across the book. One focuses on interpretation and understanding (seminar), the other on deciding what course of action to take as a result (deliberation). Together they supply a crucial key to informed voting, problem solving, and other types of knowledge-in-action. Citizens need to understand an issue before they can decide intelligently what to do about it, obviously; and they need to do both of these things with others, dialogue being the basis of thinking. Both seminar and deliberation, well planned and well led, deliver lots of learning (they are not bull sessions) and are tailor-made for a course's central curriculum objectives. For these reasons, discussion should be a main course, not a side dish, of classroom instruction.

Permit me suggest a way to read this book. Begin with Chapter 1, which introduces the book's major themes. After that, readers can get an additional overview of the book by reading the brief introductions to each of the book's three parts. Then, I suggest readers turn to Chapter 2, which gets to the nitty-gritty with a powerful model of classroom discussion called Structured Academic Controversy. After that, readers will be prepared for the elaborations that follow in Chapters 3–10. The concluding Chapter 11 summarizes the two kinds of classroom discussion featured in the book, clarifies what a centrist approach to civic education means for students and their teachers, and asserts that social studies is the logical epicenter for civic education at school.

Acknowledgments

I want to thank the friends and colleagues who read and commented on earlier drafts of one or more of the chapters in this book: Patricia Avery, Brian Barrett, Keith Barton, Terry Beck, Mary Anne Christy, Jenni Conrad, Todd Dinkelman, Gene Edgar, Carole Hahn, Sophie Haroutunian-Gordon, Diana Hess, Li-Ching Ho, Joe Jenkins, Kathy Jenkins, Joe Kahne, Bruce Larson, Peter Levine, Jane Lo, Paula McAvoy, Audrey Osler, Cap Peck, Regie Routman, Anna Saavedra, William Stanley, Hugh Starkey, Leonard Waks, and Sam Wineburg. I am especially indebted to my University of Washington colleague Debby Kerdeman and former student Lisa Sibbett for their close readings of the book proposal as well as Chapters 1 and 2. Their insightful feedback and straightforward advice over numerous conversations were invaluable. Feedback from my sister, Lynn Parker, was, as always, candid and precise. Any mistakes, of course, are my own.

I am grateful to Brian Ellerbeck, the venerable acquisitions editor at Teachers College Press, not only for this book, but also my book *Teaching Democracy* in 2003. Thanks also to Nancy Power and Michael McGann in TCP's marketing department; Pamela LaBarbiera, who copy-edited this book for TCP; Lori Tate, production editor at TCP; and to the anonymous reviewers that Brian gathered to evaluate the book proposal.

I extend a special appreciation to my longtime friend and UW colleague, James A. Banks. Jim's capacious intellect, work ethic, and warm heart are an inspiration to me. Our lunch conversations across 4 decades have shaped my views on topics ranging from health and exercise to race and democracy. His tenacious commitment to equality within the liberal democratic framework has had a huge impact on education in this country and around the world. I am gratified that this book appears in his series, and in such good company.

Thanks also to the various publishers who have granted permission to reprint Chapters 2–10 here. Details can be found on the copyright page.

Above all, I am grateful to my wife, Sheila Valencia. She is my best listener, wisest advisor, and dearest friend.

Part I

A CENTRIST APPROACH TO CIVIC EDUCATION

In Part I of the book, I argue that the political culture of the United States faces a twofold crisis, and I contend that civic education can help. I specify that shoring up liberal democracy is the proper aim of civic education, and I provide concrete models of curriculum and instruction related to this aim.

Liberal democracy is at once a conservative and progressive aim for civic education, which is to say it is an accommodating, bipartisan, centrist aim: a big tent that holds diverse perspectives and positions. This makes it a suitable aim for civic education in the K–12 classrooms of a polarized nation. The aim carves a middle way between extremes of the political left and right as well as the pedagogical left and right. The core values of this aim are freedom and equality, but also peaceful, cooperative relations among interest groups, political parties, and individuals.

Consider three ways this approach to civic education is centrist. First, it will annoy and disappoint passionate partisans, as moderation, accommodation, and compromise often do. The commitment to tolerance, for example, has long been a thorn for the left (e.g., Counts, 1932; Marcuse, 1965), and the emphasis on classroom discussion and student voice has long irked the right (Finn, 2003; Rickover, 1959). A liberal-democratic approach to civic education is centrist because liberal democracy itself is centrist. This is its nature, not a bug. This is how it evolved historically, philosophically, and sociologically since the 18th century. Second, the approach relies on argument and inquiry rather than passion and inculcation. It follows John Dewey's (1903) lead in believing that students should be taught to use their minds well—read deeply, think critically, reason with evidence, remain open to being proven wrong—but not be told to what end they should use these competencies. "Democracy means freeing intelligence for independent effectiveness—the emancipation of the mind . . ." (p. 193). This is intelligence working in tandem with autonomy. Students are helped to develop their minds and then liberated to use them as they see fit. It is up to them—observing, thinking, studying, listening—to make choices and create the future. Third, the approach values both student-centered and subject-centered instruction and treats them as one thing rather than opposing them and then attaching to one versus the other. Students see themselves in the curriculum, yes, but thanks to a disciplinary curriculum they are also exposed to worlds they could not have fathomed, past and present, near and far. Classroom discussion is mobilized both as a platform for deeper learning of disciplinary knowledge *and* as a public forum for the development of a civic voice.

Chapter 1 introduces the book's themes: liberal and illiberal democracy, knowledge and voice, and curriculum and instruction. Chapter 2 provides an elegant model of curriculum and instruction that focuses on the curriculum's central concepts, mobilizes academic controversy, and engages students in small-group deliberation culminating in free expression. Chapter 3 provides another example of classroom instruction, this one a meaty deliberation in a kindergarten classroom, while reclaiming the concept *idiocy* from the ancients.

CHAPTER 1

Introduction

Liberal democracy is a fusion of individual rights (liberalism) and popular sovereignty (democracy). Liberal democracies are made, not born. The same goes for knowledge; it is made through a social process of argumentation based on evidence, error-seeking, and the willingness to be proven wrong. Both systems—the political and the epistemic—rely on checks and balances. And schools? Schools are the best of places to educate young people in the principles and practices of liberal democracy. Schools have both the mission and the resources to develop knowledge and voice. Three distinctions organize this chapter: liberal and illiberal democracy; knowledge and voice; and curriculum and instruction. An autobiographical note concludes the chapter along with an overview of the chapters that follow.

The purpose of this book is to strengthen civic education in the United States at a time when the nation's political culture is in crisis and the need for remedy is acute. Crisis? Yes, a twofold crisis: a legitimacy crisis and an epistemic crisis. As for the first, many Americans now believe the political system is unfair (e.g., rigged, racist), and many doubt the results of elections, even certifiably fair elections. And the second: Americans have lost a shared standard of truth and, with it, shared criteria for distinguishing fact from falsehood and science from sentiment. Epistemology is the study of knowledge and truth; an epistemic crisis puts knowledge and truth in dire straits.

The legitimacy crisis has been brewing since at least the Vietnam War and the Watergate scandal of the 1960s and 1970s, augmented by the agonies of the Iraq and Afghanistan wars, globalization, and the Great Recession. But the epistemic crisis is more recent. It is due to the fragmenting effects of social media (each pod with its own truth, media trollers at the ready), which has disoriented us all, dashing our ability to concentrate and blurring the distinction between journalism and gossip. Just as devastating, we have suffered a president—a *president*—who lied brazenly, extravagantly, and relentlessly. His administration and media resonators normalized mendacity, thereby redefining the way citizens talk with one another about public policy. His disinformation campaign was not due to ineptness but a strategy designed to stun and then incapacitate the public's ability to discern truth.

3

Asked about his motive in an interview with CBS reporter Lesley Stahl, then-President Trump replied plainly: "You know why I do it? I do it to discredit you all and demean you all, so when you write negative stories about me no one will believe you" (Rauch, 2021, p. 7). His advisor, Steve Bannon, was equally candid. He clarified that Democrats were not the Trumpists' target. Instead, "The real opposition is the media. And the way to deal with them is to flood the zone with shit" (Lewis, 2018). In other words, undermine the press and overwhelm the public sphere with lies, disinformation, and fiction.

Our political culture has always rested on a foundation of legitimacy such that citizens consent to be governed—they trust (cautiously) and accept (mostly) the authority of government. Our political culture has relied also on fidelity to facts and shared criteria for distinguishing truth from fiction. These two pillars of democracy—trust and truth—are now cracked. The rupture is not looming on the horizon; it has happened. And the two pillars are joined. Their interdependence was not obvious until the crisis was upon us. As science fiction author Neal Stephenson observed, "The ability to talk in good faith about a shared reality is a foundational element of civics that we didn't know we had until we suddenly and surprisingly lost it."[1]

Can civic education help? It can. To be sure, education is only one social institution among many, and not the most powerful. Furthermore, this institution has largely sidestepped its earlier charge to cultivate democratic knowledge and character, opting instead, under pressure from all sides, to fit students to a rapidly changing economy. Still, civic education must do at least what it can do. To stretch its reach, we can sharpen its focus, clarify its aim, and make better choices among alternative approaches.

This book, for its part, focuses on civic education at *school*. Schools are not the only places where civic education occurs, of course; a good deal of it happens at home in the family and in weekend and after-school activities—in churches, synagogues, mosques, ballparks, workplaces, online groups, teams, and clubs. Attention must be paid to the civic education occurring in these places. And it is: Numerous nongovernmental organizations create and sponsor participatory civics programs in the community. But the school, whether public or private, is the most important place because education is its explicit purpose. Imparting knowledge—"reality" in its many dimensions, from history and geography to physics and geometry—is its mission. In addition to this singular purpose, schools have the needed assets: teachers, students, diversity, problems, curriculum, and instruction. This is a potent combination: an explicit purpose plus the key resources.

The school's raison d'être is its curriculum. The curriculum identifies and specifies the knowledge, skills, and virtues parents send their children to school to learn. Curriculum is the *what* of school, instruction is the *how*. In this book, I focus on two "whats": knowledge (disciplinary knowledge) and voice (self-expression, dialogue), and I show how particular instructional practices—classroom discussion along with concept development, role-playing, and direct support for reading comprehension—can help students learn them.

This, then, is a curriculum-and-instruction book, but underlying this pedagogy are what has been called the social foundations of education—the disciplines of sociology, philosophy, and history. Accordingly, attention is given to the school as a unique place in the community and, equally, to the school as a community itself. Just as a church, synagogue, or mosque is entirely different from the buildings around it, so is a school. Schools are social places, of course, but they are also *public* places. When young children come to school, they emerge from the private chrysalis of babyhood, family, and kin and step into a public space and onto a public stage. Familiar routines and roles and faces give way to a mélange of strangers and new interaction rituals. Schools have diverse student bodies, some schools more than others, but each to a meaningful extent. There may be racial, religious, linguistic, gender, and class differences there along with the accompanying differences in social status and power. Immigrants from the world over may be there, both authorized and unauthorized. There is also the hodgepodge of personalities and idiosyncrasies. Difference is there at school, and a sea of voices. The young "public" is right there in a setting dedicated to learning, growing, and getting along.

Accordingly, schools have much of what they need to educate young people in the arts of speaking and listening to other members of the democratic public, the people with whom they are joined in a social contract—a civic partnership. This is the heterogeneous "we the people." It is not an identity group, at least not in the way that term is used today; it is a *demos,* not an *ethnos.* This is a partnership where language is king; where talk, not violence, settles disputes. This is civic discourse. It is "civic" because it is about the public's business—the *demos*—and it is "discourse" because, unlike the battlefield, it is a place where "speech takes the place of blood, and acts of decision take the place of acts of vengeance" (Pocock, 1998, p. 32). Knowing one another well or believing the same thing or enjoying the same customs or being fond of one another—none of these is necessary for democratic relations. If it were, democracy would be impossible in most places.

The upshot is that a people aspiring to this ideal, to a political community of this kind, needs an education system that inducts its youth into a civic culture of speaking and listening to people they might not know or like, whose behavior and beliefs they may not warm to, with whom they may be unequally related due to histories of discrimination and servitude, and with whom they may have no occasion otherwise to be in discussion, or even in the same room, but with whom they must be involved in peaceful political deliberations—governance.

LIBERAL AND ILLIBERAL DEMOCRACY

How shall we conduct civic education? It is an ancient question that rests on another that is still more basic: How shall we live together? The answers swing from the technical to the metaphysical, and both kinds are needed (Stitzlein, 2021). The technical answers are a matter of engineering, of finding the right means; the metaphysical are a matter of finding the right ends, in which case we are concerned with not with the "how" but the "why." I will suggest now the "why," the end or aim, of civic education.

To begin, we should understand that civic education is always, in William Galston's (2001) succinct phrase, "relative to regime type" (p. 217). A country's "regime" is its form of government coupled with its political culture, including both its practices and aspirations. Primary and secondary schools around the world are expected to contribute to the civic development of their students, but the aim of civic education will depend on the sort of regime a particular country has or wants to have. Every regime has an interest in civic education, even autocratic regimes like contemporary China, Russia, and Saudi Arabia. As a case in point, Nazi Germany had extensive civic education programs, both in school and out. These were tailored to the cultivation of good Nazis. Youth were taught obedience to Hitler, patriarchy, homophobia, antisemitism, and racism (Rempel, 1989). By contrast, democratic regimes require a civic education that cultivate democratic citizens—people who have knowledge, skills, and values suitable to a liberal-democratic regime.

We should also understand that "democracy" or "democratic," as the terms are used in everyday parlance, are shorthand for what in the social sciences and this book is called "liberal democracy." This concept stems from the 17th and 18th century Enlightenment political philosophy of Hobbes, Locke, Montesquieu, and the founders of the American republic, James Madison especially. *Liberal democracy, in my judgment, is the proper aim of civic education in the United States.* It is the regime we have, it is the one we are trying to defend against authoritarian attacks, it is the one we are trying to improve (the political left and right have competing visions of improvement, of course), and it is the one that has recently been thrown into crisis.

Liberal in "liberal democracy" does not mean what it does in everyday political speech: left-of-center or progressive or (in the United States) Democratic as opposed to right-of-center or conservative or (in the United States) Republican. Instead, it refers to the philosophy of classical liberalism. This is the philosophy of individual rights and the rule of law. Both Republicans and Democrats, generally, are "liberal democrats" in this sense, for liberal democracy is the basis of the U.S. Constitution and the regime it created.

Liberal democracy is a unique and fitting aim for civic education because it is at once a traditional and progressive aim, which is to say it is a centrist, accommodating aim. It supports a big tent. It is a broad, middle way between extremes.[2] Its core values are freedom, equality, and the rule of law and, together, their offspring: pluralism, tolerance, knowledge, voice, and community—a peaceful civic·partnership among a diverse people. It is a regime that seeks to lower the temperature in the room, so to speak, in such a way that diverse groups and beliefs can live together—a different religion next door, multiple races on the same street and in the same house, queer and straight people working openly in the same office, political parties acting as the loyal opposition, not enemies, and conceding defeat when they have lost an election.

Our current crisis threatens both parts of liberal democracy. The noun part, *democracy*, refers to majority rule, free and fair elections, universal adult suffrage, and the peaceful transfer of power from one administration to the next. The modifier, *liberal*, refers, again, to individual rights and the rule of law. The latter, *law*, limits the power of government to infringe on the former, *rights*. The law also limits the freedom of individuals to harm one another. Government power is constrained, but an individual's freedom is also constrained. "Liberty is the right to do what the law permits" Montesquieu (1758, ¶ 214) famously wrote, summarizing the relationship between freedom and lawful constraint. Philosopher Judith Shklar put it differently: "Every adult should be able to make as many effective decisions without fear or favor about as many aspects of her or his life as is compatible with the like freedom of every other adult" (1989, p. 21). Parties to such an agreement, that is, members of such a community, need to grasp the relationship of freedom and constraint so that they will not, in the name of "freedom," shout "fire" in a crowded theater or poison the water supply, drive through red lights, or otherwise foul the commons, for that would be sheer "idiocy" (the premise of Chapter 3, this volume). Members will voice their opinions vigorously and take the adversarial function of opposing interests seriously, but they will do so within the context of civic consciousness and a willingness to live by the community's decisions. This is constitutional democracy. This is liberal democracy

Let's turn now to the antonym. An *il*liberal democracy has the one aspect but not the other, and the result can be brutal. An illiberal democracy has the democracy part—the adult suffrage, the majority rule, and the elections—but not the individual rights and liberties nor the laws that limit state power and the nastiness of fellow citizens. Democracy detached from liberalism is democracy without human rights—without life, liberty, and the pursuit of happiness. Such a democracy will not protect diversity; the majority can, and likely will, use its power to oppress minorities and those values and individual freedoms it finds repugnant. An election will be held, yes, but the winner will attack the press, favor one religion over others, use the police to stop peaceful protests rather than protect them, imprison political opponents, abrogate the independence of the judiciary, support vigilante attacks on unpopular groups, and so forth. It is an old, sad story. "Coups" are not generally how liberal democracies die these days. Rather, "death occurs step by step, through the steady degradation of political pluralism, civil liberties, and the rule of law, until the Rubicon has been crossed as if in a fog, without our knowing the precise moment when it happened" (Diamond, 2020, p. 37; also Zakaria, 2003).

Summarizing, a liberal democracy is a hybrid—"a fusion of the idea of the power of the people and the idea of legally guaranteed individual rights" (Crick, 2008, p. 15; also Fukuyama, 2022). It aims to create and maintain three goods: freedom, equality, and popular sovereignty.

There have been enough liberal-democratic nations for us to know that they are fragile and usually short-lived. Today, only six of the 15 most populous nations are, more or less, liberal democracies, and three of these (India, Brazil, and the United States) have slipped recently (Freedom House, 2022). But understand that any sort of democratic regime is a rare occurrence for humankind, so much so that its absence at any time or place does not demand explanation (Wiebe, 1995). Historians are surprised when liberal democracies appear, all the more so when they develop and endure. Tyranny, not liberal democracy, is the historical norm, the most common forms being theocracy, military dictatorship, and absolute monarchy—rule by clergy, colonels, and kings. (Remarkably, the third of these has often combined with the first in such a way that the monarch's authority is believed to be divine.) By the time Aristotle wrote his *Politics* (1958) over 2 millennia ago, there had been such a variety of political systems that he could set about classifying them. Among them were democracies, which he dismissed as feckless because they predictably devolved into illiberal mob rule (majority will without constitutional restraint).

Illiberal mob rule? Yes. Civic education should give no quarter to wishful thinking about "we the people." Two reasons are persuasive. First, people can and do succumb to populist demagogues who exploit and amplify their resentments and anxieties. On this, the historical record is clear. (Trump may have been a narcissistic vandal who created a neofascist cult, but he wasn't a rarity, historically.) Second, research on implicit bias and other forms of what is called "motivated reasoning" reveals that people feel first and think later. It turns out that rational thinking is the cart and not the horse. "Our explicit reasoning processes serve to rationalize behavior rather than to cause it" (Taber & Lodge, 2016, p. 62). In other words, people reason more like attorneys than judges. Our politics begin in our gut, and we have already taken sides by the time reasoning kicks in. Our thinking is motivated by preconscious passions, and hardly anyone—well, no one[3]—escapes this. Ubiquitous examples are racial bias and confirmation bias.

Taken together, these two vices—our weakness for populist demagogues and our unconscious biases—confront democracies with nearly insurmountable odds. This was precisely Madison's worry. "If men were angels no government would be necessary," he wrote in "Federalist 51" (2003b, p. 316). Government *is* necessary because "we the people" become illiberal zealots—fierce adherents to factions, each righteous in its passion and uncompromising in its goals. "A dependence on the people is, no doubt, the primary control on the government," Madison continued, moving now to a solution, "but experience has taught mankind the necessity of auxiliary precautions." These are constitutional provisions: checks and balances, bills of rights, separation of powers—all of them meant to control both the people and the government and prevent absolutism, religious violence, and oppression; or, stated positively, to preserve liberty and rights, peace, and dignity. These provisions have become common features of liberal democracies ever since. Stephen Holmes (1995) sums it up with characteristic verve:

> Citizens are myopic; they have little self-control, are sadly undisciplined, and are always prone to sacrifice enduring principles to short-run pleasures and benefits. They may even be tempted to confiscate the wealth of a few, without foreseeing how such an act will affect the living standards of most people. A constitution is the institutionalized cure for this chronic myopia: it disempowers short-sighted majorities in the name of binding norms. A constitution is Peter sober while the electorate is Peter drunk. Citizens need a constitution, just as Ulysses needed to be bound to his mast. If voters were allowed to get what they wanted, they would inevitably shipwreck themselves. By binding themselves to rigid rules, they can better achieve their solid and long-term collective aims. (p. 135)

The passage is from Holmes's book *Passion and Constraint: On the Theory of Liberal Democracy*. Passion abhors constraint, but peace, justice, knowledge, and voice demand it and can't function without it. Thomas Jefferson argued that voters also need education. He agreed with Madison that "auxiliary precautions" were needed to control Peter drunk but believed that education could sober him up. The two together—a constitution and education—may be our best hope.

This is not to say that today's liberal democracies are without grave injustice and debilitating social problems. In the United States, about one of every four children lives in poverty. Countless parents work two jobs and still have no health care. And a racial hierarchy is fundamental to the nation—explicitly at its creation and implicitly today. Don't these facts make liberal democracy an unacceptable goal? In my judgment, they do not. I take counsel from Danielle Allen and Winston Churchill. Allen (2020), a political theorist, educator, and African American whose great-great grandfather was counted three-fifths of a person when the Constitution was ratified in 1788, asked herself recently, "So why, then, do I love the Constitution?" Her answer integrates two arguments—one for constraint, the other for education—and clarifies that the Constitution does not describe a world but imagines one.

I love it because it is the world's greatest teaching document for one part of the story of freedom: the question of how free and equal citizens check and channel power both to protect themselves from domination by one another and to secure their mutual protection from external forces that might seek their domination. . . . Those who wrote the version ratified centuries ago do not own the version we live by today. We do. It's ours, an adaptable instrument used to define self-government among free and equal citizens—and to secure our ongoing moral education about that most important human endeavor. (p. 62)

Allen wants to save the baby—the ongoing struggle for freedom, equality, and popular sovereignty—rather than throw it out with the bathwater of White supremacy. Like her, I do not want to downplay the significance of the racial hierarchy on which the United Sates was built. The comparative historian of race, George Frederickson (2015), demonstrates that South Africa under apartheid, Germany under the Nazis, and the American South under slavery and Jim Crow were the only explicitly racist political regimes that can be found in history. These were formal, juridical regimes. While South Africa and Germany can be said to have reckoned with their pasts, the United States simply has not. But we cannot deny that it has moved in that direction, the prime examples being the 13th, 14th, and 15th Amendments in the 1860s following the Civil War. These formally changed the contract (Mills, 1999) and initiated a second founding (Foner, 2019). Add to these the Civil Rights and Voting Rights Acts of the 1960s. Allen's hopeful interpretation rests, then, on liberal democracy's potential for meliorism or progressivism, that is, its "practical engine of self-correction and improvement" (Freedom House, 2022, p. 3). It was liberal-democratic ideology that wrote the amendments of the 1860s and the laws of the 1960s. It was liberal-democratic ideology that recognized women's suffrage in every state in 1919, the people's right to marry whomever they pleased in the 2010s; and then, in the 2020s, it was liberal-democratic ideology that began to demand that police departments serve their communities equitably and stop killing Black men with impunity. Reactionaries continue to push back at this liberal-democratic progress, plus liberal-democrats themselves disagree; and so the struggle continues. It is this struggle that civic education features as core subject matter—the fight for the vote, for dignity, for rights, for majority rule, for law, for freedom and equality.

Winston Churchill was Peter sober when he quipped to Parliament in 1947 that liberal democracy is the worst form of government "except for all the others that have been tried from time to time." Today, as Trumpism tries to undermine liberal democracy in the United States and Putinism works to do the same in Ukraine, and other illiberal autocrats elsewhere, civic education needs to come resolutely to liberal democracy's defense.

Summarizing, I believe liberal democracy is the proper aim of civic education in K–12 schools. It is a moderate, middle way that accommodates a broad array of beliefs. It is too broad for some: too progressive, godless, amoral, and statist for many conservatives and too accommodating, capitalist, individualist, and unequal for many progressives. For committed activists at both poles, liberal democracy is easy to dismiss as weak tea. It fails to stir the passions and warm the heart. Idealism and partisanship do that; religious faith and ethno-nationalism do that; identity politics can do that. Liberal democracy, by contrast, is moderate and incremental. Because it does not champion beliefs about the purpose of life or the afterlife, it can be uninspiring. It plods along, dressed in gray, trying peacefully to solve problems while embracing tolerance, limited government, debate, and the routine transfer of power from one administration to the next.

Abraham Lincoln attempted in an early speech—in 1838 when he was just 28 years old—to make liberal democracy as inspiring as its more passionate competitors: "Let reverence for the laws . . . be preached from the pulpit, proclaimed in legislative halls, and enforced in courts of justice. And, in short, let it become the *political religion* of the nation." He knew the system was frustratingly tepid for partisans, but he knew also that liberal democracy's centrism is not a flaw but essential to its nature. The state is prohibited from limiting freedom by mandating beliefs or identities. It is obliged to disclaim partisan visions of the good life and must, generally, steer clear of moral orthodoxy. This is liberalism's commitment to neutrality (e.g., Jefferson's wall of separation between church and state). Frustrating and tepid? Yes. Essential? Yes. Since Lincoln's time the historical record has been clear: Liberal democracies have been better than the alternatives at securing the things we liberal democrats value most: freedom, equality, pluralism, tolerance, limited government, the rule of law, popular sovereignty, a shared standard of truth (the scientific method), and peace among a diverse citizenry.

KNOWLEDGE AND VOICE

This book argues for the central place of knowledge and voice in the civic education curriculum, and it pays close attention to what they are. Let's look first at knowledge, keeping in mind the epistemic crisis we now face.

Knowledge

The term *knowledge* rolls off the tongue so easily that both its meaning and method remain obscure. To select knowledge for the school curriculum, we need to be clear about what it is and how it is produced. Knowledge here is Stephenson's "shared reality." It includes both declarative and procedural knowledge: knowing *that* and knowing *how*. In the school curriculum generally and civic education particularly, I am interested in a kind of declarative and procedural knowledge called *disciplinary* knowledge. This is factual knowledge that has gone through a shared (social, mediated) process by which truth claims are formed and then published (presented, made public). The latter, publication, is important because it makes the truth claims and methods available for critique (error-seeking, evaluation), followed by correction and confirmation or falsification. Once checked and corrected as needed, the claims stand as true until new evidence comes along that raises questions and reboots the process.

Disciplinary knowledge is what psychologist Lev Vygotsky (1962) called "theoretic" knowledge and philosopher Charles Sanders Peirce (2014) called "scientific" knowledge. I believe the school curriculum needs to prioritize this kind of knowledge. Why? Not because it is the only kind of knowledge nor the best kind, but because it is the particular kind that the public, attempting to live together in a pluralistic society, needs. There are other kinds, notably spiritual knowledge that derives from prayer or revelation; ancestral knowledge that derives from kinship and lineage; and indigenous knowledge that derives from communion with the natural world since time immemorial. There are self-knowledge and intuitive knowledge as well, and there is the vast store of what Vygotsky called "spontaneous" or everyday knowledge: the experiential, sociocultural knowledge that derives from everyday living and socialization in familiar, local contexts.

So why should disciplinary knowledge be privileged in the school curriculum? The answer is that it is the kind of knowledge that establishes the standard of truth—the shared reality—on which our lives together depend. The way it accomplishes that is its method of production. Disciplinary knowledge is unique because it results from a transparent, regulated method of error-seeking, contestation, and validation. These activities "discipline" the process and its product. They occur across a broad social network of knowledge construction-and-validation communities, namely science, journalism, jurisprudence, scholarly organizations, and government. They occur also in specialized subcommunities such as historical societies and research laboratories. Here is the blind peer-review procedure at academic journals, the arguments in professional associations and guilds, the work of fact-checkers at news organizations, panels of jurors in trials, panels of judges in appellate courts, investigative journalists, and government agencies that regulate and oversee truth claims, such as the Food and Drug Administration. The school curriculum needs to center this kind of knowledge because it orders our collective life, our commonwealth. It facilitates communication and decision-making. This is as true in the public sphere as in the marketplace. It is needed for the civic partnership that allows us to live together with our diversity—our plurality of custom and belief—more or less intact. It is needed for public health (epidemics, climate change), environmental stewardship (biodiversity, land management), the rule of law, and the need for inquiry in every sphere of life. This is the knowledge, popularly known as "factual knowledge" or "objective truth," that is threatened by today's epistemic crisis. Not having shared standards for distinguishing reality from fiction ravages not only truth but the social order, robbing it of coherence, method, and a shared way forward.

The checking-challenge-review process that produces disciplinary knowledge is more or less impersonal and institutional. *Who* said something matters, of course, but *what* was said is the stuff that will be checked. The process is systemic and rule-governed. In his sober and insightful book on our epistemic crisis, *The Constitution of Knowledge*, Jonathan Rauch (2021) distills the rules to two fundamentals.

1. The empirical rule: Knowledge claims must be evidence-based.
2. The fallibilist rule: A truth claim is accepted only until new evidence debunks it; hence, truth claims live and die as evidence demands. (Until recently, Pluto was a planet.)

The process results in knowing whether it is the Sun or the Earth that moves, whether a vaccine is safe, which suspect committed the crime, why storms are getting worse, and who won the election. It is hardly a perfect system—prejudice (prejudgment) always looms, power matters, mistakes are made—but revealing and correcting these prejudices and mistakes are among its chief concerns.

This knowledge-construction and -correction process includes and is shaped by debates and struggles between multiple schools of thought and differently positioned groups. This viewpoint diversity, these multiple and competing perspectives, often arise as struggles between mainstream and marginalized knowledge. These conflicts are common rather than rare, for the knowledge-construction process is embedded in human interests and unequal power relations (Beadie & Burkholder, 2021). Provocations to mainstream knowledge enter from locations outside the established channels, challenging the canon and finding the errors or, more encompassingly, the paternalism and racism built into it. These conflicts are endemic to the knowledge-construction process, not exceptions. The process is *social*; accordingly, it happens *in* the fray, not above it.

Often these clashes take the form of challenges to truths that have hardened into orthodoxies, which categorically violate the second rule, fallibilism. In his influential account of "transformative knowledge," James A. Banks (1993) provides examples in the scholarship of W.E.B. Du Bois and Lorraine Code. Du Bois (1962) disputed settled interpretations of the Reconstruction period in U.S. history, while Code (1991) challenged settled interpretations of gender, subjectivity, and objectivity. The curricular principle that emerges from Banks's analysis is this: For a course of study to be both accurate and complete rather than one-sided and partial, which is to say for a course to be intellectually rigorous and true, multiple perspectives are a necessary ingredient. These competing viewpoints, coming both from students' lived experience and marginalized scholarship, promote intellectual engagement because they must be weighed and adjudicated: compared and contrasted, contextualized, corroborated. This is a rich stew for deeper learning.[4]

Voice

In tandem with disciplinary knowledge, this book argues for the central place of genuine personal expression in civic education. By this I mean that civic education should teach students to express their own views on academic questions and public policy, their reasoning and opinions, and give them ample opportunities to exchange these views with others—speaking, listening, responding. Of course, this includes the disciplinary practices identified earlier: error-seeking, contestation, and validation. More colorfully, this is what the great media scholar Neil Postman (1969) termed "crap detection." This is what well-planned and well-led classroom discussion can foster. And this kind of speech, this kind of reasoning-with-others, in public, is what is meant here by "voice."[5] In the chapter that follows this one, we see a well-structured, field-tested instructional model for doing just that.

This exchanging-reasons conception of voice is based in political philosophy, where it is tied to *political autonomy*—an individual's capacity to make uncoerced decisions along with the freedom to actually do so (Christman, 2020). If students are to take their place as citizens and express their best thinking about public affairs, their voice has to be cultivated right alongside the disciplinary knowledge and lived experience that will inform it. This capacity is crucial to both human flourishing and liberal democracy. These young people are just emerging from dependency, individuating from peers and parents, maturing and self-actualizing, learning to spread their own wings to pursue their own goods.

Voice is the expression of this freedom. As John Stuart Mill (1978) wrote in one of the best essays we have on freedom (and note the similarity to Montesquieu and Shklar quoted earlier), "The only freedom which deserves the name is that of pursuing our own good in our own way, so long as we do not attempt to deprive others of theirs, or impede their efforts to obtain it" (p. 12). Voice is also an expression of our sociality, because we are using our voices to speak to others who also have voices. "Politics is a communicatively constituted activity. Words are its coin, and speech its medium" (Ball & Pocock, 1988, p. 1). Language and speech are vital to the maintenance of a political culture that wants to tackle policy issues with dialogue and persuasion rather than violence and retribution. Language and speech constitute the civic partnership that keeps uncivil strife at bay, and they make possible the rule of law. Voice, more basically, is needed for consent, and the consent to be governed is the essence of popular sovereignty. Young children don't have this capacity, which is among the reasons why they are in the custody of their parents. But as youth approach their emancipation, consent is precisely what is required: an independent decision to join the civic partnership.

Fortunately, both knowledge and voice already are valued learning outcomes in most schools; therefore, neither goal is a fantasy. Of course, controversies erupt regularly over both knowledge and voice. Recall debates over the teaching of evolution in the 1920s, Afrocentrism in the 1980s, U.S. history in the 1990s, and race and antiracism today. Efforts by teachers and school administrators to constrain student voice are not uncommon, and sometimes cases go to school board meetings and even to the Supreme Court. Indeed, such cases are fixtures of the ongoing culture wars (Raskin, 2015; Zimmerman, 2002). The balancing act is dicey: Educators have to weigh multiple aims and factors, from curriculum objectives and professional integrity to student safety and parents' rights. The school curriculum is, in the main, remarkably settled, even entrenched. Still, at the smaller-grained level of course and unit design, there are myriad curricular judgments that teachers make and multiple opportunities for them to nurture students' ability to form and express reasoned opinions.[6]

An additional point is needed in order to tie this section on knowledge and voice to the prior one on liberal democracy. The knowledge-making process functions both to generate factual knowledge and to find errors. These are two sides of the same knowledge-making process: verification and falsification. And, as Rauch (2021) notes, this epistemic system resembles the checks-and-balances of the liberal-democratic political regime that Madison created. There are, then, not one but two constitutions, so to speak: one for knowledge and one for government. Both systems are social; both are fueled by multiple perspectives, argument, and error-seeking; and both run on procedural rules for turning contention into consensus—policy on the one hand, knowledge on the other. "Both systems, political and epistemic, are cumulative and constructive," Rauch writes, and both "use their turbulence as a source of stability." In both cases, multiple and opposing voices are essential, for without them our view is narcissistic. Without interlocutors and conflict, there can be no debate or exchange; and then checks and balances are impossible. Crucially, both constitutions "specify a process, not an outcome. . . . [It is] a process of contestation and resolution, leading to new questions and controversies as older ones are settled" (pp. 110–111).

CURRICULUM AND INSTRUCTION

Curriculum, as we have seen, is the *what,* the subject matter, of teaching. This book emphasizes two subject matters: liberal-democratic knowledge and liberal-democratic voice. Instruction is the *how*—how teachers teach these and how they relate to students. My work generally and this book in particular emphasize three instructional modalities: classroom discussion, political simulations, and explicit supports for reading and comprehension. While curriculum and instruction are distinct, they overlap; and three overlapping areas require educators' attention. These are thinking, bridging, and questioning.

Thinking

Education in a liberal democracy should not be confused with transmission—depositing information into the heads of students who then use their voices only to spout it back. This is where curriculum needs its partner, instruction. As John Henry Newman (1852) put it long ago, true learning "consists not merely in the passive reception into the mind of a number of ideas unknown to it, but in the mind's energetic and simultaneous action upon and towards and among those new ideas" (section 5). This suggests a simple maxim: Students must think about what they are learning if they are to learn it. Osmosis is not how people learn disciplinary knowledge. Further, knowing the answers is not sufficient; students must also know the questions that produced them. Their minds must *act* upon questions and answers. In a classroom setting, students can think *with* the teacher, the authors they are reading, and one another in discussions, finding and weighing competing interpretations, and challenging their own view of things with the views of others. As we shall see in subsequent chapters, *seminars* are discussions that do this in one way while *deliberations* do it in another. Both are species of inquiry, which is why they facilitate learning. And in a curriculum centered on big ideas (concepts), factual knowledge becomes organized in the mind in a way that is adaptive—usable in the future and, therefore, generative.

Bridging

In addition to the "energetic and simultaneous" application of the mind to the curriculum, the curriculum must be made meaningful to students in their actual lives—that is, in their lived sociocultural contexts. This is not only a matter of creating a caring and respectful climate for social relations at school. The learning of disciplinary knowledge depends upon it, too. There is ample disagreement surrounding this point, and it has ignited educators' and parents' passions for centuries. It is a worthy argument, for it features a central tension in education between student-centered and subject-centered pedagogy. John Dewey recognized that extremist camps had formed around this dyad and were doing sectarian battle by the end of the 19th century. He tried to calm the dispute in his essay *The Child and the Curriculum*. "Just as two points define a straight line, so the present standpoint of the child and the facts and truths of studies define instruction" (1902, p. 11). In other words, curriculum and instruction need to be both student-centered and subject-centered at once, one strengthening the other.

The question here is this: Should the curriculum precede the child, having been decided already by adults in faculty and school board meetings? Or should the curriculum follow from students' interests, strengths, and funds of cultural knowledge? The former hands curriculum decision-making to adults (teachers, parents, and elected school board members); the latter hands it to the "child" in her "present standpoint"—her lived experience and her present identity. Lisa Delpit (1988) argued in a seminal paper, "The Silenced Dialogue," that White progressive educators were too often ambivalent about their authority in the classroom; consequently, they were too often reluctant to exercise curricular authority over the child, especially students of color. This ambivalence operates in a perverse way, she wrote, for it functions "to ensure the maintenance of the status quo, to ensure that power, the culture of power, remains in the hands of those who already have it" (p. 285). Poor and minoritized children need to learn the middle-class codes of the school and society if they are to flourish, Delpit concluded.

The competing views among parents, educators, and policymakers on this issue are ardent and legion, but I believe Delpit is correct. She argues that for education to be liberating and to advance justice, it must build upon the familiar (the child's present identity and her sociocultural context), but open windows onto a world that is decidedly not familiar (a disciplinary curriculum). The Earth seems flat to our everyday perception. We *feel* its flatness. Should school mirror that? It should not. It should begin but not end there. The curriculum should lead outward from there, for that is "education" (from the Latin, *leading out*).

My University of Washington colleague Geneva Gay, like Dewey and Delpit, opts for both window and mirror. Gay (2018) produced a body of work on a kind of instruction called "culturally responsive teaching" that influenced a generation of schoolteachers. She advises teachers to build two-way "meaningfulness bridges" (p. 37) that link the curriculum to the child and the child to the curriculum. These bridges connect disciplinary knowledge to students' lived experience. Windows are fitted to mirrors. As we have learned from studies in cognitive science, the acquisition of new knowledge needs to be articulated with students' funds of prior knowledge. This connection defines learning and explains the "ah-ha!" moment. Here is the linking of the novel to the known, the strange to the familiar. These connections allow students to draw from the well of experiential knowledge acquired in their familiar sociocultural locations but also to venture into the world of abstract knowledge that enables them to think outside the boxes of their experience. Both "home knowledge" and "school knowledge" are needed if students are to see the not yet seen and think the not yet thought. Students might then become aware of the forces structuring their lives. Further, they might use their voices to take action (see Rubin et al., 2021).

Meaningfulness bridges need to be built with care. Prior knowledge can facilitate the learning of disciplinary knowledge, but it can also obstruct it. Here again is the problem of implicit bias and motivated reasoning. Readers are familiar with the sarcastic phrase, "Don't bother me with the facts, I've already made up my mind." Research on learning has taught us that prior knowledge can cause students of any age "to not attend to new information and to rely on existing schema to solve new problems" (National Academies, 2018, p. 5). Only through reflection, intention, and effort can such biases be managed, if then. This is one of the central challenges of teaching: striking the right balance between the child and the curriculum, between the mirror and the widow, the familiar and the strange, experiential knowledge and disciplinary knowledge.

Questioning

Voice is developed in tandem with disciplinary knowledge because the latter, disciplinary knowledge, is fueled by questioning, that is, by doubt and inquiry. Indeed, expertise in any field is largely a matter of knowing what questions the field is asking—what problems it is trying to solve now. "It is the act of inquiry," Paula McAvoy and Arine Lowry (2022) remind us, "that facilitates learning" (p. 91).

Disciplinary knowledge rests on questions, questions need responses, responses require voice (speech and expression), and voice demands exchange—dialogue. Drawing students into a dialogue with one another on the curriculum's central questions is any teacher's abiding wish and, when it happens, teaching's juiciest reward. Discussion gives students the opportunity to express themselves—their identities, hunches, questions, and truth claims—"in public." This is the opportunity to both develop a voice *and use it*. Discussion affords students the opportunity not only to express their views but to listen to others' and to determine if what they are hearing requires them to adjust their own thinking. This entails perspective-taking and, as we shall see in the next chapter, respect.

The questions under discussion are controversial because reasonable people will disagree about how to answer them. These may be questions of fact, definition, or values, and they are at the center, not the margins, of a disciplinary curriculum. This is because disciplinary reasoning—the kind of inquiry undertaken by practitioners of a discipline, the way they frame and study questions—is as much a part of the discipline as are its substantive content and findings. Consider six questions:

- Was the agricultural revolution humankind's greatest achievement or its greatest mistake?
- Why are only some social movements successful?
- Was the U.S. Civil War preventable?

- Should the Electoral College be abolished?
- Does 1619 (slavery) or 1776 (freedom) best represent the story of the United States?
- Who is, can be, and should be a citizen of this country?

Controversial academic issues like these and countless others in the social studies curriculum are a boon to teaching and learning. They spark intellectual inquiry, they provoke an exchange of views, they require multiple perspectives, they demand reading and comprehension, and they produce a more complete understanding—deeper learning.

AN AUTOBIOGRAPHICAL NOTE

In the next section, I will overview the chapters in the book. But I want first to relate a few things about myself. I was born in 1948 to White, middle-class parents in Englewood, Colorado, just south of Denver. My parents owned a small business—a "beauty shop." Dad was the manager and lead hairdresser, and Mom was the bookkeeper. It was a bustling business. My older sister and I did chores at the shop on Saturdays and some evenings. (To this day I fold towels and sweep hair in my dreams.)

My parents were active members of Englewood's United Methodist Church; therefore, so were my sister and I. Such is the "thrownness" of life. We are dropped into existence without a predetermined character and then begin to construct ourselves in interaction with what we find when we start sizing up our environment and making choices about how to be and what to do. None of us chooses the racial, cultural, or class contexts of our birth— the hand of cards we were dealt at our grand entrance—nor the available identities and ways of being that come with them. And we have already been steeped in them by the time we become aware of them.

As it turns out, my United Methodist upbringing fostered liberal tolerance of other faiths. Still, my parents worried that suburban insularity and homogeneity were threats to their children's development and to their own flourishing, too. Secure in Roosevelt's social-democratic liberalism that was still alive in Eisenhower's postwar America, they set about assembling a group of families who were somewhat diverse, that is, who attended other churches. These others—Mormon, Baptist, and Roman Catholic—were, to my sister and me, strangely different. Not frightening, but odd and interesting. Soon our parents reached farther, to non-Christians. This was a big step. There were other monotheists (a Jewish couple), polytheists (a Hindu couple), and nontheists (a Buddhist couple).

As the initial exoticism of this experiment in grassroots multiculturalism subsided, the group became ordinary friends. Our mothers were the glue, of course. They gathered monthly at one another's homes to talk and drink tea. They brought sewing projects and referred to themselves as "the sewing group." The couples gathered now and then, too, and always celebrated New Year's Eve at one another's homes. The children became ordinary friends, too, populating one another's birthday parties and gathering at the annual sewing group picnic on Labor Day, where we braced ourselves for the looming school year.

It was a thoroughly modern thing my parents did, for it assumed that our faith was but one of many. "Modern faith becomes reflexive," Jurgen Habermas wrote (2006, p. 152), because it can't ignore the fact that it exists alongside other faiths as well as secular, disciplinary knowledge. Modern societies are characteristically self-aware in this way, affording the recognition that we live in a plural world.

This modern, liberal awareness (again, "liberal" in the classical, not contemporary, sense) is tolerant and has important social and political consequences, too. Not the least of these is the idea of the secular state. Reduce religion's role in government, privatize it, and you mitigate one awful cause of religious warfare and persecution. Another consequence is the spread of liberal democracy. As we have seen, such a regime is not merely an electoral democracy in which citizens authorize elected representatives to make law and administer society; it is also an individual-rights democracy in which religious, political, racial, linguistic, and other differences are recognized as a fact of life, and their free exercise is protected by law. This ideal, in turn, becomes the basis for grassroots civil rights movements that struggle to realize it. As Gary Okihiro (1994) clarified in *Margins and Mainstreams,* the core, creedal values of the nation are animated not by those already secured within the mainstream, not by those privileged already, but by those *not* secured and *not* privileged. In their struggles for freedom and equality, these oppressed groups preserve and advance the ideals of liberal democracy. Voting, then, is not the only form of popular political participation in a society that is trying to be a liberal democracy, nor the most demanding. There are other citizens with other viewpoints and lifestyles—ideological and cultural. Relating to them, tolerating and even respecting them, even fighting for them, is part and parcel of maintaining the civic partnership that is at the heart of the liberal-democratic experiment.

I presume most of my readers are liberal democrats of whatever faction—conservative, progressive, libertarian, Republican, Democrat, independent. No doubt we agree on some things and disagree on others. Personally, I am a liberal democrat of the Social Democrat or New Deal type. Thus, my domestic political aims are left of center, making me a "liberal" or "progressive" in today's vernacular. These aims include reducing economic inequality (I believe that government's first obligation, after defense of the homeland and protection of individual rights and liberties, is the prevention of poverty); ending systemic racism, especially in police departments and schools; ratifying the Equal Rights Amendment; providing universal health care and early child education to all residents of the country; and, in pursuit of majority rule, abolishing the Electoral College. These are the ends I pursue in my political life as a citizen. As an educator, I try not to push these views, for that would be illiberal and disrespectful of my students' dignity and autonomy; rather, I try to educate students in such a way that they possess the knowledge and judgment to make their own decisions and choose their own paths. I return to this theme in the chapter that follows this one and again in the Afterword of the book, "Cultivating Judgment" (Chapter 11).

OVERVIEW OF THE CHAPTERS

When Jim Banks asked me to collect a set of my articles and essays for inclusion in his Multicultural Education Series at Teachers College Press, I searched for a strategy and turned to one of my most important mentors, whom I never met: the curriculum-and-instruction scholar Hilda Taba. Taba immigrated to the United States from Estonia where, as a woman in the 1930s, she could not get a university position. In the United States she landed a position, eventually, at San Francisco State University and worked closely with teachers in the area. Taba had an ingenious, analytic mind. One of her simple and brilliant instructional strategies is List, Group, and Label. I have worked with this strategy for decades, first as a social studies teacher and then as a teacher educator. It is an inductive method fueled by the human capacity to perceive similarities and differences and, from these, to create categories (concepts). Taking the strategy to heart, I printed a list of my publications and then cut the list into strips of paper, one entry on each, and spread them out. I then grouped and regrouped them and gave each group a name. After about a month of this, a group emerged that became Chapters 2 through 10 of this book, and then came the group's label—the book's two-part title.

The 10 chapters that follow this introduction articulate *knowledge and voice* in civic education as well as *curriculum and instruction*. These are the book's two anchors. Both dyads are partnerships, not oppositions, and they are both "sleepers" to some extent; that is, they have unassuming exteriors but lively, generative interiors. They *structure* civic education and unify the chapters of this book. Two additional chapters will complete Part I.

- Chapter 2, "Teaching Academic Controversies," features a model of curriculum and instruction called Structured Academic Controversy. It deserves to be widely used, and I have revised it over decades of using it and teaching it to new and veteran teachers. I appreciate its ease of implementation, even for novice teachers; its suitability to the most rigorous curriculum objectives; and its structured approach to reading and perspective-taking—students do these things before voicing their own position on the issue.

- Chapter 3, "Teaching Against Idiocy," demonstrates that schools, as public places, have the key assets for educating liberal democrats. And it revives the ancient term "idiot," which meant selfish, for blinkered individualists who don't see that freedom needs to be balanced with the common good if freedom is to survive.

Part II: Toward Deeper Civic Learning

- Chapter 4, "Concept Development," illustrates what it means to have a curriculum of powerful ideas rather than a curriculum of names, dates, and factoids to be memorized. What *are* concepts, anyway, and what is an instructional model for helping students build them with their own intellectual labor?
- Chapter 5, "Reinventing the High School Government Course," reimagines course design and exemplifies a curriculum of big ideas. It shows that even college-prep advanced placement courses can be designed for deep understanding rather than superficial retention. Knowledge and voice are developed in tandem, concept development is cyclical or "looped," and students do as well on the exam as students subjected to test-prep teaching and learning.
- Chapter 6, "Listening to Strangers," elaborates the seminar/deliberation distinction with two empirical cases. Middle school students participate in a seminar on Howard Fast's novel about the American Revolution, *April Morning*, while high school students deliberate a controversial state law. Key listening practices are identified.
- Chapter 7, "What Is Justice?" questions what we mean when we say "justice." Like Chapter 6, it rests on a comparison, this time between two locations of justice: in individuals and in societies. Teachers can take action to nurture the former, so that students can take action, if they choose, to nurture the latter.

Part III: Global Civic Education

- Chapters 8 and 9 turn in the direction of cosmopolitan civic education, or the quest to educate "global citizens." Chapter 8, "Educating World Citizens," looks at the recent trend to transform schools in urban areas into "international" schools. I wonder what this means and ask if students are educated in *perspective consciousness*, where they know their own cultural voice to be one among many. And are they taught that they are, above all, citizens of the nation and stewards of its interests, or that they are, above all, citizens of the world?

- Chapter 9, "Human Rights Education's Curriculum Problem," zeros in on the flimsy state of human rights education in the American school curriculum. I argue that if *human rights* is to be taught, learned, and practiced, we need a curriculum for it. More than any other, this chapter drills down on the meaning and origin of *disciplinary* knowledge—factual knowledge—as distinct from other kinds of knowledge.
- Chapter 10, "The Right to Have Rights," examines the boundaries to membership in our political culture. I do this via a review of an important book by legal scholar Angela M. Banks. Who is allowed to be a citizen of this country, who is not, and why does it matter? Here we consider the inclusionary and exclusionary aspects of citizenship status and recognize that classrooms contain both authorized and unauthorized immigrants.
- Chapter 11, "Afterword: Cultivating Judgment," is newly written for this book. In its three sections, I clarify the two essential forms of classroom discussion, seminar and deliberation, and then return to what a centrist approach to civic education means for students and their teachers. I close by arguing that the social studies curriculum is the logical home base for civic education in K–12 schooling, and, consequently, that a robust social studies curriculum must be restored to the early grades where it has been shoved aside in many places.

CONCLUSION

Education for a liberal-democratic regime, and the shared standard of truth it requires, are the theme of this collection of my work. I outline a pedagogy that focuses on three things: first, curriculum decision-making: choosing from the vast universe of possibilities the subject matter for civic education, attending closely to both disciplinary knowledge and civic voice. Second, organizing curriculum and instruction to achieve deep rather than superficial learning. Third, instruction that gets young people in the habit of speaking and listening to one another "in public" about powerful ideas and questions. The following chapter details a model that does all three. It is an elegant model and entirely practical.

Teaching Academic Controversies

As our democratic experiment falters, robust curriculum and instruction are needed in schools. This chapter shows how a popular model called Structured Academic Controversy (SAC) can be fine-tuned to teach knowledge and voice together using discussion, cyclical learning, and explicit supports for learning from text. To signal the revision, I have added a plus sign to SAC. SAC+ aims to teach civility and cooperation (its social goal), a course's central concepts and controversies (its academic goal), and the skill of deliberation along with the ability to form and express an opinion (its civic goals). The controversies it teaches are issues (questions) on which people have multiple and opposing views. These may be controversies of fact (Is it true?), definition (What is it?), or values (Is it just?). Students develop knowledge while learning to use language and information to engage with others.

> Language is one of the most potent resources each of us has for achieving our own political empowerment.
>
> —Danielle S. Allen

In this chapter, I offer an appreciation of the instructional strategy called Structured Academic Controversy (SAC) and detail the revisions I have made to it over the years. I have taught with it, using it in my own teaching. I have taught for it, teaching novice and experienced teachers to use it in their teaching. And I have contemplated its purposes, principles, and procedures. I am delighted by the depth of thinking it can provoke and reassured by the cooperation it brings about. I am impressed by the linguistic work it gets done and buoyed by its utility. I appreciate its relative ease of implementation, even for novice teachers; its suitability to rigorous curriculum goals; and its responsiveness to the demands placed on education in a liberal democracy, especially its promotion of knowledge growth, reasoning with evidence, respect, and civil discourse. Here, I review SAC's development as a cooperative learning strategy and then detail the modifications I have made to sharpen its effect. These address three outcomes: content selection for deeper learning, literacy development, and cultivating student voice. In my judgment they are important additions to the model, and they work in concert to prepare students to take their place on the public stage.

The revised SAC aims to be effective socially, academically, and civically. In a SAC, students develop knowledge while learning to use language and information to engage with others on controversies of fact, definition, and values. To its credit, SAC goes beyond mere *exposure* to multiple views on these controversies to having students actually grapple with these views. This is because in SAC, participants must role-play, exchange views, and determine if what others are saying requires them to adjust their own beliefs.

The chapter is informed by a 10-year research-and-development study of the high school government course[1] as well as my experience teaching SAC to secondary school and college students, and their teachers, for over 30 years. My graduate students across these years have been collaborators. As teaching assistants in social studies curriculum and instruction courses at the University of Washington and as co-presenters at inservice workshops and academic conferences, they have fueled my thinking about SAC—its strengths and weaknesses, its nooks and crannies.[2] Still, the conclusions presented here are my own.

COOPERATIVE LEARNING AND SAC

Before we can make sense of the revisions, let us look at traditional SAC's admirable legacy and structure. SAC was developed by two scholars of cooperative learning, David Johnson and Roger Johnson (1979, 1985, 1988). Cooperative learning is the broader concept, and SAC is a species. SAC has elements in common with other types of cooperative learning, but it is unique. Let's begin with the broader concept.

Cooperative Learning

Cooperative learning became a popular instructional strategy in the 1980s, when a disparate group of educational psychologists and sociologists turned their attention to learning in small groups or teams. Prominent among them in addition to the Johnsons were Elliot Aronson (1978), Robert Slavin (1985), Yael Sharan and Shlomo Sharan (1976), and Elizabeth Cohen (1986). Together, they found positive outcomes: increased school attendance and motivation to learn, and greater academic and social learning by a wider range of students.

Common elements across the several types of cooperative learning are positive interdependence, individual accountability, face-to-face interaction, and teacher-assigned heterogeneous learning groups. The first speaks to the need for a groupworthy task. The task *requires* the group if the work is going to get done. The goal is to accomplish the task by way of everyone doing their job and encouraging others to do theirs. The second prohibits group grades. Individuals are to be held accountable for doing their part and learning. If formal assessments are to be done, they are for individual learning. However, group recognition and rewards are common alongside individual accountability, especially when competition between groups is included. Students encourage one another in the group to succeed so that the group can earn whatever group rewards are available. The third common element is captured by Cohen's (1986) observation that the process of group interaction is "enormously interesting" (p. 3) to young people. There's something about the group dynamic that motivates students to learn to cooperate successfully and achieve the group's goal. They become a team. Further, "students who usually do anything but what they are asked to do become actively involved with their work and are held there by the action of the group. . . . Face-to-face interaction with other group members demands a response or, at least, attentive behavior" (p. 3).

The fourth similarity across types of cooperative learning concerns equity pedagogy and group composition: Teachers aim to achieve in each small group the greatest heterogeneity possible given the student population at hand. Teachers achieve this mix in small groups of two to five, purposefully mixing whatever student differences are at hand—social status, academic ability, attendance record, interpersonal skill, gender, race, religion, learning challenge, talent, personality, skill set, first language, and so forth. In this way, small groups are as heterogeneous as the whole class. Ability grouping, along with other segregating schemes, is rare because it minimizes rather than maximizes the mix, and "there is no evidence that putting low-achieving students into a homogeneous ability group is effective" (Cohen, 1986, p. 22). Further, the teacher emphasizes to students that cooperative group work is work, not play. Friends are not allowed to choose one another for small-group work—friends tend to play rather than work. Random assignment may be used to assign students to small groups in a new class where the teacher has little knowledge of students' strengths, social status, identities, and background. Groups can be purposefully mixed once the teacher is more familiar with the individuals in the classroom. Roles can be assigned (e.g., Cohen's group harmonizer, group facilitator, and group time-keeper), and everyone will have a particular part to play.

SAC

SAC shares these attributes with other types of cooperative learning, but uniquely, it joins language to cooperative learning on controversial issues. These controversies can be ethical (issues of right), conceptual (issues of definition), or empirical (issues of fact). The selected controversy is SAC's subject matter, and students play the roles as advocates for one side of the issue or the other.[3]

The entire procedure typically occurs in a single small group of four, divided into two pairs. Consequently, the teacher in a typical classroom is coordinating six or seven SAC groups at once and twice that number of pairs. SAC centers also on study of texts and other resources (e.g., maps, photos), student-student discussion, role-playing, and advocating competing positions on a controversial issue. The controversial issue can be historical or current—from "Should the Parthenon [Elgin] Marbles be returned to Athens?" to "Should our state's law on police use of deadly force be changed?" While these two examples are mainly ethical, controversies that are mainly empirical are common, too—from the historical stalwart, "Which side fired the first shots at Lexington Green?" to the current issue, "Is mass incarceration of African Americans the new Jim Crow?" And conceptual issues are ubiquitous. Was the American Revolution really a *revolution*? When does a military action become a *genocide*?

SAC is an ambitious classroom practice. The subject matter is rigorous, requiring instructional scaffolds to build the prior knowledge students lack as well as strategies to connect with the funds of knowledge they bring. The pedagogy, too, can be challenging, requiring not only small-group management but also supports for reading comprehension and productive face-to-face discussion. Furthermore, teachers must monitor their own convictions and biases, deciding whether to present as controversial an issue on which they have already reached a position (see Hess & McAvoy, 2015). Yet SAC is worth the trouble. It is pertinent to civic learning outcomes and also to disciplinary content and skill objectives (hence "academic" in its moniker). SAC is both a discourse structure and an instructional procedure. Johnson and Johnson's starting point is that when students are put in small groups and asked to interact with other students while they learn, conflicts among their preferences and perspectives are likely. Rather than avoiding such conflict, SAC mobilizes it as a learning opportunity. The Johnsons (2009) write, "Intellectual conflict is not only highly desirable but also an essential instructional tool that energizes student efforts to learn. . . . Ideas in the classroom are inert without the spark of intellectual conflict" (p. 37).

First, the teacher assigns students to mixed teams of four, which are then subdivided into two pairs. Each pair is assigned to a position on the controversy and asked to role-play advocates of that position. Next, each pair is told to prepare a presentation of its position and reasons to the opposite pair. The two partners work alone and together to study the information provided, and then together they plan a brief presentation to the other pair. After this preparation, the pairs take turns making their presentations, and then a general discussion unfolds, each pair still advocating its position and asking the other side for the key facts that support its position. What happens next is crucial: The pairs reverse perspectives. Each pair presents the other's argument to the other's satisfaction. The point here, of course, is to grasp the facts and logic used by *both* sides. Then comes the final phase of the SAC, where the two pairs join together to summarize the best arguments for both points of view and then strive to reach consensus on a position that all can support.[4]

THE REVISED MODEL

I have made three revisions to traditional SAC. Each is an addition. I call the result SAC+. These additions address content selection, reading comprehension, and political autonomy. They are needed because they address problems that arise in the course of a SAC: They help teachers select the most powerful (educative, generative) controversies for study, deepen students' understanding of the selected controversies, and develop students' capacity to make uncoerced (independent) judgments. The third modification emphasizes political autonomy over consensus, as we shall see. Altogether, and this is key, the revisions mobilize schools' unique character as mediating institutions where young people encounter the broader public. According to developmental psychologist Connie Flanagan (2013), schools are "mini-polities" where young people "work out what it means to be a citizen of the larger polity" (p. 229). Schools have the necessary assets for this work, as I have shown elsewhere (Parker, 2005, 2010). They have diverse schoolmates (more or less), problems (academic, social, and civic), "strangers" (schoolmates who aren't friends or family),[5] and curriculum and instruction (schools are educative places). For even the youngest students, school is a public place, not to be confused with a home, temple, workplace, or market. "The children I teach," wrote kindergarten teacher Vivian Paley (1992), "are just emerging from life's deep wells of private perspective: babyhood and family. Then, along comes school. It is the first real exposure to the public arena" (p. 21).

Publics come in all sizes and shapes: the classroom and school, the town and nation, the neighborhood, the peer group, the bowling alley, the pub. These are social spaces—beyond the family—where a "we" is deciding what to do about a shared problem. Language is joined with cooperation. This is Habermas's "communicative action" (1984, p. 1) and Dewey's "conjoint communicated experience" (1916/1985, p. 93). The essence of discussion, as Bridges (1979) wrote, is "to set alongside one perception of the matter under discussion the several perceptions of other participants, challenging our own view of things with those of others" (p. 50).

1. Content Selection

Despite the challenges, SAC is not too difficult to pull off, even for a beginning teacher. The structured group work is not hard to manage, and it is more or less the same procedure each time. What is difficult is *planning* a SAC, and content selection is at the center of this work. Known also as curriculum decision-making, content selection is the practice in education whereby declarative and procedural knowledge are selected for instruction. It entails choosing from a universe of possibilities a small sample of subject matter suitable for teaching and learning in a particular course and context, with students of a particular age, culture, and history. The process is problematic because class time is limited, while the subject matter possibilities are vast and the students diverse.

The Johnsons paid scant attention to the matter. Yet choosing the controversy and the concepts it features is a crucial undertaking for teachers, especially if the SAC is to be a course workhorse. Accordingly, this first revision suggests that a SAC should not be marginal to a course's central purposes or done simply to engage students. SACs *are* engaging (the Johnsons's "spark"), but this spark should be mobilized to help students achieve a course's core subject matter.

Two principles can steer this work. One involves identifying a course's most important concepts and skills; the other deepens learning through quasi-repetitive learning cycles.

Identifying Central Concepts and Skills. While content selection can mean that one topic is selected instead of another (e.g., *migration* over *region* in geography), or one perspective over another (e.g., centering the United States's founding on 1619 rather than 1776), it more subtly refers to a *relationship* among subject matters: Some subject matter is prioritized over others, and instruction is orchestrated for both. As Bruner (1960) said in an earlier era, "to learn (a discipline's) structure, in short, is to learn how things are related" (p. 7). This means that a course's subject matters needs to be orchestrated to achieve deeper learning of prioritized material and somewhat superficial learning of needed but peripheral material. In this way, depth and breadth are treated not as opposites but as partners. Let me explain, and to do this I will introduce concept development.

To achieve the vaunted curriculum of ideas rather than the pilloried curriculum of names and dates, concepts need to be the mainspring of a course. Concepts are ideas, and ideas are abstractions that apply to several or many concrete instances (cases, examples). In a conceptual curriculum, the abstract and the concrete work together. To learn a concept is to learn its critical attributes *and* to see how they operate in an array of examples. Examples will differ from one another, but each has the concept's critical attributes along with many facts (there are different kinds of music, each with lots of factual detail, yet they are all music; many kinds of government, but all are governments).

Consider *federalism*, the organizing concept of U.S. government and, by extension, the high school government course. To learn the concept superficially is to learn its definition, that is, to learn that the concept's name "federalism" refers to (1) a way of organizing a nation, (2) in which power is distributed or shared between national and subnational units of government (states, provinces). There are numerous ways to organize a nation, and federalism is the one where two or more levels of government have formal authority over the same land and people. Notice how abstract this definition is. This is because there are no examples yet. To learn this or any concept seriously requires multiple examples. *The examples are also part of the curriculum.* Without them, the concept is only a definition to be memorized, an abstraction without reality. A deeper understanding of federalism will include knowledge of a diverse set of on-the-ground examples that display the definition in an array of concrete circumstances (federalism in the United States, India, Mexico, etc.).

Reader, try this yourself. Take a concept that you regard as central to a course of study (e.g., *racism* or *freedom* in U.S. history; *migration* in human geography; *revolution* in world history; *intersectionality* in women's studies) and imagine the set of examples you would select to instantiate that idea in diverse settings. When students learn the differences across the examples but grasp the essential similarities too, they will have formed the concept.

A course can contain meaningfully only a handful of central concepts, of course, because each of them has to be exemplified if it is to be understood. The identification of these concepts and their examples becomes a primary focus for content selection. Only then, to return to SAC, does SAC become meaningful, for SAC can be deployed to teach these examples. It is put to work teaching the core ideas of the subject. Examples of federalism take us quickly to both contemporary and historical policy controversies, from state-by-state marijuana legislation back to the famed Jefferson–Hamilton conflict over the legitimacy of a national bank, and many in between: Obamacare, same-sex marriage, and abortion policy.

Skills, too, need to be selected. They need to be reduced in number from the universe of possibilities, and they need to be related to the focal concepts. *Deliberation* is the critical thinking skill that SAC teaches, along with the broader social skills of cooperation. Skills, like concepts, develop iteratively across multiple trials. To learn to deliberate (to weigh alternatives in discussion with others) requires modeling, practice, and feedback. This takes us to the second principle for content selection.

Deeper Learning Through Looping. Meaningful learning requires that a limited set of powerful ideas and skills is selected for study, and that these are studied and applied in multiple examples and scenarios. This emphasis on multiplicity is not a matter of repetition but complexity. Bransford and colleagues (2000) call it cyclical learning. Bruner (1960) had a similar idea and called it a "spiral" curriculum (p. 52). High school teachers I work with call it "looping." It entails revisiting ideas and skills in different contexts, cyclically, in order to know them differently and comparatively, and therefore deeply. Learning is deepened—made more complex and applicable—thanks to revisiting the same idea or practicing the same skill, but in multiple, novel problem spaces (examples, cases). Each cycle is different. Students see the differences, but they aren't derailed by them because they see the similarities, too, which are the critical attributes of the concept.

Returning to our illustration, teachers of the U.S. government course might plan three SAC cycles on *federalism*. Further, they could select law-related controversies that center on the delicate balance of power between the national government and state governments. In this way, *federalism* would be developed across three examples. Their similarities and differences will deepen students' understanding of the concept's critical attributes; meanwhile, myriad peripheral knowledge will be gleaned from the human and institutional dramas of each case, the branches of government involved, and the relevant clauses from the Constitution. Examples can be selected that are spread across the centuries.

1. 1819. In *McCulloch v. Maryland* the Supreme Court decides that a national bank is legal under the Constitution's "necessary and proper" clause, and that the national government is supreme over the states.
2. 1995. In *United States v. Lopez*, set in Texas, the Supreme Court strikes down Congress's Gun-Free School Zones Act of 1990 on the grounds that the federal government violates reserved powers of the states with this legislation.
3. 2005. In *Gonzales v. Raich,* set in California, the Supreme Court decides that under the Constitution's Commerce Clause, Congress can criminalize the production of cannabis and its use even if states have legalized it.

Teachers likely would remix the SAC groups in each cycle—the four-person teams and their constituent pairs—thereby looping the cooperative learning experience, the skill of deliberation, and the peer context for each student's political autonomy moment (more on this below). These learning cycles build transfer of knowledge (application) into the bones of instruction as the concept is applied to one scenario after another.

Looping multiple SACs on a perennial controversy, as in this illustration, is not a requirement of SAC pedagogy, but we can see how this kind of course design would contribute to a more complex understanding of the subject matter. Furthermore, perennial issues recur—students will face them in the future. Meanwhile, multiple SACs on unrelated controversies, which is more common, still have the advantage of sharpening students' skill of deliberation, since that (the skill as opposed to the content) is what is looped.

2. Learning From Text

We turn now to literacy development and zero in on reading comprehension. There are two reasons to do this. First, a SAC is a language-and text-dependent learning activity. A SAC cannot be pulled off successfully without students completing its reading tasks with decent comprehension. Middle and high school teachers (college professors, too) know that many reading assignments are given but few are completed, and fewer still are comprehended. Without comprehension what we get in SAC is, at best, naïve opinion formation. Second, reading comprehension is not easy for adolescents—including students admitted to advanced courses (Parker et al., 2018). We know that adolescents generally are not gaining adequate levels of literacy skill, and this directly impinges on SAC. Greenleaf and Valencia (2017) summarize the stark reality: "Few students reach literacy levels that enable them to develop interpretations, think critically about texts, make evidence-based arguments, or assemble information from multiple texts into a coherent understanding of a topic" (p. 235). Few adolescents can do it, yet that is precisely what SAC requires.

Many secondary school teachers support their students' reading, actually requiring it and bringing it to the center of instruction. What this second addition does is build this support into the structure of SAC rather than leaving it to chance. At stake is access to the learning outcomes of a SAC—its academic, social, and civic goals. SAC requires the reading *and* comprehension of informational texts so that students' opinion formation is flush with facts—juicy facts about the historical context of the controversy, the participants and their perspectives, the alternatives being considered, the interest groups behind these alternatives, and so forth. This addition to SAC attends both to text selection and comprehension.

Text Selection and Modification. A SAC is a deliberation—this is its central skill. This means that teachers must select texts that present two sides of the selected controversy. These are the positions on the controversy that students will read and discuss within the pair, present to the other pair, and then weigh as they form their own opinions on the matter. Background information on the controversy is needed. This is typically presented in a third text that both pairs read first. Often, it is a section from the course textbook or a story from a reputable news source. Or teachers can present it orally or by other means. Students do need background information on the controversy in order to make sense of the position (the "side") they have been asked to present.

Before selecting this background text or the texts presenting the two sides, teachers need first to hone the SAC question, for this focuses the reading activity: Students read to answer this question. Returning to *federalism* and the second SAC example, the Supreme Court case about guns in schools, a teacher might frame the controversy like this: "Is the 1990 Gun-Free School Zones Act, forbidding individuals from knowingly carrying a gun in a school zone, unconstitutional because it exceeds the power of Congress to legislate under the Commerce Clause?" (Oyez, 1995). But a simpler question could focus more tightly on the two levels of government: "Does the national government have the power to regulate school gun policies in the state of Texas?"

Once the question is honed, texts can be selected. For Supreme Court cases, the two sides are likely to be abridged versions of the decision and the dissent. Streetlaw.org and Landmarkcases.org are deservedly popular sources for such adaptations. But most SACs are not dealing with controversies that come before the highest court in the land, and so texts must be found elsewhere. Consider these four SAC controversies:

- Was Lincoln a racist?
- Why did the United States drop the atomic bombs on Japan?
- Should our state's law governing police use of lethal force be changed?
- Should human consumption of Chinook salmon be outlawed, reserving the fish for Orca whales who face starvation?

The first two are historical, and abridged texts for them are freely available from the Stanford History Education Group (SHEG; 2020) at sheg .stanford.edu. For many historical controversies, however, a well-chosen section from the course textbook may need to suffice for the background information because it is readily available; meanwhile, the alternative positions will come from primary and secondary texts. The latter two controversies refer to current events—one across the nation and one specific to the Pacific Northwest. The needed texts for the current controversies will be found in various media—alternative positions in editorials, op-eds, blogs, interest group websites, and background information in news reports.

Text selection is complicated by the need to modify texts so that struggling readers, along with their more accomplished classmates, actually attempt the reading and then comprehend it. Organizations like Streetlaw and SHEG often do the modifying, saving teachers the trouble. One of their most important adaptations is to shorten the text to a reasonable length, and then surround the print on a page with calming white space. This builds compliance (students will be more likely to do the reading) and comprehension, too. A reading specialist at the first school where I taught called it "reducing" the text. "If you want them to read it closely, reduce it," was her gentle command. Whether the course textbook or a primary document, reduction of the amount of print and simplification of the prose will be needed. Wineburg and Martin (2009) write,

> "The real question for teachers is not whether to use or not to use primary sources. The crisis in adolescent literacy is too grave and the stakes too high for such neat choices. Rather, the question for teachers must be: How can I adapt primary sources so that all students benefit?" (p. 212).

To summarize, when we select texts for SAC, we align them to one or more of the course's central concepts. In this way, we get the SAC to do the basic work of the course, serving its main learning goals. Second, we frame a pertinent SAC question. It presents the controversy as an open question, and it focuses the reading and group work plus the follow-up activities (writing, oral presentations). Third, we choose a text for each of the two positions—one for each pair—and, typically, we choose also a third, impartial text that is read by both pairs and gives needed background information. Fourth, we modify the texts as needed to increase the likelihood that struggling as well as proficient students will read and comprehend them. Overall, the point is to use texts to teach students about the controversy, and then to elicit students' own positions on the controversy. All this matters because middle and high school students have surprisingly few opportunities and little support to *use texts for purposeful learning in the subject areas* (Greenleaf & Valencia, 2017). Happily, SAC is a near-ideal activity for it: The purpose for reading is clear, the amount of text is limited, and the information in the text is needed for the tasks that follow—the pair presentations, the discussion, and students' decisions about how to decide the controversy.

Supporting Comprehension. For some teachers, text selection is the essence of content selection. But experienced teachers of middle and high school students know that their students' reading comprehension must be supported explicitly. It cannot be assumed that students will do the assigned reading, let alone comprehend it. Fortunately, SAC paves the way for teachers to scaffold reading comprehension because key supports are built into its structure. Once teachers enter SAC's structure, they find themselves engaging three practices that facilitate better comprehension. These three distill a good deal of reading research:

1. Before reading begins, teacher provides a purpose for reading the selected text.
2. Teacher specifies ways of interacting with the text during reading.
3. Teacher makes clear how the information taken from the text will be used after reading.

The needed support occurs in three phases. The crucial *before*-reading support occurs when teachers present an unambiguous statement as to why students need to read the text: "Read this to learn the side of the controversy you will present to the other pair and the arguments you and your partner will make." *During* reading, the teacher supports comprehension by having students work with their partner to mark up the text; talk about its position, facts, and arguments; and anticipate the arguments the opposing pair will make. This is similar to the annotation strategies students may learn, but it is active and conversational rather than passive and silent. *After* reading, the partners plan their presentation, sequencing and prioritizing the points they will make and dividing the speaking time. Then they proceed to the presentations and the reversal of perspectives, and then the pairs join together to evaluate the arguments. This takes us to the third revision.

3. Student Voice—Political Autonomy

Danielle Allen (2014) focuses on the role of language in political maturation, calling it "one of the most potent resources each of us has for achieving our own political empowerment" (p. 21).

> When we think about how to achieve political equality, we have to attend to things like voting rights and the right to hold office. We have to foster economic opportunity and understand when excessive material inequality undermines broad democratic political participation. But we also have to cultivate the capacity of citizens to use language effectively enough to influence the choices we make together. The achievement of political equality requires, among other things, the empowerment of human beings as language-using creatures.

Language development was explicitly the concern of the second revision, learning from text. Now, the third revision goes further, using language to express one's own claims and preferences. This revision promotes political autonomy, which is the capacity to make an uncoerced decision. This is required if students are to take their place on the public stage, giving voice to their own thinking about public affairs.

But this is a debatable revision. Educators argue, as they should, about whether in a liberal democracy it is more important to teach the young to make independent decisions or to work with others to reach decisions acceptable to all (consensus and compromise). Liberal democracies[6] value both, but in SAC+ I emphasize the cultivation of students' autonomy. The Johnsons, you will recall, opted for consensus. The main reason for my decision is that, especially in middle and high school classrooms, which is to say especially with teens, responsible individuation from peers and parents is a developmental imperative. Adolescents need opportunities to clarify their own values and take responsibility for their own convictions, not rejecting peers or family but growing their own wings, finding their own voice.[7] Language is essential: articulating one's own thinking and listening to others' thinking. As Flanagan (2013) shows in *Teenage Citizens*, this is the critical period of life when political ideas are born. Nurturing independent judgment during this period will embolden adolescents to follow neither the crowd nor the demagogue, but to think for themselves.

Consequently, this revision adds another step to the SAC procedure, and it skips over the consensus prompt that ends the Johnsons' model (see Figure 2.1).

Figure 2.1. The SAC+ Model

1. Students are assigned to teams.
2. Teams are divided into pairs, and each pair is assigned a position and directed to study their text(s) in order to prepare a presentation on the pair's position, reasons, and supporting facts.
3. Pairs study their text(s) and prepare a presentation. Comprehension is not assumed but is encouraged and facilitated by the teacher.
4. Pairs present to one another, listening carefully to the arguments given.
5. Pairs reverse perspectives, feeding back what they have heard to the satisfaction of the other pair.
6. Discussion still in roles: the two pairs join to summarize the best arguments for both points of view.
7. Genuine discussion. Students are invited to drop the assigned positions and see if the team can reach a decision on the question or, if not, clarify the points of disagreement. Each student clarifies and expresses his/her/their own position and argument.

In SAC+, students are led quickly into the issue's contested space. This occurs at steps 1 and 2. Before they have studied the controversy, they are placed in a team and divided into pairs representing competing positions on the issue. They are told they will be presenting their position and argument to the other pair, and then are given time to study the issue and prepare an argument. This enacts what I call the "engagement first" principle (Parker et al., 2018): Steps 1 and 2 engage students and create a need-to-know the background of the controversy and the position-specific information and reasoning that they will read at step 3. There is a kind of productive anxiety (Cohen's "the action of the group"). During the paired presentations and what follows in steps 4–6, students are responsible for articulating and listening to one another's reasons.

Then comes the final step, where students are given the opportunity to drop the position to which they were assigned. At this point, students search for their "own" position and reasons. They decide whether to stick to the assigned position they had been presenting and defending, or abandon it in favor of the one argued by the opposing pair, or a hybrid or something altogether different. They may have developed some investment in the assigned position by now (this is common); or if they had a pre-SAC position on the issue, they may seize the opportunity to assert it now if they still favor it. Either way, students might switch from a defensive stance (in role) to an inquisitive one (free of role). They might become curious about what position to adopt as their own now that they know something about the controversy, enough to be a reasonably informed participant in that space—a legitimate player. This is an accomplishment. With the pairs now having studied the texts, presented, and listened to one another, the discussion can be an intelligent one, and individuals' opinion formation can take off from there. "Do we need to agree?" someone asks, just to be sure. "No, you don't," is the reply.

The prompt "Feel free to drop your assigned position. What do you really think?" creates a moment where students may abandon the assigned position and reasons. They are not asked to do so; they are provided the opportunity to do so. Consequently, the opportunity is fresh, a sort of reset moment. Following the structured role-playing of preparing, sharing, and listening to positions, there is an opening. Why? The listening-and-feedback process at steps 4 and 5 matters. This is what Waks (2010) calls "giving ear to" the other argument and "waiting in suspense . . . with attentive expectation or anticipation" (p. 2744). Having prepared, presented, and defended a position, and then giving ear to the "other" position, not one's "own"; and then, on top of this, being liberated from the assigned position—all this may leave the student wondering just where his or her "own" mind is on the issue. This is the fertile political autonomy moment.

It is important to see that respect is implicated along with language. Both come with the territory of exchanging reasons. Listening to one another is initially structured in steps 4–6 but then listening is transformed when the role requirement is dropped at step 7. Listening continues at step 7 as students gather material from one another to form their own opinions, but they are free now to believe what they will, and they listen to determine if what others are saying requires them to adjust their own reasoning. They sort through what others are thinking-saying as they shape their own thinking-saying. Laden (2012) shows that this kind of responsiveness is inherent in reasoning. This is why exchanging reasons promotes mutual respect. When I give you my reasons and ask you for yours, I acknowledge that you, too, are a thinker, a reasoner, an agent, not a cardboard character. Sharing reasons implicitly recognizes the inner life, the dignity, of our interlocutors.

Using SAC+ to cultivate voice *rather than* consensus-building skills is debatable, as noted. Learning to speak one's mind, expressing one's preferences and objections, is crucial to young people's maturation as individuals and citizens. Voice is *the* elemental form of civic engagement and empowerment. But both independence and cooperation are necessary, and they operate in tandem. After all, we think better about problems when our partners are capable of thinking for themselves. Schools should cultivate both as part of their civic mission. As we loop students through a number of SACs, we can alternate at step 7 so that students are directed one time to reach a consensus (per the Johnsons) and, next time, to express to one another (the "public stage") their own view. Or we could do both in the same lesson: press for consensus during the discussion, and press students to argue for their own position during follow-up communication: writing and presentations. At any rate, the combined effect of teaching for consensus *and* autonomy is sure to make for more robust deliberations as the course progresses.

CONCLUSION

As our democratic experiment falters, strong civic pedagogies are needed in schools. SAC+ is one such pedagogy. It aims to teach cooperation (its social goal), a course's central concepts and controversies (its academic goal), and deliberative skill along with political autonomy (its civic goal).

Time for teachers' instructional planning and collaboration is the key resource here. Ideally, teachers will talk with one another about the handful of concepts that could effectively anchor a course, the handful of related controversies and texts that will be targeted for study, and the learning cycles that will deepen learning. All this is too difficult *and too interesting* to be done alone. Argument is needed to get it right.

SAC+ is not a value-free pedagogy. It promotes five goods especially: knowledge, critical thinking, literacy, multiple perspectives, and student voice. More generally, SAC+ values liberal democracy and the principles that define it—popular sovereignty, equality, liberty, pluralism, evidence-based reasoning (science), and respect. The latter, respect, underpins the listening, speaking, and argument—the language and relationship—that constitute deliberation. This same cluster of values rejects indoctrination and coercion, for these negate critical thinking and liberty, and they are fundamentally disrespectful. Accordingly, SAC+ is centrist in the manner of Dewey's (1902) middle way. It is a pragmatic path between the extremes of traditional and progressive pedagogies. Students are encouraged to make up their own minds rather than toe a line. This makes a deliberative pedagogy like SAC+ too radical for some conservatives (e.g., Kurtz, 2021) and too conservative for some radicals (e.g., Gibson, 2020). On one side are those concerned that students will be drawn away from their parents' values or that social studies education will be politicized; on the other are those concerned that so-called impartial deliberations perpetuate inequities by concealing them. This is a juicy controversy, worthy of looped SACs+ in a teacher education course.

Let me return, finally, to the appreciation with which I began. Incisive research by early cooperative learning researchers was important and consequential. A sustained school reform movement was launched, instruction was reimagined along the lines of social interdependence theory and equity pedagogy, and educators were shown that they could have their cake and eat it too: School attendance and academic achievement were strengthened thanks to the dynamic social interaction of diverse students, not sacrificed to it. In this chapter, I presented principled modifications to sharpen the effect of the earlier model. These address problems that will surely confront teachers who want to implement it: choosing and then framing the right controversy, getting students to understand it by reading and talking about it, and helping them form and express their own views.[8]

CHAPTER 3

Teaching Against Idiocy

This chapter peers into the classroom discussions of a beloved kindergarten teacher and, thereby, into the tension between individual freedom and civic virtue. And it reclaims the term "idiocy" from its usage in ancient Greece. Idiocy in its origin is not what it means today. In Athens, when a person's behavior became idiotic—selfish and unmindful of the commonwealth—then the person was believed to be like a rudderless ship, of no consequence except for the danger it posed to others. Here we have a powerful contrast: the private individual and the public citizen. Public citizens do not materialize out of thin air. They are not born already grasping the knotty principles of toleration, impartial justice, limited government, equality, or the difference between liberty and license. Without civic education they are not inclined nor able to deliberate public issues with others whose beliefs or cultures they may dislike. Accordingly, we can appreciate teachers' skillful and purpose-driven use of classroom discussion to educate students for citizenship.

Idiocy is the scourge of our time and place. Idiocy was a problem for the ancient Greeks, too, for they coined the term. "Idiocy" in its original sense is not what it means to us today—stupid or mentally deficient. The word carrying its recent meaning is deservedly and entirely out of usage by educators, but the original meaning needs to be revived as a conceptual tool for clarifying a pivotal social problem and for understanding the central goal of education.

Idiocy shares with *idiom* and *idiosyncratic* the root *idios*, which means private, separate, self-centered—selfish. "Idiotic" was in the Greek context a term of reproach. When a person's behavior became idiotic—concerned myopically with private things and unmindful of common things—then the person was believed to be like a rudderless ship, without consequence save for the danger it posed to others. This meaning of idiocy achieves its force when contrasted with *politēs* (citizen) or public. Here we have a powerful opposition: the private individual versus the public citizen.

Schools in societies that are trying in various ways to be liberal democracies, such as the United States, Mexico, and Canada, are obliged to develop public citizens. I argue here that schools are well-positioned for the task, and I suggest how they can improve their efforts and achieve greater success.

41

DODGING PUBERTY

An idiot is one whose self-centeredness undermines his or her citizen identity, causing it to wither or never to take root in the first place. Private gain is the goal, and the community had better not get in the way. An idiot is suicidal in a certain way, definitely self-defeating, for the idiot does not know that privacy and individual autonomy are entirely dependent on the community. As Aristotle (1958) wrote, "Individuals are so many parts all equally depending on the whole which alone can bring self-sufficiency" (p. 6). Idiots do not take part in public life; they do not *have* a public life. In this sense, idiots are immature in the most fundamental way. Their lives are fundamentally out of balance, disoriented, untethered, and unrealized. Tragically, idiots have not yet met the challenge of "puberty," which is the transition to public life.

The former mayor of Missoula, Montana, Daniel Kemmis (1995), writes of the idiocy/citizenship opposition, though he uses a different term, in his delightful meditation on democratic politics, *The Good City and the Good Life:*

> People who customarily refer to themselves as *taxpayers* are not even remotely related to democratic citizens. Yet this is precisely the word that now regularly holds the place which in a true democracy would be occupied by "citizens." Taxpayers bear a dual relationship to government, neither half of which has anything at all to do with democracy. Taxpayers pay tribute to the government, and they receive services from it. So does every subject of a totalitarian regime. What taxpayers do not do, and what people who call themselves taxpayers have long since stopped even imagining themselves doing, is *governing*. In a democracy, by the very meaning of the word, the people govern.

Alexis de Tocqueville (1969), writing over 150 years before Mayor Kemmis, also described idiocy. All democratic peoples face a "dangerous passage" in their history, he wrote, when they "are carried away and lose all self-restraint at the sight of the new possessions they are about to obtain" (p. 540). Tocqueville's principal concern was that getting "carried away" causes citizens to lose the very freedom they are wanting so much to enjoy. "These people think they are following the principle of self-interest," he continues, "but the idea they entertain of that principle is a very crude one; and the more they look after what they call their own business, they neglect their chief business, which is to remain their own masters."

Just how do people remain their own masters? By maintaining the kind of community that secures their liberty. Tocqueville's singular contribution to our understanding of idiocy and citizenship is the notion that *idiots are idiotic precisely because they are indifferent to the conditions and contexts of their own freedom.* They fail to grasp the interdependence of liberty and community, privacy and puberty.

Similarly, Jane Addams argued in 1913 that if a woman was planning to "keep on with her old business of caring for her house and rearing her children," then it was necessary that she expand her consciousness to include "public affairs lying quite outside her immediate household." The individualistic consciousness was "no longer effective":

> Women who live in the country sweep their own dooryards and may either feed the refuse of the table to a flock of chickens or allow it innocently to decay in the open air and sunshine. In a crowded city quarter, however, if the street is not cleaned by the city authorities, no amount of private sweeping will keep the tenement free from grime; if the garbage is not properly collected and destroyed a tenement house mother may see her children sicken and die of diseases from which she alone is powerless to shield them, although her tenderness and devotion are unbounded. (p. 1)

Addams concluded that for women to tend only to their "own" households was "idiotic," for to do only that would prevent women, ironically, from doing just that at all. One cannot maintain the familial nest without maintaining the public, shared space in which the familial nest is itself nested. "As society grows more complicated," she continued, "it is necessary that woman shall extend her sense of responsibility to many things outside of her own home if she would continue to preserve the home in its entirety."

Leaving aside individuals, families can be idiotic, too. The paradigm case is the Mafia—a family that looks inward intensely and solely. A thick moral code glues the insiders together, but in dealing with outsiders who are beyond the galaxy of one's obligations and duties, anything goes. There is no organized cooperation across families to tackle shared problems (health, education, welfare), no shared games, not even communication save the occasional "treaty." There are no bridging associations. Edward Banfield (1958) called this *amoral familism* and articulated its ethos as "maximize the material, short-run advantage of the nuclear family; assume that all others will do likewise" (p. 83).

Amoral familism is certainly not restricted to the Mafia. Social scientists who examine popular culture find no shortage of it today. Perhaps the best contemporary example in the United States, because it is both so mundane and so pervasive, is the SUV craze. Here, the suburban family provides for its own safety and self-esteem during such mobile tasks as commuting to work and running household errands, but it does so at others' expense. When criticized for putting other drivers and passengers at risk, for widening the ozone hole, and for squandering nonrenewable resources, SUV drivers often justify their behavior by speaking of their "rights" or the advantage of "sitting up higher than others." But they focus especially on family safety (Jain, 2002). It is my right to do whatever I choose, goes the argument, with the added and supposedly selfless rationalization of protecting "my" family from dangers real and imagined. To draw the line of obligation so close to the nuclear family is idiotic because it undermines, as Addams and Tocqueville argued, that family's *own* safety along with everyone else's.

We could continue this survey of idiocy from its individual and familial forms to its large-scale enactments in ethnocentrism, racism, or the nationalistic variety, wherein a nation secures its own needs and wants in such a way that the world environment—every human's nest—is fouled, whether by conquest or by dumping poisons into the air and water. But let me instead conclude this section with a puzzle: How did idiocy grow from an exception in the Greek *polis* to a commonplace in contemporary, economically developed societies? Numerous social scientists have asked just this question. Karl Marx (1965) saw idiocy as the inevitable by-product of capitalism, wherein accumulating profit becomes an end in and of itself and nearly everything—from labor to love—is commodified toward that end. Robert Bellah and his colleagues (1985) located idiocy in a deeply pervasive culture of rugged individualism. John Kenneth Galbraith (1998) focused on the mass affluence of contemporary North American society, in which, for example, beef cattle are consumed at such a rate as to flood the environment with their waste, while farmland is misdirected to their feed. As Galbraith wrote, "Few people at the beginning of the nineteenth century needed an adman to tell them what they wanted" (p. 2).

SCHOOLS AND IDIOCY

Capitalism, individualism, and affluence are a powerful brew. But what about the education sector of society? Do schools marshal their human and material resources to produce idiots or citizens? Does the school curriculum cultivate private vices or public virtues? Can schools tame the rugged individualism and amoral familism that undermine puberty and foul the common nest?

Actually, schools already educate for citizenship to some extent, and therein lies our hope. By identifying how schools accomplish at least some of this work now, educators can direct and fine-tune the effort. The wheel doesn't need to be reinvented; it is at hand and only needs to be rolled more intentionally, explicitly, and directly toward citizenship. There are three assumptions that propel this work and three keys to its success.

The first assumption is that democracy (rule by the people) is morally superior to autocracy (rule by one person), theocracy (rule by clerics), aristocracy (rule by a permanent upper class), plutocracy (rule by the rich), and the other alternatives, mainly because it better secures liberty, justice, and equality than the others do. Among actually attainable ways of living together and making decisions about common problems and projects, democracy (that is, a republic, a constitutional democracy) is, as Winston Churchill said, the worst form of government except for all the others.[1] Democracy is better than the alternatives because it aspires to and, to varying degrees, is held accountable for securing civil liberties, equality before the law, limited government, competitive elections, and solidarity around a common project (a civic *unum*) that exists alongside individual and cultural manyness (*pluribus*). That democracies fall short of achieving these aspirations is obvious, and it is the chief impetus of grassroots social movements that seek to close the gap between the actual and the ideal. Thus, Martin Luther King Jr. demanded in his 1963 March on Washington address not an alternative to democracy but its fulfillment:

> We have come to our nation's capital to cash a check. When the architects of our republic wrote the magnificent words of the Constitution and the Declaration of Independence, they were signing a promissory note to which every American was to fall heir. . . . We have come to cash this check, a check that will give us upon demand the riches of freedom and the security of justice. (2001, pp. 81–82)

The purpose of the Civil Rights Movement was not to alter the American Dream but to realize it. When a democracy excludes its own members for whatever reason (slavery, patriarchy, Jim Crow, etc.), it is "actively and purposefully false to its own vaunted principles," wrote Judith Shklar (1991, p. 12). Here is democracy's built-in progressive impulse: to live up to itself.

The second assumption, if schools are to educate for citizenship, is that there can be no democracy without democrats. Democratic ways of living together, with the people's differences intact and recognized, are not given by nature; they are created. And much of the creative work must be undertaken by engaged citizens who share some understanding of what it is they are trying to build together. Often, it is the unjustly treated members of a community who are democracy's vanguard, pushing it toward its principles. "We know through painful experience that freedom is never voluntarily given by the oppressor; it must be demanded by the oppressed," King (1963, p. 80) wrote in the "Letter from Birmingham Jail." The framers of the U.S. Constitution may have been the birth parents of democracy, American style, but those who were excluded, then and now, became the adoptive, nurturing parents.

The third assumption is that engaged citizens do not materialize out of thin air. They do not naturally grasp such knotty principles as tolerance, impartial justice, the separation of church and state, the need for limits on majority power, or the difference between liberty and license. They are not born already capable of deliberating about public policy issues with other citizens whose beliefs and cultures they may abhor. These things are not, as the historical record makes all too clear, hardwired into our genes. (Ask any school principal!) Rather, they are social, moral, and intellectual achievements, and they are hard-won. This third assumption makes clear the enormous importance of educating children for democracy.

On the foundation of these three assumptions, taken together, educators are justified in shaping curriculum and instruction toward the development of democratic citizens. In poll after poll, the American public makes clear its expectation that schools do precisely this (Hochschild & Scovronick, 2002).

SCHOOLS ARE PUBLIC PLACES

As it turns out, schools are ideal sites for democratic citizenship education. The main reason is that a school is not a private place, like our homes, but a public, civic place with a congregation of diverse students. Some schools are more diverse than others, of course, but all schools are diverse to some meaningful extent. Boys and girls are both there. Jews, Protestants, Catholics, Muslims, Buddhists, and atheists are there together. There are African Americans, European Americans, Mexican Americans, Asian Americans, and many more. Immigrants from the world over are there in school. This buzzing variety does not exist at home, or in churches, synagogues, or mosques, either. It exists in public places where diverse people are thrown together, places where people who come from numerous private worlds and social positions congregate on common ground. These are places where multiple social perspectives and personal values are brought into face-to-face contact around matters that "are relevant to the problems of living together," as John Dewey put it (1916/1985, p. 200). Such matters are mutual, collective concerns, not mine or yours, but *ours*.

Compared to home life, schools are like village squares, cities, crossroads, meeting places, community centers, marketplaces. When aimed at democratic ends and supported by the proper democratic conditions, the interaction in schools can help children enter the social consciousness of puberty and develop the habits of thinking and caring necessary for public life. They can learn the tolerance, the respect, the sense of justice, and the knack for forging public policy with others *whether one likes them or not*. If the right social and psychological conditions are present and mobilized, students might even give birth to critical consciousness. This is the kind of thinking that enables them to cut through conventional wisdom, such as peer pressure, and see a better way.

This, then, is the great democratic potential of the public places we call schools. As Dewey observed, "The notion that the essentials of elementary education are the three R's mechanically treated, is based upon ignorance of the essentials needed for realization of democratic ideals" (1916/1985, p. 200). Used well, schools can nurture these essentials, which are the very qualities needed for the hard work of living together freely but cooperatively and with justice, equality, and dignity. Schools can do this because of the collective problems and the diversity contained within them. Problems and diversity are the essential assets for cultivating democratic citizens.

THREE KEYS

But how actually to accomplish this? Three actions are key. First, increase the variety and frequency of interaction among students who are culturally, linguistically, and racially different from one another. Classrooms sometimes do this naturally. But if the school itself is homogeneous or if the school is diverse but curriculum tracks keep groups of students apart, then this first key will be all the more difficult to turn. It is not helping that resegregation has intensified in recent years, despite an increasingly diverse society. White students today are the most segregated from all other races in their schools.[2] (On this criterion, they may be at the greatest risk of idiocy.) Still, race is not the only source of diversity among students. School leaders must capitalize on whatever diversity is present among students—be it race, religion, language, gender, or social class—and increase the variety and frequency of opportunities for interaction.

Second, orchestrate these contacts so as to foster competent public talk—deliberation about common problems. In schools, this is talk about two kinds of problems: social and academic. Social problems arise inevitably from the friction of interaction itself (Dewey's "problems of living together"). Academic problems are at the core of each subject area.

Third, clarify the distinction between deliberation and blather and between open (i.e., inclusive) and closed (i.e., exclusive) deliberation. In other words, expect, teach, and model competent, inclusive deliberation.

I lay out the pedagogical details of teaching deliberation in Chapters 2 and 5 of this volume and in my earlier book *Teaching Democracy* (Parker, 2003). Here are some highlights.

Deliberation exploits the assets afforded by schools: problems and a diverse student body. Deliberation is discussion aimed at making a decision across these differences about a problem that the participants face in common. The main action during a deliberation is weighing alternatives with others in order to decide on the best course of action. In schools, deliberation is not only a means of instruction (teaching *with* deliberation) but also a curricular goal (teaching *for* deliberation), because it generates a particular kind of social good: a democratic community, a public culture. The norms of this culture include, first, engagement in cooperative problem-solving.

This is in contrast to avoiding engagement either by being idiotically consumed by private affairs or by electing others to do the deliberation and then relapsing into idiocy for the 4 years between elections. Other norms include listening as well as talking, perspective-taking, arguing with evidence, sharing resources, and forging a decision together rather than merely advocating positions taken before the deliberation begins.

Deliberation is ideally done with persons who are more or less different from one another; for pedagogical purposes, therefore, deliberative groups—schools and classrooms—should be as diverse as possible. Teachers and administrators can expand the opportunities for interaction by increasing the number and kind of mixed student groups. These groups should be temporary, because separating students permanently, for whatever reason, undermines both individual and civic health. What the participants have in common in these mixed groups is not culture, race, or opinion, but the problems they face together and must work out together in ways that strike everyone as fair (Aronson et al., 1978; Pettigrew, 2004).

THE SOCIAL CURRICULUM

Probably the best-known example of young children deliberating their shared social problems comes from the kindergarten classroom of Vivian Gussin Paley. In a number of books, Paley has captured the look and feel of actual classroom-based deliberation, and she shows how entirely possible it is to do such work in everyday classroom settings, even with the youngest children. In *You Can't Say You Can't Play* (1992), she tells how she facilitated a lengthy deliberation about whether to establish the classroom rule stated in the book's title. She engages the kindergartners in an ongoing discussion about the desirability and practicability of having such a rule. She tells them, "I just can't get the question out of my mind. Is it fair for children *in school* to keep another child out of play? After all, this classroom belongs to all of us. It is not a private place, like our homes" (p. 16). The children find this a compelling question, and they have lots to say. Paley brings them to the discussion circle again and again to weigh the alternatives. "Will the rule work? Is it fair?" she asks. Memories and opinions flow. "If you cry, people should let you in," Ben says. "But then what's the whole point of playing?" Lisa complains. Paley sometimes interviews older children to ascertain their views and brings them back to her kindergartners. Trading classes with a 2nd-grade teacher, Paley tells those children: "I've come to ask your opinions about a new rule we're considering in the kindergarten. We call it, 'You can't say you can't play.'"

These older children know the issue well. Vivid accounts of rejection are shared. Some children believe the rule is fair but just won't work: "It would be impossible to have any fun," offers one boy. In a 4th-grade class, students conclude that it is "too late" to give them such a rule. "If you want a rule like that to work, start at a very early age," declares one 9-year-old (p. 63).

Paley takes these views back to the discussion circle in her own classroom. Her children are enthralled as she shares the older children's views. The deliberation is enlarged; the alternatives become more complex. In the Socratic spirit, she gently encourages them to support their views with reasons, to listen carefully, and to respond to the reasoning of other children, both classmates and older children.

High school deliberative projects exist, too. Perhaps the most widely documented are the Just Community schools conducted by Lawrence Kohlberg and his associates (Mosher et al., 1994; Power et al., 1989). In these projects, democratic governance becomes a way of life in high schools. These projects aim to transform the school culture—its hidden or implicit curriculum—and in this way to systematically cultivate democratic citizenship. Even if the values of justice, liberty, and equality are well explored in the academic curriculum, the students are quick to perceive whether the school itself runs on a different set of values. They will learn the latter as the real rules of the game.

Students in Just Community schools participate in the basic governance of the school. They deliberate on everything from attendance policy to the consequences for stealing and cheating. Today, students might consider whether, as a move against resegregation, cafeteria seating should be assigned randomly.

The Just Community high schools and the kindergarten deliberations of Vivian Paley together suggest five conditions of ideal deliberation.

- Students are engaged in integrated decision-making discussions that involve genuine value conflicts that arise in the course of relating to one another at school. These value conflicts may concern play and name-calling in an elementary school; cliques and taunts in a middle school; and cheating, attendance, and segregation in a high school.
- The discussion group is diverse enough that students have the benefit of exposure to reasoning and social perspectives different from their own.
- The discussion group is free of domination—gross or subtle—by participants who were born into privileged social positions or by those who mature physically before others.
- The discussion leader is skilled at comprehending and presenting reasoning and perspectives that are missing, countering conventional ideas with critical thinking, and advocating positions that are inarticulate or being drummed out of consideration.

- Discussions are dialogic. Discussants engage in conversation
  about their viewpoints, claims, and arguments, not in alternating
  monologues.

THE ACADEMIC CURRICULUM

Citizens need disciplinary knowledge just as much as they need deliberative experience and skill. The suggestion to engage students in dialogues on the shared problems of school life is not an argument for "process" without "content." It is not an argument for lessening emphasis on subject-matter learning. To the contrary, making decisions without knowledge—whether immediate knowledge of the alternatives under consideration or background knowledge—is no cause for celebration. Action without understanding is not wise action except by accident. The Klan acted; the Nazis acted; bullies act every day.

Consequently, a rigorous liberal arts curriculum that deals in powerful ideas, important issues, and core values is essential alongside deliberations of controversial public issues. Moreover, if deliberation is left to the school's social curriculum only—that is, to the nonacademic areas of student relations and school governance—then students are likely to develop the misconception that the academic disciplines are settled and devoid of controversy. Nothing could be further from the truth. The disciplines are loaded with arguments and debates, and expertise in a discipline is measured by one's involvement in these discussions. A good teacher, in this view, is able to engage students, in developmentally appropriate ways, in the core problems of the subject matter.

Historians, for example, argue about everything they study: about why Rome fell, why slavery lasted so long in the United States, and what forces contributed to the fall of the Soviet Union. What historians do is develop theses—warranted assertions—about such matters. They defend their claims with their interpretations of the evidentiary record. Political scientists likewise don't know with certainty why in the past few years the United States has abandoned the UN Charter and embarked on rugged unilateralism, nor do they "know" a host of other things: whether nation-states will survive their contest with globalization or why the current cohort of 18-to-25-year-olds has proven so unengaged in politics.

Engaging students in deliberations of academic controversies is arguably the most rigorous approach to disciplinary education available. Its advantage over drill-and-cover curricula, whether of the middle-track pedestrian variety or the Advanced Placement version, is that it involves students in both the substantive (facts and theories) and syntactical (methods of inquiry) dimensions of the disciplines (Schwab, 1964). At the same time, such engagement prepares them for the reasoned argumentation of democratic living.

Fortunately, some resources are readily available that help teachers and curriculum leaders decide which issues are appropriate for study and then lay out several alternatives for students to consider. Two of the best low-cost resources for the high school social studies classroom, especially history and government courses, are published by the National Issues Forum and by Choices for the 21st Century.[3] Each organization produces a series of booklets with background information on a pressing problem (contemporary or historical) and three to four policy alternatives. Both engage students in the kind of deliberation that develops their understanding of one another, the array of alternatives, the problem itself, and its historical context.

The authors of these materials have developed the policy alternatives. Consequently, students are given (and don't have to generate themselves) grist for the analytic mill. Students can evaluate the authors' diagnosis of the problem and judge their representation of stakeholders on the issue. Then they can deliberate about the options presented. The provision of alternatives by the authors scaffolds the task in a helpful way, modeling for students what an array of alternatives looks like and allowing them to work at understanding them and listening to one another. After such experiences, students are ready to have the scaffold removed, investigate an issue of their own choosing, and create their own briefing booklet.

THE THREE Rs?

I would like to see a national campaign against idiocy, and I believe schools are ideal sites for it. Put differently, schools are fitting places to lead young people through puberty and into citizenship. Schools are the sites of choice because they have, to some extent, the two most important resources for this work: diversity and problems.

I realize that this view is apt to be too optimistic for some readers. After all, schools are products of society and are embedded in it. They are not autonomous places where massive social forces can be stopped with a lesson plan. Still, schools are not insignificant sources of social progress. At some level, everyone seems to believe this. It is the reason that curriculum debates are often the most impassioned to be found anywhere in society. My view is that the three R's—mechanically treated and tested with puritanical fervor—are not sufficient for the realization of democratic ideals. A proper curriculum for democracy requires both the study and practice of democracy.

TOWARD DEEPER CIVIC LEARNING

Part II of the book delves further into curriculum and instruction and aims for deeper civic learning. This entails a curriculum that is centered on powerful concepts rather than rote memory of disparate facts (Chapter 4), especially in the one civics course taken by nearly every student in the United States (Chapter 5), and engaging students in productive face-to-face discussions (Chapter 6). Finally, I reflect on two meanings of justice—just individuals and just societies (Chapter 7). As in Part I, classroom discussion is the featured pedagogy. There are two reasons for this: First, discussion is collective inquiry; several viewpoints are set alongside one another so that our own view of things is challenged by those of others. This deepens learning. Second, strategic content selection focuses the discussion on a course's most important subject matter, its central objectives, thus making discussion the main course rather than a side dish.

Discussion pedagogy has its critics. Whether *deliberation*, the kind of discussion featured in Chapters 2 and 3 and again in Chapter 5, or *seminar*, which will be introduced as deliberation's necessary partner in Chapter 6, these dialogue-based instructional models have drawn criticism from both the right and left. From the right comes skepticism for instructional models that take time from curriculum coverage and direct instruction by the teacher. Discussion is seen as a time-wasting diversion where students express and debate opinions rather than learning facts on which to base them. In this way, it "can become a major distraction from teaching the substance of history and related subject matter" (Rochester, 2005, p. 654). From the left comes a different concern—that discussion is yet another form of domination, another arena in which entrenched inequalities proceed as usual. As numerous feminist scholars have shown (e.g., Sanders, 1997), the issues that are selected for discussion and the group dynamics that occur during their consideration can reinforce rather than disrupt relations of domination and acquiescence. Some critics from the left have become so discouraged about the pedagogical potential of discussion that they want to abandon it altogether.

Summarizing, the right says *don't* go there; it's a waste of time. The left says you *can't* go there; it's a charade. Both views can be helpful if treated as cautionary tales. The right reminds us that subject matter (content) must be a primary concern. Fortunately, deliberation and seminar are not vacuous bull sessions; quite the opposite, they are structured to be content-intensive. The principal task in planning classroom discussion is choosing the most important and generative disciplinary questions, concepts, and texts. The left's criticism will remind teachers to exercise judgment—to be judicious about the questions chosen for discussion, proactive about potential student discomfort, and strategic in the use of instructional supports so that discussions are rigorous, caring, and productive.

Some questions are not appropriate for classroom discussion, of course. But that's no reason to abandon it, particularly when it's in such short supply already. Abandonment would only perpetuate current classroom habits: teachers talking too much, students talking too little, and, overall, the loss of a rich, "thinking curriculum" (Resnick & Klopfer, 1989).

CHAPTER 4

Concept Development

In Chapter 2, we saw that concepts are the mainspring of a powerful school curriculum and any rigorous approach to teaching controversial issues. But what are concepts, why are they key to deeper learning, and how are they taught and learned? These questions are the focus of this brief chapter. Concepts are ideas. They exist in the head, not in the world. But, crucially, they organize what is in the world. Consider the concepts race, equality, island, mesa, chair, monarchy, *and* liberal democracy. *Each is a category that holds multiple, concrete examples. Some concepts, like* island *and* chair *are well-defined; there is agreement on their meaning. Others like* race *and* equality *are disputed. Either way, concepts furnish the mind, and they travel: When students learn powerful concepts, their understanding of the world expands and they can tackle novel problems more knowledgably.*

"Whoa! Pluto's dead," said an astronomer at the California Institute of Technology in Pasadena. He was watching a webcast of the vote. "There are finally, officially, eight planets in the solar system" (Inman, 2006). The vote had been taken at an August 2006 meeting of the International Astronomical Union (IAU) in Prague, the scientific group that decides such things. What happened? Had the concept of *planet* changed so that poor Pluto was no longer a member of that category? Or had something about Pluto changed so that it no longer fit the definition?

It was a little of both. Since Pluto was discovered in 1930, causing subsequent generations to memorize the Sun's planets in terms of their nine-ness, more and more has been learned about Pluto—its shockingly small size, for example (smaller even than Earth's moon), and its own shockingly large moon, Charon, at half the size of Pluto. This new knowledge caused questions to be raised about Pluto's membership in the category *planet* by the end of the 20th century. But in 2006 the astronomers came at it from the other direction, too. The IAU remodeled the definition of *planet* such that Pluto could no longer be included unless its moon also counted as a planet, placing the planetary number at 10 and opening the cosmic door to many more "dwarf planets," as they are now called. Not only was Pluto too small relative to its moon, the IAU said, but it did not dominate its neighborhood—its orbital region in the solar system—in another key way: From here on out (or until the concept's attributes are again revised), planets must have clear orbits that are swept clean of other astronomical bits and pieces thanks to the planet's own superior force. Pluto's orbit is anything but swept clean.

In sum, Pluto used to be a planet; that is, it used to be classified as a member of the category or class called "planet." But it is no longer. Not only did Pluto itself change, so to speak, as scientists' knowledge of it grew, but the critical attributes of the concept *planet* were revised, too. The new definition, says astrophysicist Alan Boss of the Carnegie Institution, "is much more scientifically palatable" (Inman, 2006). Consequently, Pluto has gone from being an example of *planet* to being a "nonexample" because it lacks some (not all) key attributes that examples of the concept must possess.

TEACHING AND LEARNING CONCEPTS

What the case of Pluto illustrates for us about social studies teaching and learning is twofold. First, concepts, whether *planet, peninsula, terrorism,* or *democracy,* are social constructs. That is, they are constructed—made by humans, not found in nature. Second, concepts change. Fundamentally, concepts are social agreements, and these change as human thinking about the world changes. They change also as power relations in societies shift and realign. Here is the classic example: During Galileo's time, early in the 17th century, priests were deciding what was what, as they had for centuries. They had the authority and the power to back it up. The clergy based their decisions on church doctrine, not on observations and experiments. Accordingly, when Galileo wrote that he observed through his new telescope that Earth's moon was not perfectly round and smooth but had mountains and valleys, and that he agreed with Copernicus that the planets were moving while the sun stood still, he was brought before the Inquisition, tried for heresy, and forced to recant. Now, however, 4 centuries after the "scientific revolution," the IAU, not the Pope, decides on Pluto. It really was a revolution. The whole edifice of knowledge and knowing changed.

Understanding that *concepts are constructs* has inspired generations of new and old teachers alike to help their students construct them by their own intellectual labor. *Concept formation* is the classic strategy made famous by venerated Estonian American curriculum scholar Hilda Taba et al. (1971). This strategy has students build a concept inductively by noting the similarities across a handful of carefully selected examples. (There it is, that's the strategy in a nutshell.) Their teacher selects examples that display the variation possible within the concept, but each example has all the critical attributes required by the concept's definition. Students form (construct, build) the concept when they identify these common attributes. This is *concept formation*. Let's turn to its partner, *classifying*.

CLASSIFYING

Classifying is the method by which students apply, test, and refine the concept they have formed, and by this method deepen their understanding. Classifying is needed when students encounter a task where they must decide whether a new case is an example or not. Does the new case fit the definition? That is the question. Students must recall the critical attributes of the concept and determine whether those attributes are present in the new case.

The new case is bound to be different in some ways—large or small—from the examples studied initially when the concept was formed. Accordingly, students need to examine the differences *and decide if any of them matters as far as that concept's critical attributes are concerned.* That decision-making process is called classifying. In Pluto's case, a celestial body that once fit the definition of *planet* no longer did. The reason was that Pluto changed (well, not really, but scientists' ability to observe it changed), making it no longer fit the critical attributes. Also, the critical attributes of the concept were modified at a meeting of the group of scientists that is in charge of specifying them.

There are four kinds of classifying, and teachers of students of every age and circumstance are wise to know and be able to use them all. There are subtle differences among the four in the thinking they require of students. Note how the cognitive demand shifts slightly from one to the next.

1. Deciding whether a new item is an example (The teacher asks, "Is this an example of [the concept]?")
2. Distinguishing examples from nonexamples ("Which of these is an example of [the concept]?")
3. Producing examples ("Find or create an example of [the concept].")
4. Correcting nonexamples ("What changes are needed to make this an example of [the concept]?")

The four types of classifying can be used both before and after concept formation. Teachers use them *before* concept formation for the purpose of diagnostic assessment; that is, determining the extent to which students have already formed and can apply a particular concept. A 4th-grade teacher may be thinking that a class needs a concept formation lesson on *peninsula.* But she first assesses their understanding of the concept. She decides to use the first type of classifying. Pointing to Florida on the wall map of the United States, she says, "I'm curious. Who can tell us whether this piece of land here in the state of Florida is a *peninsula*? Put a thumb up if you think it is, a thumb down if you think it isn't, and a thumb sideways if you don't know or aren't sure." In a class of 25, the teacher sees two thumbs up, two down, and 21 sideways.

She then elicits their reasons. Without hearing the reasons, she has learned nothing much. "Those of you with your thumbs sideways, why?" Some say they've never heard the word before. Another thinks a peninsula "is more like a lake." And so forth. The two thumbs up actually don't know the concept, it turns out. They're claiming Florida is a peninsula, but for all the wrong reasons. The two thumbs down think it is not a peninsula, but their reasons reveal they haven't thought carefully about the concept either. Hence, the teacher decides to work up a concept formation lesson. Thinking about a good set of examples, she chooses Florida, the Yucatán, Iberia, and the Malay peninsula.

When classifying is used *after* instruction on a concept, it is for the purpose of deepening students' understanding of the concept by providing them the opportunity to *use* it—to apply it to new cases. Of course, if students haven't formed the concept, they will be unable to apply it. Noticing this, the teacher will determine that their understanding of the concept is too weak to simply move on to the next topic; hopefully, the teacher will provide more classifying practice or reteach the concept.

Let's consider a second example. A 5th-grade class will be learning the concept *democracy*. It is one of the central concepts for understanding U.S. history, the common social studies subject matter of the 5th grade. Their teacher has diagnosed his students' preinstruction understanding of this idea by asking them a few simple diagnostic questions:

What is democracy? (asking for the critical attributes of the concept)
Is the United States a democracy? Why? (classifying type 1)
Can you think of another example of democracy? (classifying type 3)

In this way, this teacher learned that his students have little understanding of democracy save naïve notions of voting and elections. Accordingly, he plans an introductory concept formation lesson.

First, he assembles three or four examples of democracy that will be the building blocks of the concept. He decides to use the governments of the United States, Mexico, and Canada because the textbook has information on them readily available. For the fourth example, he wants something less bookish, more experiential. He selects the democratic classroom meeting his students have each Monday morning.

Using the concept-formation strategy, students will build an understanding of democracy from the bottom up (inductively) by studying each example, comparing and contrasting them, and then summarizing how they are alike. The similarities among examples are the critical attributes of the concept (they are the things that make these examples of the same concept). The critical attributes common to the United States, Mexico, Canada, and their classroom meetings are these: the majority rules (laws are made by all citizens or their representatives), minority rights are protected, and laws are written down. These are the three attributes students eventually should summarize under the name *democracy*. Is the resulting concept as complex as the one formed by college political science majors? Of course not, but it would be an achievement for 5th-graders. Do students understand that these attributes are ideals rather than realities? Probably not yet, but they now have a foundation on which they can begin to draw that distinction.

SOME EXAMPLES

There are loads of opportunities for concept formation and classifying in social studies classrooms. Concepts are ideas that may deal with concrete places, persons, objects, or events (like *planet* and *peninsula*) or with less concrete/more abstract ways of thinking, feeling, and behaving (like *democracy, imperialism,* and *justice*). Here are several more concepts and some examples of each that would be appropriate for study in, say, the 3rd and 4th grades.

Justice (fairness)

Taking turns
Writing and publishing rules
Applying rules equally to everyone

Island

Kauai
Cuba
Singapore
Sri Lanka

Technology

Steamboat
Pony Express
Airplane
Computer chip

Community

Mesa Verde
Washington, DC
Cairo
Selma, Alabama

Public Issue

Should citizens be required to vote?
Should zoos be banned?
Do we need a new rule that says, You Can't Say You Can't Play?

Migration

Oregon Trail
Ellis Island immigration station
The Great Migration
Angel Island immigration station

Holiday

Cinco de Mayo
Thanksgiving
Veterans Day
New Year's Day

In high school, concepts such as *imperialism, democracy, revolution, poverty, terrorism, nationalism, race, religion, capitalism, racism, federalism, colonialism, globalization,* and *civil war* need to be taught and learned. And, crucially, so do the concepts central to reasoning: *inquiry, evidence, argument,* and *thesis.* These are hefty concepts, but probably no more so for the teenager than *island* and *community* are for the 8-year-old. And the templates for teaching and learning them—concept formation and classifying—are more or less the same. When the final unit of a year-long U.S. history course has students develop a thesis on the question, "Why are only some social movements successful?" they are prompted to revisit the social movements they have studied across the course (examples could be U.S. independence from England, woman's suffrage, abolition, labor unions, the Civil Rights Movement) and to apply and, if necessary, revise their understanding of a central concept in history, *social movement.* The same is true when the government teacher asks, "How democratic is the U.S. Constitution?" Here, their understanding of *democracy* is at issue, and the U.S. Constitution is the case to which they are applying it.

CONCLUSION

Is Pluto a planet? Is Florida a peninsula? Is the United States a democracy? Teachers who understand what concepts *are* can better keep their eyes on the prize: centering their teaching on deep and enduring conceptual learning rather than superficial coverage of a string of facts and events. A curriculum centered on ideas has generative power. Ideas are mental tools: they are portable and consequential. Not only do we take them with us wherever we go, but we use them to make sense of what's happening and to decide when and how to take action. As Pluto's fate reveals, making and remodeling concepts is a key social and scientific activity, always relevant. Helping students build them inside their own heads is at the core of a teacher's work. For this reason, teachers, even new teachers—if they wish to be examples of the concept *teacher*—need to have a thorough understanding of concepts and how to teach them.

CHAPTER 5

Reinventing the High School Government Course

The high school government course is the principal site of formal civic education in the United States today. Most students take it just before or after their final course in U.S. history, a good sequence. If they are seniors and citizens of this country, they become eligible to vote while taking this course. With colleagues at the University of Washington, the George Lucas Educational Foundation, and teachers and school leaders in several school systems, I conducted a multi-ear research-and-development study aimed at renewing this course. We created a model that students found engaging and challenging. The first section of the chapter introduces the course, the second describes the research and design principles, the third describes the political simulations that are the spine of the course, and the fourth examines design issues that emerged across the years: the importance of identifying core concepts and skills and the struggle to help students read, that is, to learn from texts.

The U.S. government course is a staple in the American high school curriculum. Most high schools offer it, and most graduates took it in one form or another (National Center for Education Statistics, 2009). Consequently, the course—in terms of institutional investment and student enrollment—is arguably the main site of formal civic education in the country. This chapter presents the final, or 2.0, curriculum of a multiyear research and development initiative aimed at innovating this course. My team's pedagogic approach centers on a rigorous form of project-based learning (PBL) in which each project is a weeks-long political simulation. Political simulations are among the "six promising approaches" to civic education identified by a recent consensus panel (Campaign for the Civic Mission of Schools and the Leonore Annenberg Institute for Civics, 2011, p. 6); however, they are unequally distributed to students based on their racial and socioeconomic characteristics (Kahne & Middaugh, 2008). The curriculum presented here was implemented in both well-resourced suburban and poorly resourced, poverty-impacted urban public schools. It includes instructional supports that increase the likelihood of success for the range of students who now enroll.[1]

This chapter is addressed to high school government teachers as well as to civic educators more broadly, including curriculum developers in district and state offices and in civic education organizations. My goal is to present this curriculum and pedagogy along with my reflections on both, so that readers may adapt them, if they wish, to their own efforts to renew the government course and other high school social studies courses.

The team chose to work with the advanced placement version of the course, called AP U.S. Government and Politics (APGOV). We had several reasons. First, it is a popular AP course. It ranks fourth or fifth in annual enrollment of the nearly 40 AP courses offered. Since the late 1990s, the number of students taking it has increased rapidly, now standing at around a quarter million (College Entrance Examination Board, 2014). Second, and contributing to the increase, AP is being "democratized" (Lacey, 2010, p. 34); that is, the demographic profile of participating students is changing rapidly. This is due to a number of factors, including a deliberate expansion effort by the Department of Education in cooperation with the College Entrance Examination Board (College Board), the association that creates and administers AP tests and courses (see Wakelyn, 2009). Recently, an "excellence for all" trend has brought advocates of school tracking alongside advocates of detracking, making bedfellows of two groups of school reformers that traditionally pursued different goals: social efficiency on the one hand and social justice on the other (see perceptive accounts of the trend by Schneider, 2011, and Labaree, 2010). The effect of this union is to give many more students access to AP courses, which both groups have championed as the "gold standard" (e.g., Mathews, 2009) of the American high school curriculum. As more students, including historically underserved students, enroll in APGOV, *our* aim is to improve its quality.

A third reason for choosing to work with the AP version of the course is that it affords the opportunity to test our pedagogical approach on a most challenging platform. As the saying goes, "If you can innovate here, you can innovate anywhere." This is due to the daunting structural constraints that come with AP: a very large topical array; a breadth-oriented, high-stakes summative test; and the test-prep pedagogy for which AP courses are generally known.

Our initiative had five goals: (1) to improve the authenticity or real-world value of the course, (2) to increase student engagement in the course, (3) to improve the "meaningfulness" of student learning while (4) achieving same or better pass rates on the AP test as students in traditional APGOV classrooms, and, finally, we (5) wanted the increasing number of students now enrolling in APGOV not only to enter but to succeed in the course—both to learn and to enjoy.

In the next section, we describe our research and the design principles by which the course was developed. Following that are descriptions of the five political simulations that became the heart of the course, plus their constituent tasks and a note on the organization of the curriculum. The final section discusses key implementation issues that have arisen across the years—key because these issues are fertile and unlock a range of further issues. They are linked to the design principles described in the first section and concern (1) the centrality of simulations, (2) content selection, and (3) helping students learn from texts.

METHOD AND DESIGN PRINCIPLES

We employed a research-and-development methodology called design-based implementation research (DBIR). DBIR is, by definition, concerned with problems of practice. Its primary goal is to improve practice. Its secondary goal is theory building, which includes problem redefinition as the work proceeds and the refinement of central categories—the three design principles presented below plus learning from text, which is developed in the discussion section. The seminal work on DBIR was done by Brown (1992) and has been refined since by Penuel, Fishman, and others (e.g., Penuel et al., 2011). Brown argued that classroom innovations should be developed collaboratively by teachers, researchers, and school leaders; Penuel and his colleagues underscored this point and clarified that DBIR is committed to "using research to solve practical problems" (Penuel et al., 2011). This requires the research to be plainly and directly "practice centered" (Penuel et al., 2011, p. 332). Accordingly, we designed an innovation and then iteratively implemented, tested, and refined it in classrooms. We did this across three school districts in the years 2007–2014.

Our team was a multidisciplinary group of learning and curriculum researchers, APGOV teachers, political scientists, and social studies curriculum coordinators. Our teacher collaborators became designers and curriculum makers working with others on the team to create and implement a PBL-APGOV curriculum and then to gather data on the implementation and to revise the curriculum annually. The revisions were aimed at solving problems as they emerged and improving the next implementation. This iterative design-implement-revise process, grounded in actual problems of practice, is the essence of DBIR.

We began in a relatively well-resourced suburb with a robust AP culture, an expressed interest in PBL, and the institutional stability to accommodate the upheavals of innovation. It was, in a word, a "greenhouse." The superintendent was a forceful instructional leader; professional development was thoughtful and routine; teachers were respected and held to high professional standards; and there was a social studies curriculum coordinator—a mid-level manager who could liaison with other mid-level managers (e.g., the AP director) as well as teachers and building principals. Also, because the district was at the forefront of efforts to democratize AP courses, we could situate our work in schools that had a high number of AP newcomers mixed in with students who were AP "veterans."

Then, in the third year of implementation, we extended the DBIR to two poverty-impacted urban school districts. Both were democratizing AP, but both faced the difficulties common to underresourced city schools (Rothstein, 2004). Now, we were attempting to innovate within not only the constraints of AP but also the constraints of school systems that were facing the hardships of urban poverty and the particular stresses of urban school politics (e.g., the testing regime, the discourse of "failing schools," overburdened building principals). Table 5.1 summarizes the 7-year DBIR process.

Results have been detailed elsewhere (Parker et al., 2011, 2013). Generally, students in the PBL-APGOV course did as well or better on the AP test than students in comparison groups, and students found the course and projects personally meaningful. End-of-course statements such as these are common from students: "I've been exposed to all these new things that I've never heard of before, or hadn't understood exactly . . . As I've said before, my parents aren't very big with politics. So, I am interested a lot more now in political issues." And "It has made me more aware of where our money goes, who makes the rules, the decisions, and how things actually work."

Rather than explore these results in this chapter, we want to describe the course itself, the projects, and the emerging issues. Accordingly, we turn now to the design principles that guided our initial course development as well as the annual revisions. The first was suggested by our teacher collaborators, who had some familiarity and experience with PBL and political simulations (e.g., moot court, mock election). The second and third were derived in team deliberations during the planning year from the learning research of our teammate John Bransford (e.g., Bransford et al., 2000). The three principles are (1) rigorous projects as the spine of the course; (2)

Table 5.1. Research and Development Across 7 Years

School year	District type	Districts/schools/teachers	Version
2007–08	Planning sessions	1/2/4	
2008–09	Suburban greenhouse	1/2/4	1.0
2009–10	Suburban greenhouse	1/2/3	1.1
2010–11	+ Poverty-impacted urban #1	2/3/3	1.2
2011–12	+ Poverty-impacted urban #2	3/8/8	1.3
2012–13	+ Poverty-impacted urban #1 & 2	3/6/6	1.4
2013–14	+ Poverty-impacted urban #1 & 2	3/7/7	2.0

quasi-repetitive project cycles, where projects build on one another cumulatively; and (3) engagement that creates a need to know. We elaborate on each below. The issues that we address in the discussion stem from them as well. The first principle is the basis for next two.

Rigorous PBL

In the opening paragraph, we used the term *rigorous* to describe our approach to PBL. Because *rigor* has become a buzzword, we must clarify our usage. In our model, which we call Knowledge in Action, rigorous PBL has four characteristics. First, projects carry the full subject-matter load of the course. They are not culminating activities that come at the end of an instructional sequence, nor lively interludes inserted periodically into traditional recitation. Rather, projects encompass and fuel teaching and learning throughout the course. Projects are central, not peripheral; they are "the main course, not dessert" (Larmer & Mergendoller, 2010).

A second attribute of rigorous PBL is that the projects are "authentic," by which we mean they are related clearly to life outside school—to politics and governance in the United States. Therefore, they invite the kind of "authentic intellectual work" that is both complex and personally meaningful (King et al., 2009). Wright-Maley (2015) referred to a simulation's authenticity as verisimilitude, related to *veridical* or *veritas*—truthful. This is a critical attribute of simulations, for there is the expectation that a simulation will simulate (accurately represent) some aspect of reality, although in a simplified way. As Myers (1999) explained, this is the attribute that links simulations to children's imitative play.

A third attribute is the specification of meaningful learning as a goal. This is typical of PBL (Larmer & Mergendoller, 2010; Ravitz, 2009), but it is in contrast to the superficial learning for the test that is often associated with AP courses. A National Research Council study (2002), for example, found that "the inclusion of too much accelerated content can prevent students from achieving the primary goal of advanced study: deep conceptual understanding of the content and unifying concepts of a discipline" (p. 1). A focus on meaningful learning means more than a great many topics covered quickly and then followed by a high-stakes test—a default definition of rigor that we call "breadth-speed-test" (Parker et al., 2013). Furthermore, a focus on meaningful learning goes beyond authenticity. Meaningful learning also is, we specify, deep and adaptive learning. The chief characteristic of deep knowledge is that it is differentiated; students understand a concept through multiple examples or cases. For example, *federalism* is a core concept in U.S. government and politics. To understand it deeply is to know different examples of the concept at work—in the debates over health care policy today, the battle over slavery in the mid-19th century, or the Jefferson-Hamilton debate over the legitimacy of a central bank during the founding period—and to know what the various examples have in common. Closely related to deep knowledge, adaptive learning is the kind of learning that supports additional learning in the future. Adaptive learning refers to knowledge that is applicable or actionable or, as educational psychologists prefer to say, "transferable" to situations encountered later despite the fact that future scenarios will differ from the ones first encountered. The multiple examples already in the learner's mind allow additional examples to be graspable, despite their novelty. (We base this meaningfulness criterion, including transfer, on Bransford's research on cyclical learning [Bransford et al., 2000, 2006] as well as Taba's [1962] and Bruner's [1979] seminal work on concept development.)

A fourth attribute of rigorous PBL is an appropriate assessment that serves as an external, summative measure of student achievement. In our case, this is the APGOV test. It is written not by members of our research team but by a committee of political scientists who teach the entry-level college course. These professors work with assessment experts from the College Board. As in any AP course, this test looms over the course, galvanizing the attention of teachers, students, and a small industry that produces texts, flash cards, and test-prep guides. The standard for the course and test is that they match what students get in the corresponding college course. This is what gives AP its name: Students who pass the test may be placed in the subsequent course at college without having to take the introductory course. They "place out of it," as the saying goes.

We believe these criteria together make a rigorous form of PBL. Projects do the course's heavy lifting. The resulting student learning has real-world applicability as well as complexity and flexibility. And student achievement in the course is assessed by a challenging, external measure. These criteria could be designed into non-AP courses, but as we said, the AP platform already exists, enjoys a positive reputation among numerous constituencies, and is in need of pedagogic innovation if it is to express a conception of rigor that goes beyond breadth-speed-test.[2]

Looping for Depth

The chief practical problem we faced was how to achieve deep, adaptive learning in a course notorious for broad scope—many, many topics stuffed into a small space. The situation easily sponsors test-prep pedagogy (rushed "coverage") and, consequently, superficial learning. Using popular phrases, it can descend into a "pancake course" that is "a mile wide and an inch deep." One experienced APGOV teacher quipped that all a teacher can do is "duck and cover." The course description published by the College Board lists six topics, with the percentages of multiple-choice questions devoted to each on the AP test:

1. Constitutional underpinnings (5–15%)
2. Political beliefs and behaviors (10–20%)
3. Political parties, interest groups, and mass media (10–20%)
4. Institutions of national government: Congress, presidency, bureaucracy, federal courts (35–45%)
5. Public policy (5–15%)
6. Civil rights and civil liberties (5–15%)

In contrast, meaningful learning requires that a limited set of generative ideas and skills is selected for study and that these are studied, used, and refined through multiple examples and scenarios. Meaningful learning also requires a kind of instruction that allows for cyclical repetition or spiraling (Bransford et al., 2000, 2006; Brown, 1992; Bruner, 1979; Taba, 1962). This entails revisiting ideas and skills in different contexts in order to know them differently, comparatively, deeply. Our collaborating teachers named this "looping." Deep learning, then, necessitates curricular decisions about which ideas and skills are worthy of cyclical treatment but also an instructional procedure that permits this quasi-repetition without sacrificing pass rates on the test. Deliberative content selection addresses the what of meaningful learning while looping addresses the how (see Parker & Lo, 2016a). Working together on this problem, deliberating across multiple meetings and years, our team eventually concluded that five concepts should be looped throughout the projects:

1. Limited government
2. Separation of powers (federalism, three branches, checks and balances)
3. Constitutionalism (rule of law, precedent)
4. Civil rights and liberties
5. Institutions linking citizens to government (elections, interest groups, political parties, media)

In the projects and their component tasks, students return to these ideas, but in different ways and settings, in order to build differentiated understandings while having multiple opportunities to apply or try them out in diverse scenarios. This is our approach to achieving deeper knowledge.

An example of looping content within and between project cycles is the recurrent instruction on federalism throughout the course. Federalism is the separation (and often sharing) of powers among levels of government. The concept is notoriously difficult for high school students. Many of them recognize government and politics only at the national level (the president, Congress, the army), and the problem is compounded by the homonymic nature of the word *federal*: It signifies one of the levels of government (national) but also a form of government consisting of multiple levels of government that divide and share power (national, state). To help students develop the concept, it is featured early in the first project cycle, "Founders' Intent." Students take roles as delegates to the Constitutional Convention of 1787— men who held federalist or antifederalist sentiments. Accordingly, the idea is constructed experientially (students interacting in roles) and on the basis of a contrast (always a useful aid to concept development). Students then deliberate controversial policy issues in these roles. The first is the historic Jefferson–Hamilton debate: Is the national government authorized to create a bank? Next is a contemporary issue: Should states be allowed to legalize marijuana use when it is prohibited by the federal government? Should the federal Supreme Court be able to overrule local governments whose voters want to ban same-sex marriage?

To loop federalism between, in addition to within, project cycles, the curriculum has students revisit the concept in other simulations. In "Elections," students in various roles interrogate or advocate the platforms of the two major political parties, with Republicans generally promoting states' rights and Democrats generally supporting national policies. Federalism is looped again in "SCOTUS," when students, as lawyers or justices, argue states-rights cases, and again in the final project cycle, "Government in Action," when students, now as political consultants, decide which level of government their client—an interest group—should approach to achieve its policy goals.

Besides determining which substantive content to loop, we needed to determine which skills or "syntax" (Schwab, 1964) to loop. Using the same deliberative process, the team eventually decided on five skills for looping:

1. Constitutional reasoning (reasoning about policy on the basis of the Constitution)
2. Deliberation (discussion to decide among alternatives)
3. Perspective-taking (e.g., trying on diverse political ideologies and social positions)
4. Political autonomy (making uncoerced decisions, e.g., consenting to be governed, voting for candidate X)
5. Close, interpretive reading of core texts (e.g., Constitution, *Federalist 10*)

The first skill, constitutional reasoning, dominates the others. It is the kind of reasoning needed for arguing about public policy in any role, both in this course and in U.S. political life. The research team observed that when students were arguing from their assigned roles in the simulations (e.g., as a congressperson favoring *x* policy or a judge favoring *y* interpretation of the law), they often relied on their personal values rather than knowledge of the Constitution and the roles to which they had been assigned. This was true especially of students who entered the course with paltry knowledge of the Constitution and law, but youth generally are more familiar with their own preferences, experiences, and opinions than they are with the jurisprudential framework of the nation (Flanagan, 2013). Accordingly, they were inclined to perform their roles from a personal stance rather than the stance of the roles they were playing or knowledge of the Constitution. Observing this, teachers began to deliberately frame the distinction, explaining this law-related form of reasoning and coaching students in its use.

In order to build greater potential for deep learning into the structure of the course, the five simulations revisit a single master course question (MCQ): "What is the proper role of government in a democracy?" Students are introduced to the MCQ at the beginning of the course. As they proceed through the projects, they loop back on the question and try to generate stronger, progressively more-knowledgeable responses. We understand this approach as inquiry-based learning, but of a sort that is stretched through the entire course. The course doesn't contain inquiries so much as it is an extended inquiry on this question. By unifying the projects, the MCQ gives the course just one overarching focus. Furthermore, the MCQ is authentic. It animates not only the founding era but today's party platforms and congressional stalemates. The researchers and teachers settled on the question in the first year of this DBIR, revised it after the first implementation year, and then returned to the original in the third.

Engagement First (Need-to-Know)

The third design principle is engagement first. Schwartz and Bransford (1998) explored *when* to use texts and lectures within the total repertoire of instructional methods. Their question was: At what point in an instructional sequence are they most effective? There was no doubt about the value of reading and listening to information and explanations—the question was how to optimize their value. Schwartz and Bransford concluded that there is an optimal readiness for learning from textbook readings or lectures after some understanding has been generated in other, more involving ways. They called this "a time for telling" (p. 475). Our third design principle, therefore, is that engagement in project work (e.g., being assigned to the role of a legislator with the task of forming and advancing a legislative agenda) should normally precede telling (e.g., an in-class lecture or assigned reading on how Congress works). The purpose of this sequencing is to create a need-to-know so that the information students gain from reading or listening is required to perform well in the role and to construct a deep and adaptive understanding. The telling has somewhere to go because there is already something going on. Students are already engaged in a drama where the information is needed; the telling explains or clarifies what is going on. "When telling occurs without readiness," Schwartz and Bransford wrote, "the primary recourse for students is to treat the new information as ends to be memorized rather than as tools to help them perceive and think" (p. 477). This is a powerful distinction.

Accordingly, this third design principle reverses an entrenched habit of schooling. This habit could be called "engagement later," where the experiential, interactive activity comes after new information has been presented. In its most basic form here, engagement first means that students are assigned to roles before they know enough to perform them well, which creates a need-to-know. Of course, this is not easy to pull off. As Brown (1992) wrote, it takes "clinical judgment" for a teacher to orchestrate this kind of instruction. "Successful teachers must engage continually in on-line diagnosis of student understanding" (p. 169).

A straightforward example of the engagement first principle is the Structured Academic Controversy (SAC) activities that are distributed throughout the course. These SACs are an adaptation of a cooperative learning structure developed by Johnson and Johnson (1985). A SAC provides students with two opposing courses of action on a controversial policy issue and has them argue for one or the other, but eventually learn both. At the beginning of the procedure, the teacher assigns students to four-person teams. Each team is divided into two pairs, and each pair is assigned to one side of the controversy, playing the role of advocates of that position. Each pair needs to study its position and reasoning, using material that has been gathered by the teacher, and prepares its argument for presentation to the opposing pair. Next, the teams reassemble for the presentations. Afterward, as a test of their listening and questioning, the pairs reverse perspectives, now giving the argument of the other pair until that pair is satisfied that the argument was grasped. Following this, the teams discuss the issue with the aim of coming to a consensus or a disagreement, whichever the case may be. A SAC appears in the first project on the earlier-mentioned national bank controversy of 1791. One pair presents the federalist argument put forward by Washington's Secretary of the Treasury Hamilton, while the other pair studies the antifederalist position put forward by Secretary of State Jefferson.

In our adaptation of SAC (see Chapter 2, this volume), there is an additional step. Our SACs not only use a pedagogical structure for engaging students in deliberation of controversial policy issues, they also are opportunities for students to develop political autonomy. SACs in this course emphasize a moment at the end of the procedure when students are asked to drop their roles and then share their own opinions on the issue. We call this a political autonomy moment (PAM). Thanks to engagement first, students' own views are informed by the competing views that have been presented and re-presented by the pairs and then deliberated in teams—students' horizons have been broadened in this way—after which they are given the opportunity to drop the roles and express their own, genuine views. It is in the contrast between the role-playing and the role-dropping that a PAM comes to life (see Lo, 2015: Lo & Parker, 2016).

To summarize, three design principles guided our initial course development and the annual revisions. Political simulations do the heavy lifting of the course; quasi-repetitive project cycles build on one another, cumulatively deepening students' understanding of core concepts and skills; and immediate engagement in simulations creates a need to learn new information.

CURRICULUM

We now turn to the projects and their component tasks. Please note the six embedded SACs. We end this section with a brief description of the curriculum guide.

Projects and Tasks

"Founders' Intent" (3 Weeks). The course opens with an introductory simulation, Founders' Intent. Students are introduced to role-playing and to the system of limited government and divided powers that the Constitution creates. Students are delegates to the Constitutional Convention. In these roles, they engage in three deliberations on controversial constitutional issues. First, and quickly (it is a review cycle for students who typically had U.S. history a year earlier), they decide whether to approve the Constitution, thereby animating the federalist and antifederalist arguments over the division of power between national and state governments. Second, still in these roles, but now in SAC teams, they deliberate a federalism controversy from the past (e.g., the national bank). Third, again in SAC teams, they deliberate a contemporary federalism controversy (e.g., federally mandated health care insurance). This last task loops back on federalism, now in a contemporary light, and introduces the role of political parties, which underscores their purpose: winning elections and gaining power. Students loop conceptually through federalism and textually through the Constitution and *Federalist 10*.

- Task 1: Ratification—As delegates to the Constitutional Convention of 1787, students debate its ratification.
- Task 2: Historical SAC—Students deliberate, in the same roles, a historical federalist/antifederalist debate (e.g., the National Bank of 1791).
- Task 3: Modern SAC—Students deliberate, in the same roles, a modern-day federalist/antifederalist debate (e.g., marriage, drug, health, immigration policy).

"Elections" (6 Weeks). This is a simulation of a presidential election and the second scenario in which students wrestle with the master course question, "What is the proper role of government in a democracy?" Students become

candidates, voters in swing states, journalists in media organizations, and leaders of interest groups and political parties. Through a series of tasks—from throwing hats in the ring to the general election—students learn about public opinion, political ideology, polls, campaign finance, and voter characteristics. They also learn the relationships among interest groups, political parties, and the media as they attempt to navigate and influence the campaign. After campaign platforms are presented, students vote to elect the next president of the United States.

- Task 1: Warming Up to the Race—Students play roles in a presidential primary election (includes SAC: Should voting be required?).
- Task 2: Navigating the Campaign Trail—Students begin the process of campaigning for the primary election.
- Task 3: Primary Election—Students vote on their primary candidates.
- Task 4: Gearing Up for the General Election—Students regroup to campaign for the general election (includes SAC: Should the Electoral College be abolished?).
- Task 5: General Election—Students finish the campaign and elect the next president of the United States.

"SCOTUS" (4 Weeks). Once the president is sworn in, students witness the impact of the election on the Supreme Court of the United States (SCOTUS), members of which are appointed by the president. In this simulation, students take roles in the judicial branch of government as attorneys and judges and specifically in appellate courts: circuit courts of appeals and then the Supreme Court. Students learn about and practice judicial argumentation and constitutional reasoning as they experience the way courts define and implement public policy, often dealing with issues of civil rights and liberties. Students also learn how judges and lawyers navigate the pressures of public opinion, media, and interest groups. Throughout the project, students experience the interdependence of the three branches, such as judicial review and the impact of the presidential election on appointments to the Supreme Court.

- Task 1 (optional): Trial Court—As jurors, judge, attorneys, etc., students conduct a mock trial (so as to learn the differences between trial and appellate courts).
- Task 2 (and optional Task 3): Moot Circuit Court—As lawyers and justices, students conduct one (or two conflicting) moot circuit courts on a landmark Supreme Court case.
- Task 3 (or 4): Moot Supreme Court—As lawyers and justices, students conduct a moot Supreme Court on a landmark Supreme Court case.

"Congress" (4 Weeks). The fourth project cycle is a simulation of Congress. Students are legislators and learn not only how a bill becomes a law but how politics influence public policy. In committee compromises and floor debates, students navigate political pressures—from constituencies, political parties, and interest groups—for and against particular legislation. This project loops back on the party platform promises that presidential candidates made in the "Elections" project and the bicameral system set up by the Constitution in "Founders' Intent."[3]

- Task 1: Constituency Research—Students take roles as members of Congress and research their constituency and legislative agendas (includes SAC: Should elected representatives be trustees or delegates?).
- Task 2: Write and Submit Bills—Students research and draft bills that would help their constituencies.
- Task 3: Committee Markup—Students work in committees to pass/block bills written by other members of Congress.
- Task 4: Floor Session—Students conduct a floor debate to pass bills that have made their way out of committee.

"Government in Action" (5 Weeks). In this culminating project, students are consultants to interest groups that have strong positions on immigration policy. Applying knowledge from the previous projects, students study their client's position and what makes the group a serious contender in the political arena. Their job is to draw up a wise political action plan that will help their client advance its agenda through the political system—through the branches of government and the bureaucratic agencies—thereby learning how interest groups work with government to create, implement, and evaluate public policies.

- Task 1: Meeting the Client—As consultants, students meet the interest group they will advise.
- Task 2: Prepare for a Press Conference—Students work to answer key questions about their client's policy agenda (includes SAC: Is the federal bureaucracy a boon or a threat to democracy?).
- Task 3: Litigation Techniques—Students use litigation (and the courts) to help influence public policy.
- Task 4: Presidential Influence—Students write a letter to the president that outlines a political action plan that will advance their client's agenda.
- Task 5: Congressional Testimony—Students testify persuasively to a Congressional committee on behalf of their client.
- Task 6: Political Action Plan—Students propose a comprehensive political action plan for their client's public policy agenda.

A Note About the Curriculum Guide

Our original teacher collaborators were advantaged by in-depth understandings of the content (e.g., federalism, branches, interest groups) and instructional strategies (e.g., role-playing, SAC). They had internalized these during the process of developing the curriculum and teaching the course. On the basis of this prior knowledge, they were able to implement the tasks within each project cycle reasonably well. As new teachers were brought into the DBIR, we learned that more assistance was needed—broadly in terms of the three design principles and narrowly in terms of conducting a SAC and managing group work. Consequently, we developed a 1-week professional development workshop along with a detailed procedures document for each project cycle. Our interest is not having teachers adopt our approach and carry it out faithfully; to the contrary, and respecting the professional judgment of teachers, we invite them to consider this approach and adapt it as needed.

The procedures documents for each simulation provide teachers with guides that frame the course for students; that is, they orient students to the course organization, the simulations, the engagement-first principle, and the relationships among tasks. Additionally, these documents provide the purposes and outlines of project activities, suggested materials, and need-to-know homework reading assignments. Still more detailed lesson plans are provided as well, but only for the first two projects. These are scaffolds that are then withdrawn from the next three projects as teachers devise their own supports. The goal of developing these daily plans was illustrative, to provide more explicit instructional guidance and classroom tools for teachers to use. Because this level of detail is dependent on resources (e.g., textbooks, supplemental texts), which are far from standard across schools and districts, these lesson plans simply illustrate that these kinds of daily plans need to be made locally.

DISCUSSION

Let us summarize and then highlight three issues. The curriculum is organized into five projects. Each is a political simulation that emulates real-world political processes. Since projects are the spine of the course, virtually all the information and skills students need for success in the course and on the AP test are embedded within the projects. Students take roles as political actors and consultants, and generally they are engaged in role activity before they encounter new information, so that the information is needed in order to play the role competently. The simulations are organized in such a way that students loop back on key concepts and skills as well as a master course question. Consequently, students have multiple opportunities to apply and refine them in various scenarios. This quasi-repetitive cycling is the mainspring of the course. Its goal is to help students achieve differentiated (complex, rather than simple) understandings of core concepts and skills and have multiple opportunities to try them out in action.

The aim of the curriculum is adaptive knowledge of U.S. government and politics. This is knowledge that is actionable in the future—transferable and applicable to novel contexts and problems. Another aim is to provide an engaging and successful learning experience for the wider array of students now being admitted to AP courses.

Issues

We now raise three practical issues that are related to the design principles. These should be useful to teachers, teacher educators, and curriculum developers who want to try this approach to the APGOV course or adapt aspects to other social studies courses, whether AP or not. Some teachers, we know, are teaching a one-semester rather than full-year government course and may want to select just a couple of projects and, perhaps, shorten them; others may be teaching a non-AP version of the course and will have more latitude to teach a curriculum not bounded by the AP test.

Rigorous PBL. Related to the first design principle is this question: Can PBL be done in the government course (and other high school social studies courses) without one or more of the four standards of rigorous PBL? That is, can projects sometimes be a side dish or dessert? Can the authenticity requirement be dropped or moderated? The meaningful learning requirement? The external assessment of student learning? We believe the first and fourth of these standards are negotiable but not the second and third. These two add real-world value to learning; furthermore, they assure that the knowledge and skills achieved are applicable and generative—that they support more learning later and in different contexts, such as college, work, and civic life.

Looping for Depth. Related to the second design principle is a crucial question: Which concepts and skills are loop-worthy? Looping is not an end in itself. Like PBL and the use of simulations, looping is a means to achieve other ends. The chief end is meaningful learning—knowledge that is personally and socially meaningful (authentic) but, in addition, differentiated and adaptive (deep). Restating the issue, which concepts and skills are worth learning to this extent, and how can educators go about identifying them? This is important because, in our judgment, quite a lot of PBL discourse suffers from a knowledge deficit. There is much agreement on the how—projects should be authentic and engaging, students should be active and collaborative, and there should be public audiences and products. But there is somewhat less concern for the substantive and syntactical content of projects: Project work should result in learning exactly what? Which understandings and skills should projects aim to teach deeply? Responding to this question takes educators to the heart of curriculum planning: content selection.

The issue is exacerbated in an AP course, where so much content selection has been done already by the College Board committee before a teacher even enters the scene. Nevertheless, teachers need to judge which of the many topics are central enough and generative enough to be worthy of iteration. These are the stars, so to speak, the gravitational centers around which other topics rotate like orbiting planets and moons. As shown earlier, our teachers returned to this issue across numerous meetings and, eventually, settled on the short lists of concepts and skills presented earlier (for elaboration on this process, see Parker & Lo, 2016).

Engagement First. Related to the third design principle is a three-part issue. First, how firm is the principle that students should be engaged in project activity *before* new content is taught, and second, what resources will students need in order to access that new content? A surprise for us was that the second part of this issue led to a third: Assuming that those resources are present and available (never a certainty in poverty-impacted urban schools), how can teachers and students be encouraged actually to *use* them for learning? This concern relates directly to our emphasis on rigor—on assuring that students learn powerful content and skills through PBL, not simply engage in interesting activities.

But first, how firm is the engagement-first principle? We believe it is best to treat it as a hard-and-fast rule, rarely to be broken. Routinely, students should be engaged experientially in an action arena in which new information is needed to explain and clarify what is going on. This way, students and teachers alike find themselves in a different modality of school learning based on the earlier-mentioned "time for telling" (Schwartz & Bransford, 1998) research. Students in the first year of this DBIR, especially the AP veterans, found this new modality frustrating (Parker et al., 2011). They reported that if they don't acquire new information before the activity, then "we don't know what we're doing." In end-of-course interviews that first year, we asked students to advise us on how the course components could best be sequenced for learning. Many preferred that the course stick to the traditional model to which they were accustomed: First introduce the new information in a PowerPoint lecture—"floaties," as they put it—so that the project activities can then proceed with less floundering in the deep end of the pool. We did not want to revert to this familiar routine of schooling because the new information, presented in a vacuum, would have nowhere to go except into a memory bank, undermining our goal of deep and adaptive learning. Nor did we want to ignore students' frustration. The engagement-first principle does *not* mean that students should be thrown into the deep end of the pool without floaties.

Because some amount of floundering and ambiguity is inherent in authentic intellectual work, we didn't want to reduce it entirely, but we did want to make PBL-APGOV more enjoyable and less frustrating for more students. Consequently, our teacher collaborators began to deliberately orient students to a different way of doing school. This was the framing referred to earlier. Of course, it was easier for teachers to do this in the second year, as they themselves were now familiar with the whole course. As a result, students at the end of year 2 reported greater comfort with the engagment-first design. They knew the needed information would come once the action was under way. For example, "I knew every time we started a project cycle what the basic layout of it would be . . . what we were going to be doing."

Now to the second and third parts of the issue. Resources containing the needed information were, indeed, present and available. Generally, this was the course textbook, teacher-prepared handouts, and various Internet resources. However, teachers assigned reading casually (e.g., "Read Edwards, chapter 3" was written on the board), and students mostly avoided it. This became an obstacle to achieving our goals, for it meant that resources other than the teacher were not being tapped, and students were not adequately learning needed information and concepts. Role performance suffered, looping for depth was undermined, and the full burden of information provision was borne by the teacher alone. This was especially problematic for the AP newcomers, who entered the course not only with less prior knowledge about government and politics than their AP-veteran classmates but also with dispositions toward reading and doing homework that required increased and explicit support from their teachers, not indifference or sympathetic workarounds.

Therefore, we assembled a small set of powerful yet practical strategies to support students in using and learning subject matter from texts. They are summarized in the following list (see Valencia & Parker, 2016). Each is based on the assumption that the particular ideas and information in the text to be read are actually needed for project activity and course success.

1. Teachers have read the text selection that is to be assigned, and they know what information it will convey and how that information is related to both the project activity and the AP test.
2. This allows them explicitly to state the purpose for the reading assignment when giving it. For example, "Read this to find out the meaning of the term *iron triangle*. Be ready to give multiple examples that show you understand it."
3. Information from the text is used subsequently in a project task. Literacy researchers (e.g., Valencia et al., 2014) have demonstrated

that text–task alignment is a boon to getting students both to do
and to comprehend assigned reading.
4. Underscoring the fact that learning from the text is actually
necessary, teachers do not cover the same material in a class lecture.

As a result of purposeful reading and its application, students can engage with the projects in more rigorous and substantive ways and perform
well on quizzes, too.

CONCLUSION

Bringing attention simultaneously to action-oriented learning through simulations and to learning from texts is unusual. These two concerns typically
occupy separate universes of educational research, practice, and innovation.
Adding rigor to the mix introduces yet a third dimension. It is important to
recognize that the three blended naturally in this work. We didn't force the
combination; it arose organically by "using research to solve practical problems," which required this DBIR initiative to be plainly and directly "practice centered" (Penuel et al., 2011, p. 332).

If we have succeeded at anything in these pages, it was to present a
map of a particular way of approaching the high school government course.
Certainly, "the map is not the territory" (Korzybski, 1958, p. 498). Still,
we hope to have presented a map that is readable and that indicates enough
of the territory that readers can adapt various aspects of the approach to
their own work, should they want to. The territory will not be unfamiliar
to most readers; political simulations, especially, are a long-standing feature
of government courses.

We know that there are other valuable and viable ways to improve the
quality of the high school government course, and we welcome them. We
admire, for example, the CityWorks curriculum of the Constitutional Rights
Foundation, Project Citizen of the Center for Civic Education, Street Law's
Landmark Cases, and Sandra Day O'Connor's *iCivics*. The importance of
the initiative presented here, we believe, is to show that a rigorous, authentic, and meaningful government course is possible even on a crowded, accelerated platform where the vast array of topics colludes with the high-stakes
test to produce, too often, a "pancake course" where the only apparent op-
tion is to "duck and cover." We worry that without innovation, this course
becomes merely a step on the college entrance credentials ladder rather than
a profound, adaptive civic learning experience.

By featuring political simulations as the spine of the course, including
the embedded SACs, we were able to enact three of the six promising practices (numbers 1, 2, and 6 below) identified by the Campaign for the Civic
Mission of Schools (2011):

1. Learning information about local, state, and national government
2. Opportunities to debate and discuss current events and other issues that matter to students
3. Service-learning opportunities
4. Participation in extracurricular activities
5. Opportunities for decision-making and governance experiences
6. Participation in simulations of civic processes

In this way, our initiative is linked not only to a reputable, external, deliberated measure of achievement (the AP test) but also to a set of reputable, external, deliberated standards for civic learning (the campaign's). Most important, because the "excellence for all" movement is detracking access to APGOV in many school systems, we are able to offer a version of the course that, in our judgment, is more worthy of the students now enrolling.

CHAPTER 6

Listening to Strangers

The literature on classroom discussion often shortchanges itself by treating discussion as only an instructional method. While discussion is an effective instructional means to curricular ends (teaching with discussion), the capable practice of discussion should also be a curriculum objective in its own right (teaching for discussion), the latter because listening and speaking to others about powerful ideas and public problems is crucial to the education of liberal democrats. This is civil discourse, where political argumentation flourishes and gets policies made. In this chapter, I distinguish two knowledge-and-voice approaches to classroom discussion: deliberation and seminar. We became familiar with the first of these in earlier chapters thanks mainly to SAC, a structured deliberative discussion model with tremendous utility. Seminars, as we shall see, are about interpreting a worthy text. They aim at deeper understanding of a problem rather than, as in SAC, a decision about what course of action to take. Together, deliberation and seminar make an ideal couple.

Citizens have powers. . . . Strangers are the best source.

—Danielle S. Allen

Eighth-grade students in a suburban Denver public middle school are reading Howard Fast's *April Morning*, a novel about the American Revolution and the early skirmish at Lexington. Beyond reading it, they are having a series of seminars on the book. In this one, they are comparing developmental passages: the coming-of-age of the book's young protagonist, 15-year-old Adam Cooper, and the coming-of-age of the young American nation. A disagreement emerges on the question of the transition from teenager to adult. Does that happen when teens rebel against their parents/England, or when they have to decide how to govern themselves following the struggle for independence—whether the United States's or their own? The argument is revealing. The discussants are the same age as Adam. They are growing, experiencing their own skirmishes, and more.

At another public school, a high school in downtown Denver, a different sort of argument is orchestrated. Students in grades 11 and 12 are discussing not a story, but a policy question facing the people of Colorado: Should physician-assisted suicide be legal? They have read a thick packet of background reports on the controversy and are holding their first discussion on the policy question before them: Not is physician-assisted suicide right or wrong, but should the practice be legal in Colorado for those who choose it? A good disagreement develops in this setting, too. The first student to speak doubts that doctors can be trusted with such a law. Won't they "kill off" people they don't like, she asks?

The literature on classroom discussion, with some exceptions, has not cared much about purpose. This may be due to its habitual treatment of classroom discussion as an instructional method—a means—thereby confining discussion's role to the strategic and instrumental. On this account, discussion is a lively method by which curriculum objectives such as literary interpretation, historical understanding, and mathematical problem-solving might be achieved. Although discussion does serve as a means to other ends (teaching *with* discussion), the capable practice of discussion can be considered a curriculum objective in its own right (teaching *for* discussion).

Considering the multiple purposes of classroom discussion, we can draw three distinctions. The first is the one just now introduced between discussion as an instructional strategy and as a curriculum objective (Parker & Hess, 2001). This distinction has us ask not only how discussion can enable the learning of other things, but also how the ability and disposition to discuss are themselves legitimate things to learn. The second is between two purposes, both political: discussion for the purpose of democratic enlightenment (knowing) and discussion for the purpose of democratic engagement (doing). Both are directly tied to public will formation and self-government (Parker, 2008). The third distinction is between two classroom discussion models: *seminar*, in which the purpose is democratic enlightenment, and *deliberation*, in which the purpose is democratic engagement. The middle-school discussion is a seminar, the high school discussion a deliberation. The two discursive forms in tandem can fertilize the mind and cultivate democratic political community—at least, this is their potential and what makes them interesting and worth the trouble (Parker, 2006).

Schooling and teaching contribute to political socialization, of course (Gutmann, 1999; Hahn, 1998). I argue here that classroom discussion contributes a particular kind of deliberate political socialization. This kind is democratically enlightening as well as politically engaging; it educates young people in the liberal arts of speaking and listening to other members of the democratic public—people with whom they may have little in common and whom they may not like but with whom, nonetheless, they are politically joined. This is the heterogeneous "we the people" who are citizens and comrades—not a species or an identity group, not *homo sapiens* or an *ethnos,* but a *demos.* This idea of civic partnership, introduced in ancient political theory and reconstructed in the 17th century by Hobbes, was then specified by Jefferson (1787/1954), who wrote that "the people themselves are [government's] only safe depositories" and, therefore, that "influence over government must be shared among all the people" (pp. 148–149). The upshot is that a society aspiring to political community of this kind needs an education system that inducts young people into a civic culture of speaking and listening to people they might not know or like, whose behavior and beliefs they may not warm to, with whom they may be unequally related due to histories of discrimination and servitude, and with whom they may have no occasion otherwise to be in discussion, or even in the same room, but with whom they must be involved in political discussions—governance—on the public's problems.

In this chapter, I concentrate on the democratic possibilities of classroom discussion itself. My thesis is that classroom seminars and deliberations can play a central role in an education that aims to prepare students for, and actually engages them in, what Danielle Allen (2004) called "talking to strangers." The key advantage that a program of classroom discussion affords, I will argue, is that these strangers are not confined to the imagination as they are when the *polis*—the entire self-determining political community or nation—is conjured; rather, they are, to a meaningful extent, right there onsite. The student body is bodily present (Miller-Lane, 2005). By "to a meaningful extent," I mean to signal the political and pedagogical possibilities of classroom discussion in actually existing schools that are, no doubt, unequal because of segregation by race and class. This chapter is situated, then, in a progressive discourse of what actually existing schools might accomplish as distinct from a resigned discourse of what they cannot.

My plan is to elaborate the two examples of classroom discussion introduced in the opening paragraphs, then to follow that with three sections in which I detail Allen's contribution, interpret seminar and deliberation in light of her work, and offer suggestions for listening to strangers within seminars and deliberations. In addition to Allen, I rely on Dewey and Habermas—not their differences, but their convergence around a communicative discourse theory of democratic citizenship.

SEMINAR AND DELIBERATION

There are 28 14- and 15-year-old students in the seminar on *April Morning*. They are seated in one large circle. Their teacher reviews some of the problems and progress made in the prior two seminars on this book and then reads from the chalkboard this seminar's opening question: How does Adam's coming of age compare to that of the nation? She reminds students of the five seminar "expectations" that have been established so far: Don't raise hands, listen to and build on one another's comments, invite others into the discussion, support opinions by referring to passages in the book, and tie what you know about the history of the Revolution to your interpretation of the book. Later, she reflects, "The seminar allows the opportunity for 30 individuals who have all prepared on the same essential questions to draw out deeper meaning in the text. When you have 30 minds working together, it works better than when you just have one" (Miller & Singleton, 1997, video marker 0.21). This teacher has worked with her students on seminar skills, procedures, and goals. Consequently, by this point, she can sit outside the circle and watch the students, the norms, and the opening question together do the work of seminar. Next is an excerpt at the point at which a disagreement arises over the coming-of-age question. At issue is whether rebellion or self-government marks the passage to adulthood:

Middle School 1 (Asian male): I don't think they became adults until actually after or near the end of the war because *then* they had to think of how they were going to govern themselves . . . since now they were out of Britain's rule and they didn't have a government clearly established yet, and they didn't know what they were going to do. They had to start thinking about their country.

MS2 (White female): (Agreeing) I think they really haven't become adult yet. They are working toward that and trying to think of better ways to fight. They're still rebelling against King George and the British. They won't ever become adult until they lay down the government of their country and stuff like that, later on, many years later.

MS3 (White female): (Disagreeing) But the fact that they *realized* that they were, that what the king was doing was wrong, was part of them becoming adults. Because they found out that they didn't like something, and they acted on it. So, I think that's part of becoming adult.

MS2: Well, I think that's *part* of becoming adult. But that's like what a teenager would do. If a teenager thought their curfew was too early, they would rebel against their parents. That's kind of what the country was doing. And then later on they'll become more mature and adultlike.

MS3: So you're saying that it's right in between?

MS2: Yeah, it's during the teenage years. (Miller & Singleton, 1997, 0.27–0.28)

This short excerpt reveals a disagreement on the meaning of adulthood. One interpretation is set alongside another, and students bring criteria to bear from both the text and from their own experience. The skirmish at Lexington did not qualify as adult behavior for the boy and first girl because "they are still rebelling." Not until the colonists begin the task of building a postrebellion government (a constitution, a social contract) do they cross the line from teenager to adult. Indeed, this interpretation sits well with many adults (teachers and student-teachers) with whom I have examined this excerpt. They believe, from their own experience and that of their friends, and from their reading of history, that rebellions may end one relationship but do not constitute another.

Also, we see that the disagreement between the two girls is one that their relationship seems barely able to contain, as revealed in the final two statements: "So you're saying that it's right in between [being a teenager and an adult]?" asks MS3, perhaps hoping for, and suggesting, more common ground than actually exists. "No" is what MS2 means to say in response. It's not "in between" teenager and adult. "It's during the teenage years." She had made her position clear a few moments earlier: Like teenagers, the colonists were rebelling. They hadn't become adults yet, and they wouldn't "until they lay down the government of their country . . . many years later." "Yeah," she demurs, instead of "No." But then she restates clearly: "It's during the teenage years."

Let's turn to the deliberative example, in which students are trying to decide on a policy for a public controversy. Like a seminar, a deliberation is a discussion in which several viewpoints are set alongside one another so that, as Bridges (1979) said, "Our own view of things is challenged by those of others" (p. 50). Unlike the seminar, however, the deliberative discussion is geared toward making a decision about what to do—about which alternative or hybrid of two or three is the fairest and most workable as a policy that will be binding on all. In the case of physician-assisted suicide (PAS), the question in this class is whether it should be permitted by law. This experienced discussion leader, like the seminar leader, has prepared students for the discussion. They have read a good deal of background material, including data from countries that allow PAS, and she painstakingly clarifies norms for the discussion. The task before them, she explains, is to reach a "deeper understanding of the issue," and the method is to have a "best-case fair hearing of competing or differing points of view" (Miller & Singleton, 1997, 1.7). In this way, she slows the movement toward decision, directing students in a more careful consideration of the problem and a "fair hearing" of alternative solutions. The aim of the discussion, however, remains decision-making, not enriched understanding for its own sake. Accordingly, the discussion is a deliberation, not a seminar. This is a distinction, despite all the overlap, that rests on the *purpose* of speaking and listening. I return to this point later.

The norms, which she elicits from students as she asks them to reflect on prior discussions, are posted on the chalkboard: Hear all sides equally, listen well enough to respond and build off one another's ideas, back up opinions with reasons, and speak one at a time. During the discussion, the teacher takes special care to help participants weigh each alternative thoroughly. "Let's think about this reason some more," she says often. "Who has a different reason why this might or might not be a good thing to do?" To get the discussion started, she asks for someone to state a reason for or against legalizing PAS in Colorado. A Latina girl volunteers that she is against it because it could lead to abuses.

High School 1 (Latina female): I for one am against PAS because I believe it could lead to abuses. And I think it's not fair to society to say that some terminally ill people can take their life when doctors could just go unplug some people from life support because it costs too much to keep them in hospitals or whatever. I don't think it's right to do that to society. . . . I think that doctors can take advantage of the fact that they can do this, that they can kill off people, and I think that they'll turn around and say we don't want these people because they don't look right or whatever and just go off and kill them off, and I just don't think that's fair.

HS2 (African American female): What do you mean that they'll try to get rid of someone by pulling the plug? Isn't that up to the person who is terminally ill?

HS1: It should be, but not always. It could lead to the fact that doctors could just do what they wanted.

HS3 (White female): The right to decide that you want PAS is a right for *you* to decide. The doctor doesn't decide that and say, you know, you're costing too much money and we're going to pull the plug. It's a right for you to decide.

HS1: I understand. But it could lead to that. I'm sure now it's not that way, but in the future it could . . .

HS4 (African American male): I don't believe in it. . . . Life is precious and it is given to us by God and no one should decide when to end your suffering. . . . [The physician] would be helping them murder themselves. . . . Why take life when life is given to us? (Miller & Singleton, 1997, 1.16–17, 1.24–25).

The teacher points out the value tension that has emerged between human life and individuals' freedom to choose. Additionally, she names and clarifies the "slippery slope" argument raised by the first speaker: A well-intentioned action taken today can have unintended negative consequences down the road. "Let's stick with this [slippery-slope argument] a little longer," she prompts after several exchanges, and asks what material from the background reading might apply. "What did you read that would support the argument that abuses will surely come and the law will be used unequally?" One boy cites statistics from the Netherlands, where PAS is legal, on the number of lives that were terminated without request. Another adds that dying patients have sometimes felt pressured to end their lives to save money for their families.

LISTENING TO STRANGERS

What kind of political training is this? Such a question requires that we first ask who these discussants are to one another. Certainly they are classmates: students assigned to the same instructional group by school administrators and the jumble of social forces they negotiate—neighborhood schools and desegregation law, school funding inequities, immigration, racism, multiculturalism, and so forth. But although students are, as classmates, "thrown" together bureaucratically by an administrative calculus, they are acquaintances, too (more or less). They have been together in classroom and school settings (cafeterias, ballfields, bathrooms, hallways) for some time; they have some knowledge of one another, or believe they do. According to the Oxford English Dictionary (Oxford University Press, 1989), *acquaintance* is "personal knowledge; knowledge of a person or thing gained by intercourse or experience, which is more than mere recognition, and less than familiarity or intimacy." The accompanying usage example given in the OED emphasizes the definition's final clause. It is from O'Neill's 1922 play *Anna Christie*: "Are you trying to kid me? Proposing—to me—for Gawd's sake!—on such short acquaintance?" On this understanding, some students will be less than acquaintances, perhaps not even recognizing one another, and others may be more: siblings or cousins, boyfriends and girlfriends, and "best friends."

Much is to be gained, however, by noticing the *lack* of familiarity and intimacy that comes with the territory of public schooling. This is why the public school—the common school—can be seen to be the best available site for democratic political education. There are two reasons, and both stem from the fact that a school is not a private place, like our homes, but a public, civic place. First, this public arena is, by definition, a diverse congregation, or, less elegantly (and less theistically), a jumble. Some schools are more a jumble than others, but all are to some meaningful extent. (Nearly as antidemocratic as segregationist practices are those that fail to recognize whatever diversity is present.) Boys and girls are both there. Jews, Protestants, Catholics, Muslims, Buddhists, and atheists may be there together. There are racial and class differences, and immigrants from the world over. This buzzing variety does not exist at home, church, synagogue, or mosque. It exists in places where people who come from numerous private worlds and social positions are thrown together for a purpose, such as schooling.

Of course, the diversity of the student body in any school is circumscribed by the segregated—and now resegregated (Fry, 2007)—U.S. society at large. American schools are mirrors of a segregated society, not autonomous islands; they express the asymmetries that are inscribed in the social system generally—inequalities of recognition and respect on the one hand, and of distribution of material resources on the other. Although public schools may be more diverse than most other social spaces in the student's life, the "buzzing variety" within them is not what it could be. (Imagine, for example, if they were random samples of the society at large.) Poor children do not generally go to school with affluent children, and Blacks and Whites do not typically attend together. Orfield (2001) found that Whites on average attend schools where less than 20% of the students are from all other racial and ethnic groups combined. Blacks and Latinos on average attend schools with 54% students of their own group.[1]

The second reason that schools may be the best available sites for democratic political education is that, owing to the congregation of students at school, there are inevitably "the problems of living together" at school (Dewey, 1916/1985, p. 200). These are mutual, collective concerns—not "mine" or "yours," but "ours." There are mainly two kinds of problems at school: social and academic. Social problems arise over resources, policies, classroom assignments, injustices and inequalities, and the friction of interaction itself: egos and social positions rubbing up against one another in discursive space. Academic problems are at the core of each discipline, and expertise in a subject is defined largely by one's knowledge of them. A strong curriculum plunges students into them in pedagogically measured ways.

In tandem, diversity and problems are the two key assets for democratic political education. For Dewey (1916/1985), "progress" comes "through wider relationships," and isolation stunts growth. But I want to highlight the democratic potential not only of the presence of these two assets but also of the relative lack of *acquaintance*—the OED's "familiarity or intimacy"—among students, even among those similarly positioned. This lack, I propose, can be seen as a third asset. Allen's (2004) work lends a good deal of help. What Dewey (1916/1985) named "a mode of associated living, of conjoint communicated experience" (p. 93), Allen, who follows Ralph Ellison, Hannah Arendt, and Aristotle rather than Dewey, named "political friendship" (p. 165).

POLITICAL FRIENDSHIP

Politics is many things, but mainly the activity surrounding the power to govern: "getting it, keeping it, opposing it, subverting it, squandering it, and so on" (Frazer, 2007, p. 250). Typically, it involves relating to—persuading, mobilizing—people we don't know well, if at all. Allen (2004) called these fellow citizens not acquaintances but, sharpening the point, "strangers" and argued that "political friendship" among them is the particular "mode of citizenship" needed for our times (p. 165). Political friendship is based not on knowledge, familiarity, or intimacy, for "one doesn't even have to like one's fellow citizens in order to act toward them as a political friend" (p. 140). Were liking one another necessary, democracy would be impossible. This matters, because the kind of relationship *citizens* need, as distinct from ordinary friendship based on emotional closeness, occurs at what Allen called "the midway point between acquiescence and domination" (p. 121). Equity, then, is political friendship's core, not affinity or intimacy. We arrive back at a more interesting and powerful understanding of the heterogeneous "we the people"—citizens who don't know one another but who are and must be, if shared problems are to be addressed and solved, equal before the law and one another's civic regard. They are bound together, not culturally so much as politically, by the problems they face in common.

Political friendship rests not on equity alone but also on political trust. Allen's (2004) concern is that *distrust makes impossible any serious sense of solidarity among citizens.* Distrust "paralyzes democracy," she argued, because citizens feel insecure with one another. "Trust in one's fellow citizens consists in the belief, simply, that one is safe with them" (p. xvi). There is a cognitive dimension to trust: One believes that one's own vulnerabilities won't be exploited. There is an emotional dimension, too: One feels unafraid though vulnerable before one's fellow citizens. Assuming that everyone feels vulnerable from time to time (interpersonal vulnerability) and that members of historically oppressed groups feel vulnerable nearly all the time (intergroup, subordinate-status vulnerability), then political trust is elemental, along with equity, in political friendship.

Habits of political trust are as long in formation as habits of political distrust are long enduring. Allen displays these in the vivid historical centerpiece of her work, the "battle of Little Rock," the events surrounding the desegregation of Central High School in September 1957. In her account, the events, images, and personal sacrifices of that month were a mirror held up to the American public sphere, and the consequence of that reflection was a reconstitution of the United States—figuratively, the inauguration of a second constitution. The public habits of the *ancien régime* had been exposed; White majority tyranny was revealed more viscerally to a wider audience. White women were seen cursing 15-year-old Elizabeth Eckford, the sacrificial student, while White men stood vigilant over the threatened White spaces—the school, but also the bus stop where Elizabeth waited to return home after being refused entry. With these images in mind, equity and trust become utopian goals and political friendship an unapproachable ideal.

But Allen finds an opening. Her strategy is to jettison any hope or desire for "oneness" as an aspect of, or a beacon for, "we the people." The images from Little Rock in 1957 displayed "the two-ness of citizenship" (p. 13) in the United States and put to rest the illusion of oneness (as in the pledge's "one nation . . . indivisible"). Though Whites and Blacks were members of the same democracy, "each was expert in a different etiquette of citizenship:

dominance on the one hand and acquiescence on the other" (p. 13). Allen's "talking to strangers," then, rests not on an idealization of unanimity, not even consensus, for that scheme exaggerates equality while requiring repression of emotion and suppression of facts. It "idealizes the wrong thing," she writes, "and fails to establish evaluative criteria for a crucial democratic practice—the attempt to generate trust out of distrust" (p. 85).

Wholeness is the metaphor that Allen substitutes for oneness. No dictionary, she noted, treats "one" as a synonym for wholeness; nowhere does "one" mean full, total, complete, all. In the social imaginary of "we the people," wholeness carves out a space for imagining a political solidarity that falls at that midway point between acquiescence and domination, where equity and trust among strangers might coexist. To mature as a citizen—to claim one's "majority"[2]—one needs to talk with the strangers with whom one has been thrown into the polity. Talk about what? About those problems of living together that actually require conjoint attention: Health, safety, education, work, and membership (e.g., immigration policy, see Chapter 10 this volume) are the classic examples. Under the United States's "first constitution," so to speak, to claim one's majority as a citizen was both culturally and politically to assimilate into and, thus, acquiesce to, another kind of majority—the White majority. But thereafter, after the illusion of oneness had been revealed at Little Rock, to claim one's majority was to practice standing on equal footing with strangers.

LISTENING TO STRANGERS AT SCHOOL

What kind of work can seminars and deliberations in school do for the project of cultivating political friendship among strangers? What kind of role can they play in advancing this "timely mode of citizenship?" Let's consider this from two angles: the collaborative intellectual and emotional work involved in seminar and deliberation and its potential for engendering political trust.

Both seminar and deliberation are species of collaborative inquiry, and their desired curricular outcomes—understanding and right action, respectively—rely on the expression and consideration of diverse views. They rely just as much on powerful texts. In a seminar, participants together interpret an essay, book, play, or painting, and they speak and listen to *learn*. Seminars encourage students to see the world more deeply and clearly thanks to the selection of the text, the opening question, and the multiple interpretations and experiences that are brought to bear by discussants. Deliberations encourage discussants to think together, with and across their differences, too, but now the discussion is aimed at *deciding*, and the text is a controversial public issue. Discussants are finding, studying, and weighing alternatives in order to decide a course of action—a public policy.

Seminars and deliberations display the distinction between the world-revealing (enlightening) and world-changing (engaging) functions of classroom discussion. When a group seeks understanding together, it works to create, plumb, and clarify meanings and explanations. When it forges a decision, it weighs alternatives and tries to decide among them. Seminars don't try to make material progress in the world, but deliberations do. Deliberations are concerned with action in the world under the always local and often urgent conditions of a public—a "we," a jumble of difference facing a shared problem—needing to make a decision (Parker, 2006).

The work of seminar and deliberation needs to be done *with others* for several reasons. First, the problem—whether understanding or deciding—is shared; accordingly, the decision-making should be shared (the democratic ethos). Second, inquiry is a public matter that, when vigorous, is loaded with open disputation as to who has got it right (the scientific ethos). Third, the array of alternative interpretations (in seminar) and solutions (in deliberation) that a group generates will be broader than one could accomplish working alone (the collaboration ethos). Fourth, within that broader array will be alternatives stemming from social perspectives—and these from social positions—that are more or less different from one's own, thereby developing the participants' social knowledge while contributing to a better solution (the pluralism ethos). All four aspects—democracy, inquiry, collaboration, and pluralism—rely on a decentered and discursive image of political life, what Habermas (1996) called "decentralized self-governance" (pp. 21–30).

To summarize, seminar and deliberation are discourse platforms that emphasize and express the learning and doing sides of politics, respectively. These are only emphases, for the two overlap. Much is learned in deliberations (the alternatives must be studied), and much is done in seminars because the work of textual interpretation is carried out in a thick soup of communicative action. Together, seminar and deliberation aim for what we could call *enlightened political engagement* (Nie et al., 1996; Parker, 2003). The knowledge-deepening, evidence-oriented, horizon-broadening functions of seminars on well-selected texts provide an enlightened platform for public decision-making, and vice versa.

PRACTICES OF LISTENING TO STRANGERS

But can equity (political friendship's core) and political trust (its safety net) be nurtured in classroom discussion? The two discourse models in question are pertinent for reasons that by now should be clear. Additionally, both of them operate within defined normative and pedagogic space. Earlier we saw both teachers establish norms for the discussions. They ranged from "listen to and build on one another's comments" and "invite others into the discussion" to "hear all sides equally" and "speak one at a time." This *is* equity and trust education. Obstacles will arise that will frustrate discussants and the most experienced discussion facilitator. There will be both "troubling speech" and "disturbing silence" (Boler, 2004). Speakers and viewpoints will be marginalized, and the myriad difficulties of discussion pedagogy will surface. But these are the problems that require teaching for discussion—making it a curriculum objective in its own right—not abandoning the effort. Framing equity and trust as lessons to be taught and learned places them within the realm of the possible. As Dewey (1916/1985) wrote, "Since a democratic society repudiates the principle of external authority, it must find a substitute in voluntary disposition and interest; these can be created only by education" (p. 93).

Central to teaching for discussion is teaching for listening across difference. Listening deserves to be singled out for several reasons, but a key *political* reason is that democratic community based on Allen's "wholeness" principle requires it. Equitable and trustworthy conjoint living is a matter not only of being heard but also of hearing others. Agency resides in both roles—speaker and listener—and needs to be educated if the necessary habits are to be cultivated. Which habits should be educated and how?

In the aftermath of the September 2001 attacks on New York and Washington, Thich Nhat Hanh was asked what he would "say" if he had a chance to "speak" to Osama bin Laden. Hanh is the Vietnamese Buddhist monk with whom Martin Luther King Jr. famously announced his opposition to the Vietnam War in 1966. I bring up Hanh here because he was a leading exponent of meditation as a practice of relaxed (not clinging to the usual categories) and open-ended (less expectant) listening. His response to his interlocutor:

> If I were given the opportunity. . . . , the first thing I would do is listen. I would try to understand why he had acted in that cruel way. I would try to understand all of the suffering that had led him to violence. It might not be easy to listen in that way, so I would have to remain calm and lucid. I would need several friends with me who are strong in the practice of deep listening, listening without reacting, without judging and blaming. In this way, an atmosphere of support would be created for this person and those connected so that they could share completely and trust that they are really being heard. After listening for some time, we might need to take a break to allow what has been said to enter into our consciousness. Only when we felt calm and lucid would we respond. (Hanh, 2001)

The first thing the monk would do is *not talk*. Even then, listening would be difficult, he imagines, despite the depth and duration of his own training at doing precisely that. Accordingly, he would deploy strategies: remaining calm enough to increase the likelihood of being attentive to what is being said, taking a break to allow what has been heard to be absorbed, and asking friends whose listening he admires to be with him.

This example is extraordinary, but for present purposes, it serves to indicate the role of agency in listening—that a listener (1) needs actually to *do* something and (2) *can* do something to pave the way for a more capacious and genuine hearing.

This is not so much the case when we are having conversations with intimates, of course, which is precisely the point when it comes to cultivating citizenly relations among acquaintances and strangers, where intimacy is neither the bond nor the goal. "A polity will never reach a point where all its citizens have intimate friendships with each other, nor would we want it to," Allen (2004) wrote, citizenship, after all, "is understood not as an emotion but a practice" (p. 156). She then suggested "guide-lines" by which a listener might "prepare the way for the generation of trust." Following are three. They may differ from Hanh's (or not); that is the subject of another paper. Hers are specifically interrogative; two are requests the listener makes of the speaker, and one is a distinction she asks the listener to draw. Each, she said, rests on a commitment to equity and trust.

- Ask whether the speaker has spoken as a political friend.
- Separate a speaker's claims about facts from the principles on which her conclusions are based; assess both.
- Ask who is sacrificing for whom, whether the sacrifices are voluntary and honored; whether they can and will be reciprocated. (p. 158)

These are practices, not promises. Allen called them only "some new habits to try on." Inequality and distrust will continue, and marginalizing speech and silence will persist. But as practices, they encourage agency over resignation and cynicism and make a seedbed in which political friendship might grow among strangers.

Inspired by Hanh's "friends" and Allen's "guidelines," I have experimented with an additional set of listening practices. My contexts are teacher education courses in which new and experienced teachers are learning to facilitate seminars and deliberations, neighborhood meetings where public problems are addressed, and faculty meetings where we are (on the seminar side) interpreting a problem or (on the deliberative side) deciding what to do about it. In the first context, I am mainly teaching these strategies to others, both by explanation and demonstration, and in the other two contexts, I am attempting to "try them on," as Allen said. This particular set of practices aims to allow more listening by reducing the listener's aggression, that is, the speed and vehemence with which the listener's interpretive categories close in on the speaker's statements. Each strategy, then, involves some sacrifice of the listener's comfortable ground. Each is a stance a listener might take in discussion. After Narayan (1988), I call them reciprocity, humility, and caution (Parker, 2006). I will describe them in the first person.

Reciprocity is the stance that ventilates the listener's ego. Like the others, it capitalizes on the two democratic assets that schools afford: diversity and problems. It centrally involves the effort to take the perspective of another. When I engage this practice, I intentionally privilege the speaker's vantage point and listen knowing that the speaker understands better than I his or her social position, experiences, emotions, and beliefs. This is a powerful move, for it urges me to not become attached to my initial reaction to the speaker's experience.

Humility is the stance that undermines the listener's arrogance. If I am humble while listening, I listen from the point of view that I am most likely missing something—that my understanding is incomplete and the categories that I listen with are probably faulty and, at any rate, not as tightly woven as they seem. I remind myself that I am an outsider to the speaker's experience, always, and sometimes a cultural outsider, too. There is more that I must learn, and what appears to be a mistake on the part of the speaker would probably make more sense if I had a better grasp of the details, the emotions, the situation, and the speaker's history and social perspective.

Caution is the stance that moderates the listener's discursive speed and recklessness. If I am cautious when listening, I move slowly, taking care not to report every thought that comes to my mind. I engage carefully so that I am not denying or dismissing the validity of the speaker's point of view or manner of talking.

The point of such practices is not to avoid challenging a speaker substantively or disagreeing, for that would infantilize the speaker and prevent the productive kind of discussion for which seminar and deliberation are designed. The point, rather, is to generate a greater degree of equity and the assurance that a speaker's vulnerabilities won't be exploited.

Whether practices or habits of this sort can effectively be taught is another matter. It may well be that attempts to teach such practices inevitably trivialize the profundity of learning to make way for another.[3] It may be, too, that attempts to "try on" such habits only disguise the myriad dominations and acquiescences that are proceeding apace while easing the guilt of the more privileged discussants. On the other hand, would-be listeners require some sort of scaffold, and an education in these practices may prove helpful to that end. I am drawn to Allen's (2004) pragmatism: "We need ideals for improving things that are not yet good enough and will never be perfect" (p. 86).

CONCLUSION

I hope to have presented three ideas. First, seminar and deliberation are public discourse structures suitable to the cultivation, in schools, of political friendship among "acquaintances" and "strangers" who have little in common save shared problems. The two models emphasize distinct conjoint activities—understanding and decision-making—and together aim for democratically enlightened political engagement.

Second, diversity and problems are essential assets for such an education. Without them, there's too little conflict and no widening of relationships around things that matter; accordingly, there's not much to discuss. Public schools possess these two assets in greater amounts than most other cultural locations, and this is their key advantage for democratic education. But there is another. Public schools not only are *public* environments; they are, unlike shopping malls and ballfields, intentionally *educative* environments in which these assets can be mobilized toward desired ends through the means of curriculum and instruction.

Finally, "citizens have powers" (Allen, 2004, p. 168), and they are obliged to deploy them. Even as liberal democracies extend the right to vote and other civil rights to citizens previously denied them, these empowering moves ignore the matter of exercising that power. Opportunity is not to be confused with action. Habermas (1995) is direct: Inclusion "says *nothing* about the actual use made of active citizenship" by anyone (p. 268). To actually practice citizenship for the purpose of public will formation and social betterment, citizens must claim their majority. This mode of living together is one that takes shape, not in a founding moment tucked neatly into history textbooks, but in the circulating flows of public discourse. On this account, listening and speaking to strangers about powerful ideas and public problems—that is, *governing*—signals a citizen's coming of age. Simultaneously, it works to reclaim and reconstitute the democratic public sphere as a fertile site for political critique and action.

CHAPTER 7

What Is Justice?

The development of a sense of justice—of fairness and right and wrong—takes a village, but how does that work? What is justice, and how does it develop? I explore these questions here, and my method is comparative. I examine perspectives from two disciplines—psychology and sociology. The first centers on individual psyches and their ability to take the perspective of others. The second centers on the social structures that envelop these psyches. The first offers a respected and powerful theory of just individuals, the second a respected and powerful theory of just societies. But each is dated and has a blind spot. "Individualists" emphasize the sovereignty and autonomy of persons, as if individuals were not actually the products of different ways of organizing society over which individuals have little control. "Structuralists" emphasize the underlying systems and institutions that determine how individuation takes place, as if these structures were not interpreted differently by different individuals and altered by their agency. How should we think about this dyad, individual justice and systemic justice? This is where I turn to the discerning synthesis of a brilliant philosopher, activist, and social movement leader, Martin Luther King Jr.

> "How can you advocate breaking some laws and obeying others?" The answer lies in the fact that there are two types of laws: just and unjust.
>
> —Martin Luther King Jr.

What if we seriously were to commit ourselves to educating children and youth to become enlightened and engaged liberal-democratic citizens? With all the social and psychological forces compelling them (and us) toward a life of comfortable idiocy, this would be an extraordinary aim. Were we to be successful, it would be an extraordinary achievement. What would that work entail? How would it look and feel? The present chapter delves into one aspect of that project: the task of educating just citizens. These are citizens who are principled and compassionate, who refrain from harming or exploiting others, and who believe it is their duty both to protect just institutions and to prevent injustice. "To sit passively by while injustices are committed, or democratic institutions collapse, in the hope that others will step in, is to be a free rider," writes Will Kymlicka (1999, p. 14). The idiocy of free-ridership becomes clear even to free-riders when they realize that, having not looked out for their neighbors, there comes a day when there are no neighbors left to look after them. This is the point made by the Protestant pastor Martin Niemöller (2022) when asked how the Nazis accomplished what they did, first taking over a country (Germany), then wreaking havoc on other countries and engineering the Holocaust. Niemöller said it happened this way:

> First they came for the socialists, and I did not speak out—because I was not a socialist. Then they came for the trade unionists, and I did not speak out—because I was not a trade unionist. Then they came for the Jews, and I did not speak out—because I was not a Jew. And then they came for me—and there was no one left to speak for me.

There are a number of promising ways of educating for justice. One way to organize them is to sort them into two groups: those oriented to engagement itself (participation) and those oriented to enlightenment (knowledge). One aims to engage students in decision-making and action on shared problems. The other aims to help students form particular understandings of justice (e.g., that "injustice anywhere is a threat to justice everywhere" [King, 1963, p. 77]). An instructional approach drawn from the first group is the Just Community (Power et al., 1989). Here, students become involved in school and classroom governance, deciding with one another how they will treat one another, what norms and values will govern their behavior together. There are examples of this approach from across the school grades. They center on encouraging students, whether kindergartners or 12th-graders, to deliberate with one another the norms and values of group life that will govern their conduct with one another. This requires a basic shift in the school climate and decision-making apparatus, to be sure. Students come to *experience* popular sovereignty firsthand, and on their own grounds.

An approach drawn from the second group is the Socratic seminar, which, as we saw in the prior chapter, is a method of shared inquiry into the ideas, issues, and values expressed in powerful works of art, literature, and music. For example, high school students might read and discuss King's "Letter from Birmingham Jail" (1963) and attempt, by exploring one another's interpretations, to understand how King distinguishes between just and unjust laws. They could turn next to another famous jail scene, the dialogue about Socrates' final days as depicted by his student Plato in the dialogue *Crito* (1992a). Socrates' friend Crito visits him in his cell shortly before he is to be executed by drinking poison. "I can get you out of here; I've bribed the guard," offers Crito. Socrates replies that he'll accept the offer of escape only if he and Crito can, after thinking it through together in dialogue, agree that this would be the right thing to do, the just thing to do. Both King and

Socrates display the highest imaginable respect for, and understanding of, the law. Both are in jail because of it. The behavior of each rides on his sense of justice. One was assassinated, the other executed. Each holds up a mirror in which students, if they are inquisitive and imaginative and have good discussion partners and a capable seminar leader, might clarify their own conceptions of justice.

I admire both approaches. But we should not overlook the fact that deploying either one of them presupposes that we have grappled with the meaning of the concept *justice*, that we ourselves have attempted to think it through, that we have searched for an understanding of what it means to do the right thing. Whether teachers choose to steep their students in the ideals and strategies set forth in accounts of inspiring individuals, who under the most difficult circumstances struggled to advance justice, or to engage students in decision-making in which they must work out just solutions to the problems of living together—whichever way teachers go, even if they go both ways, they cannot go far or well without an understanding of what they are attempting; that is, without a working theory of justice.

This chapter is devoted to that, to helping readers draw out and reflect upon their preconception of justice and, perhaps, to clarify and rebuild it somewhat by considering multiple perspectives on the subject. Toward that end, I provide two reasonable yet contrasting viewpoints: One is mainly a psychological conception of justice, the other mainly sociological. The first centers on individual psyches, the second on social structures. The first is concerned with the cognitive-moral development of individuals, in which moral development is viewed as part and parcel of intellectual-cognitive development; the second is concerned with the moral condition of whole societies, in which the moral development of individuals is viewed as an appendage to the way society is organized. The first worries about how just individuals such as King and Socrates got that way (and Jane Addams, Gandhi, Thich Nhat Hanh, and so on), concentrating on their psychological development. The second worries about how different social systems are organized to privilege certain groups—the ruling class or culture of power— while subordinating others. *The first offers a theory of just individuals, the other a theory of just societies.* The first will be more palatable to most readers, perhaps, because individualism is the dominant ideology of contemporary American life. It preexisted our births; we were born and grew up and formed our ideas and values within it. Few of us can escape that fundamental bias in our thinking. Even if we were protected from it in families and faith communities (and even that is unlikely), these institutions still couldn't keep out television, pop radio, and the market economy. The social historian Richard Sennett (1974) writes, "Few people today would claim that their psychic life arises by spontaneous generation, independent of social conditions and environmental influences. Nevertheless, the psyche is treated as though it has an inner life of its own" (p. 4).

There is a fundamental tension here. Each view has a blind spot: "Individualists" emphasize the sovereignty and autonomy of persons, but they do so as if individuals were not actually the products of different ways of organizing society over which individuals have little control. Meanwhile, "socialists" emphasize the underlying social situations that determine how and to what ends individuation takes place, but they do so as if these situations themselves were not interpreted and dealt with differently by different individuals and transformed continually by the theories and actions of these individuals. Each in its own way ignores the other. In *The Ethics of Ambiguity*, the French existentialist Simone de Beauvoir (1948) tries to capture the way we might feel this tension in our lives—in the conditions of our daily living: "It is in knowledge of the genuine conditions of our life," she reminds us, "that we must draw our strength to live and our reason for acting" (p. 9). These conditions are the basic material we work with, the daily delights and burdens of existing with one another. But at the heart of these conditions she finds a tragic ambiguity: We experience ourselves as sovereign subjects, agents taking action within and against the social structures that surround and engulf us—from the family to schoolhouse, the workplace, legal and economic systems—yet also as objects crushed by these forces, "crushed by the dark weight of things" (p. 7). We understand ourselves as unique, choosing persons, yet we know we are positioned as a cultural, socioeconomic, and racial "type," formed in and by a particular social milieu riddled with unequal power relations. We feel that our actions make a difference, yet we know that the circumstances of our activity are not of our choosing. We assert ourselves and effect change, yet also we are helpless.

To make the distinction between the two frames vivid, I will provide a striking case of each. From the psychology corner, I feature moral development theory as it was worked out by the developmental psychologist Lawrence Kohlberg and his colleagues. From the sociology corner, I feature historical-materialist theory as it was developed by the sociologist Karl Marx and his colleagues. Each is controversial, and each has much to say about justice, one through the individualist lens and the other through the socialist lens. Each has been contested by legions of critics (and upheld by legions of advocates).[1] I am not concerned here with summarizing these criticisms or offering an additional criticism of my own. Rather, by setting them beside one another, because each is provocative and coherent, we might perceive the criticism of one by the other and thereby clarify what we mean by justice and what we intend to do when teaching for it.

JUST INDIVIDUALS

Following the assassination of Martin Luther King Jr., a group of children ranging in age from 8 to 16 years was asked, "When the killer is found, how do you think he should be treated?" The older children thought the killer should receive a "fair trial" and be punished "according to the law." Younger children thought the killer should receive specific, usually extra-legal punishment (Siegel, 1977). For example, the killer should be "turned over to the Negroes and let them take care of him." And, "Let Mrs. King kill him," and "Dr. King was killed by him so the same thing should happen to him." In response to the questions, "Why do you think Dr. King was shot? What made the person do it?," the older children more often gave answers indicating abstract political thinking (e.g., "He was killed because he tried to do something for the Negroes"), while the younger, less abstract, more concrete thinkers typically personalized the shooting (e.g., "He hated King" and "Because a riot might have went on in his neighborhood and wrecked his home, and he thought Dr. King started it"). Specific punishments and personal motives are concrete representations of the event, whereas the ideal of justice mediated through a fair trial and the rule of law is abstract.

This study illustrates one of the truisms of developmental psychology: As children mature, their reasoning evolves from preconcrete to concrete and then from concrete to abstract, and this movement incorporates both the physical and social worlds—that is, their reasoning about which of two glasses contains more soda pop as well as their reasoning about what should happen to someone who accidentally spills one of them. From about age 2 until about age 6, most children "follow" rules; that is, they obey them through imitation, not understanding. By ages 7 to 10, most children are understanding in a rudimentary way that rules are important regulatory mechanisms in social life. On the playground, for example, changing the rules after a game has begun can be just cause for a fight. The accusation "That's not fair!" is wielded confidently by many children of this age. By adulthood, some people (around half) develop into fully abstract thinkers capable of reasoning in complex terms about a fair trial, due process, equal opportunity under the law, and the like. In *The Moral Judgement of the Child* (1965), Jean Piaget writes: "All morality consists in a system of rules, and the essence of all morality is to be sought for in the respect which the individual acquires for these rules" (p. 13). How does this concrete-to-abstract journey progress? Why do some people travel the full course while others do not?

Several philosophies tell us that justice is latent in the soul—the seed for justice is already planted in human nature. Buddhism is based on this view, as is Western philosophy in the lineage of Socrates. It follows pedagogically that what is already there can be *drawn out* in good teaching-learning settings, but not imposed. Piaget and Kohlberg extended and qualified that tradition within the discourse of cognitive developmental psychology, both providing evidence (Kohlberg's data were both cross-cultural and longitudinal) for the view that individuals become more just as they proceed through stages of development. But what is the underlying idea of justice that accompanies this concrete-to-abstract evolution in our thinking as we grow and develop? We will understand it first implicitly by examining Kohlberg's theory of cognitive moral development; that is, we will derive it from Kohlberg's stage-wise description of the natural evolution of a sense of justice. Then we will understand it explicitly by examining the decision-making method employed at the highest level of development in Kohlberg's scheme.

First, we should understand that cognitive developmentalism is one of several psychological theories about how humans know and learn. Other theories, to name only two, are behaviorism and biological maturationist theory. Kohlberg argued that cognitive developmentalism overcomes a dichotomy between these two by asserting a dialectical, or interactive, model of human development (Kohlberg & Mayer, 1972). This model considers human knowing to be a function of the increased capacity to know that results from the interaction of an always-changing individual and an always-changing environment.

Second, we should understand that Kohlberg was a Piagetian. Piaget's well-known theory holds that one's way of learning and knowing develops naturally and hierarchically through an invariant sequence of stages. No one skips a stage, but development can be arrested at any stage. Each stage is a qualitatively distinct, integrated thought system, and each is more complex, inclusive, and thus more powerful than the preceding stage. Upward stage movement occurs as one constructs a satisfactory response to the experience of disequilibrium—confusion or being stuck on a problem or dilemma one is facing. There are plenty of problems, naturally, because the friction of a person and an environment interacting engenders all manner of conflict as the person struggles to understand what is happening and to respond. According to Piaget, the only satisfying escape from confusion is further cognitive development: The way out of the present disequilibrium is the construction of a new way of knowing within which the conflict dissolves and equilibrium is restored. Each predicament becomes, thereby, fertile ground for the next resolution, and one's way of making sense of the world is thus "drawn out." Both the knower and the known develop in such a way that objects (whether toys, bottles of soda pop, parents, friends, or games) are known anew by a new knower—what Kegan (1982) calls *the evolving self.* Eventually, this evolving self

> can construe the world propositionally, hypothetically, inferentially, abstractly. It can spin an "overall plan" of which any given concrete event is but an instance of "what might be." This rebalancing, often the hallmark of adolescence, unhinges a concrete world. Where before the "actual" was everything, it falls away like the flats of a theater set, and a whole new world, a world the person never knew existed, is revealed. The actual becomes but one instance (and often a not very interesting instance) of the possible. (p. 38)

Imagining Alternatives

The implications of the evolving self for enlightened political engagement—
that is, knowledge, voice, and action—are my chief concern here. To re-
peat, "Any given concrete event is but an instance of 'what might be.'"
The present situation, the status quo, "becomes but one instance . . . of the
possible." The evolved self is not likely to take the given social situation as
anything other than one setup among an array of possibilities. Perceiving
a perniciously racist and segregated society, the freedom marchers of the
Civil Rights Movement imagined an alternative. Perceiving a rapidly global-
izing marketplace in which corporate heads were making the new game
rules, protestors of the World Trade Organization imagined an alternative.
Perceiving the fantastic rich-poor gap in the United States today, pockets of
opposition across the country are imagining alternatives.

Kohlberg's theory of moral imagination and moral reasoning, as we have
seen, was an extension and qualification of Piaget's interactive, stage-wise
conception of intellectual development. As an individual's reasoning about
the physical world evolves, Kohlberg argued, so does his or her capacity for
reasoning about the world of people and relationships and, in particular,
justice (Kohlberg et al., 1984a, 1984b). Before we can regularly consider
others' perspectives in our reasoning about issues of fairness, our mode of
perception and judgment must be developed beyond egocentricity, beyond
idiocy. We must be capable intellectually of accommodating the other as
another subject: another thinking, feeling agent. In Piaget's terms, the tran-
scendence of the infant's unabashed egocentrism requires the set of abilities
called "concrete operational thought," central to which is *reciprocity*, or the
ability to see two dimensions of a problem simultaneously. So the concrete
stage makes possible an advance from justice-as-obedience to justice-as-
equal exchange. Further cognitive development, from concrete to abstract
reasoning, permits yet another qualitative advance in our sense of justice
from *concrete* reciprocity to *ideal* reciprocity (Kohlberg, 1971). This entails
imagining yourself in another's role and considering what you would want
from that perspective. This is represented in the colloquialisms "putting
yourself in the other person's shoes" and understanding where someone is
"coming from." As the evolving self develops the intellectual capacity for
ideal reciprocity, the Golden Rule is for the first time comprehensible not
as an admonition to treat others as they treat you (concrete reciprocity)
but to treat them as you would want to be treated if you were they. Now
we can take the perspective of others with less egocentric and ethnocentric
distortion. Now, too, principled reasoning such as that expressed in the
U.S. Constitution or the Seneca Falls declaration of the rights of women or
King's "Letter" can at last be comprehended.

Perspective-taking is an act of moral imagination: One cannot actually
walk a mile in another's shoes, but one can try to imagine his or her life

conditions. It is in this light that King (1963) wrote in the "Letter": "Injustice anywhere is a threat to justice everywhere. . . . Whatever affects one directly, affects all indirectly" (p. 77). And it is in this light that Thich Nhat Hahn (1988) said, "You cannot just *be* by yourself alone. You have to inter-be with every other thing" (p. 4). Imagining oneself in another's place is the moral opposite of egocentricity and ethnocentricity. It is the key to moving from idiocy to puberty.

From Idiocy to Puberty

Kohlberg's research (Kohlberg et al., 1984a, 1984b) indicates that at each cognitive stage individuals have a distinct conception of right and wrong embedded in a distinct capacity for role-taking or taking the perspective of others. At stage 1, individuals are behaving rightly if they are obedient and escaping punishment. At stage 2, they can take the perspective of another person, but only in the limited sense of fair exchange. Here, two wrongs can indeed make a right, and "What's in it for me?" is compelling logic. "You scratch my back and I'll scratch yours" and "an eye for an eye" are slogans of fairness according to a stage 2 reasoner. Common among children in middle school (and not that rare in adults), stage 2 morality compels us to do what is necessary to please *ourselves*. Write Mosher and colleagues (1994), "The fundamental goal at stage 2 is to maximize personal gain and to minimize losses in any interaction with others. Greed, self-protectiveness, and opportunism are part of this way of thinking" (p. 43).

At stage 3, our morality becomes conventional. We become social beings. Our view of right and wrong shifts from the instrumental hedonism and concrete reciprocity of stage 2 to a view that is bound up with "what others think"—peers and family members, the neighbors, the people at church or temple, youth group members, teachers, and other adult mentors. This is an important advance, as any parent knows, yet it is its own cause for concern. A different sort of problem emerges, often with the force of a locomotive. Now, peer pressure and the drive to conform govern one's view of right and wrong. *Right action is that which pleases others.* Kohlberg calls this "good boy/good girl morality" because it heralds the shift to thinking about right and wrong in terms of group norms and approval.

Conventional morality continues at stage 4, but the reference point can shift from the concrete peer group to abstract, imagined groups such as "my country" or "humanity." Now individuals are concerned about how various groups in society define right and wrong and how the laws and moral grid of the overarching political community—the larger public—hold society together into a moral commonwealth that, paradoxically, protects diversity. This is an enormous advance over the prior stage of development. Pluralism and tolerance make sense for the first time, and the rule of law is revered as the glue that makes diversity and liberty, *pluribus* with *unum*, possible. Fixated at this stage of development, however, is the adult who believes that the law is necessarily right. Not until individuals' reasoning has developed to the postconventional fifth stage are they freed from reading the status quo—for example, the law—as if it were a moral commandment. At the fifth stage she is capable of principled reasoning and, therefore, the ability to evaluate a law or any other social situation in its light.

Individuals who are locked into stage 4 reasoning will not likely conceive two types of law as did King in the "Letter": just and unjust. Instead, they might espouse a law-and-order idea of justice: Rather than deriving their conception of law from justice, they will derive their conception of justice from the law—extant law. They will assume that the law mirrors justice. On this view, moral people obey the law; immoral people do not. Individuals operating at the stage 4 conception of justice will be entangled, therefore, in the status quo, be it just or not. Consequently, an interest in moving the law forward toward justice (i.e., a commitment to envisioning different ways of organizing society that might advance the common good while leaving our differences intact) is not likely to arise because these individuals are confined to maintaining conventions without the additional, transcendent capacity to interrogate their assumptions and contrast them with alternatives that may be more just. By contrast, individuals who have moved to postconventional reasoning have moved from law-obeying (right or wrong) to law-making or principled reasoning.

Both national and cross-national data (Kohlberg et al., 1984a, 1984b) show that preconventional reasoners (stages 1 and 2) are oriented rigidly to obedience and punishment avoidance. They have virtually no concern for group welfare or the common good—not because they are mean people but because their moral reasoning has not developed sufficiently. Most, but not all, of these reasoners are children. Conventional reasoners (stages 3 and 4) are also oriented rigidly, but now to systems of law that are considered fundamental to group welfare and social order, both the immediate group (stage 3) and the abstraction called "society" (stage 4). These reasoners have advanced beyond morality as law-obeying and punishment avoidance to morality as law maintenance. Relatively few persons are cognitively and morally capable of anything beyond this conventional rationality—capable, that is, of understanding King's response when he was asked by the White pastors, "How can you advocate breaking some laws and obeying others?" His reply: "The answer lies in the fact that there are two types of laws: just and unjust" (1963, p. 82). Postconventional reasoners can, in other words, figure out two things: (1) which laws need to be maintained and which need to be changed, and (2) what is the right thing to do when there are no laws. As Tapp and Kohlberg (1971) found, postconventional reasoners

> viewed rules and laws as norms mutually agreed on by individuals for maximizing personal and social welfare. They judged laws should be obeyed either

because of rational considerations or because they are coincident with universal principles of justice. The perspective offered a coherent, responsible guide to social change and the creation of new norms: [Norms] that served no purpose or were unjust should be changed; those that violated fundamental individual rights and universal moral principles could be legitimately broken. (p. 85)

This language, "preconventional reasoners" and "conventional reasoners," is a convenience. A stage of development is not fixed. Individuals move in and out of stage behavior as their social contexts change.

What Educators Can Do

Moving from this explanatory theory of cognitive-moral growth to an education theory, Kohlberg and his colleagues (Power et al., 1989) reasoned that not all social contexts are equal, that they act differently on the evolving knower, some encouraging more development than others. Which social conditions best support growth toward postconventional principled reasoning? Kohlberg concluded, and this is the essence of his education program, that *frequent and extended involvement in discussions of genuine value conflicts would promote development.* Let's be clear about these conditions.

First, whereas Kohlberg's earlier work (e.g., Blatt & Kohlberg, 1975) used discussions of hypothetical value conflicts or dilemmas, his later work (Power et al., 1989) used discussions of authentic value conflicts derived from the activities of the group. Second, the discussion group needs to be heterogeneous in its members' stages of development so that all discussants may have exposure to reasoning and social perspectives different from their own, thereby increasing the likelihood of genuine exchange and, therefore, intellectual conflict and disequilibrium. Third, a discussion leader is needed who can comprehend and present reasoning at various levels. In school settings, this is typically the teacher. Along with diversity in the student group, the leader can increase the likelihood that each student encounters reasoning that effectively probes and challenges his or her own. Fourth, the discussion group needs to be free of coercion, because perspective-taking requires the social conditions of genuine dialogue. (One cannot assume domination-free discussion. Doing so perpetuates inequities by denying them.) Finally, because justice is "drawn out" rather than "driven in," these discussions need to be dialogic. That is, discussants need to be engaged in conversation and debate about one another's reasoning rather than ignoring others' reasoning while reiterating their own arguments—a phenomenon Berkowitz (1981) called "alternating monologues."

To summarize, the evolving self is an increasingly imaginative and empathic self who—thanks to social and intellectual attainments that are the product of particular kinds of mind/society interactions—is successively better able to take into consideration others' perspectives in determining what is fair and what is not. *Such development can be encouraged.* The key is a combination of problems and value conflicts (never in short supply in social life!) and competent deliberation on them with the persons with whom we are experiencing these problems and conflicts.

Kohlberg's work has contributed greatly to our understanding of these matters (and for this reason I am featuring it here), but the complementary work of many others could be considered as well. Let us look briefly at just one of these now: the theorizing on justice by John Rawls (1971). His work targets specifically the problem of social equity in fair deliberation.

Reversibility

The notion of justice-as-perspective-taking, coupled with the five conditions of discussion described just now, make rather clear what this conception of justice entails both as a concept and as a set of pedagogical practices. To teach for justice on this view, a teacher could have students grapple with the advanced moral reasoning of the likes of Socrates, Gandhi, Hanh, Addams, and King (e.g., in Socratic seminars, dramatizations, book clubs, etc.) *and* expose students to one another's reasoning, right there in the classroom, in discussions of classroom rules and problems (the Just Community approach). But let us try to clarify further the conception of justice that undergirds both sets of practices.

Rawls in *A Theory of Justice* (1971) lays out an account of social justice based on a novel approach to social contract theory. Social contract theories typically posit, as a thought experiment, an imagined "initial choice situation" (a "state of nature") as a means by which social justice, given the constraints and affordances of human nature, might be imagined. Two of the most famous of these thought experiments were composed by the Enlightenment philosophers John Locke and Jean-Jacques Rousseau. Rawls criticized both of them for imagining flawed initial-choice situations that would not engender fairness in the arrangements agreed to therein. Rawls then advanced his own initial-choice situation that maximizes the likelihood of fair agreements. In his, people make decisions about social problems (e.g., who gets what; how lawbreakers should be sanctioned) behind a veil of ignorance. In this thought experiment, the veil prevents participants from knowing the roles they occupy, including their social positions and accompanying advantages and disadvantages, once the veil is lifted. The veil thereby erases inequity and forces impartiality into the discussion since the discussants do not know if, after the veil is lifted, they will be strong or weak, rich or poor, man or woman, Black or White, immigrant or native, captain or corporal, able or disabled, Gentile or Jew, European or Asian, ex-convict or senator, and so forth. A decision made under such circumstances is more likely to be fair because participants choose in such a manner that they can live with the choice after the veil is lifted and they find themselves in a particular situation.

Kohlberg (1979), citing Rawls, calls this justice as reversibility, or ideal reciprocity. Reversibility, as we have seen, means "changing places with." It is the criterion of justice implied by the Golden Rule: You cannot figure out what is the right thing to do until you consider being on the receiving end of your actions; that is, "it's right if it's still right when you put yourself in the other's place" (Kohlberg, 1979, p. 258). Reversibility requires both dialogue and impartiality as conditions for working out social justice. Kohlberg spells out Rawls's meaning as *ideal* perspective-taking or "moral musical chairs." This means "going around the circle of perspectives involved in a moral dilemma (a value conflict) to test one's claims of right or duty until only the equilibrated or reversible claims survive" (p. 262). Claims that are not reversible, that are not fair from all perspectives, are dropped from further consideration.

Rawls uses a cake-cutting example to illustrate reversibility at work. The just citizen who is put in the role of cake-cutter would cut it knowing that another person would be asked to distribute the pieces, thus placing the cutter on the receiving end of any indiscretions in the cutting. Knowing that the distribution of pieces of cake would be blind, it makes no sense to be anything but scrupulously fair in the cutting.

As the capacity for taking the perspective of others with less egocentric distortion develops, our ability to know others as they are and to imagine their suffering increases. We "develop" our way out of the idiocy that makes other people nothing but projections of our own mind or objects to be used to make us happy, safe, or rich.

JUST SOCIETIES

King (1963) writes in the "Letter": "I am sure that none of you would want to rest content with the superficial kind of social analysis that deals merely with effects and does not grapple with underlying causes" (p. 78). This statement propels us from considering how principled postconventional reasoners got that way—how they *develop*—to a consideration of "underlying causes" set not in the variables of psychological growth but in the material conditions of life, the way social systems are organized.

It is important, then, to challenge the psychological approach to justice with a socioeconomic approach. The former is convincing in its conception of justice as perspective-taking (imaginative reversibility; the Golden Rule; what Buddhists call compassion, or exchanging oneself for others [Khyentse, 1993]), and its explanation of why only a few of us develop to the postconventional morality of a King or a Socrates. However, the psychological approach lacks a critical *sociological* treatment of morality, which is to say an analysis of the interaction of values, knowledge, history, and the social positions and groups in which people actually live, such as race, ethnicity, religion, place (e.g., urban/rural), gender, and social class. The last of these today gets only sporadic attention, and bell hooks (2000) is blunt: "Nowadays it is fashionable to talk about race or gender; the uncool subject is class" (p. vii). Let us turn, then, to approaches that talk directly about class. An exemplar is the socioeconomic approach of Karl Marx (1965), called *historical materialism.*

Marx's scholarship is imbued with an abiding concern for justice. Its central focus is domination of the poor by the rich and exploitation of workers by owners. This is not a morally neutral stance. And it is clear that Marxism's prognosis of a socialist transformation of society was not merely put forward as objectively inevitable, but desirable. Stuart Hampshire (1977) captured this moral concern:

> For me socialism is not so much a theory as a set of moral injunctions, which seem to me clearly right and rationally justifiable; first, that the elimination of poverty ought to be the first priority of government after defense; secondly, that as great inequalities in wealth between different social groups lead to inequalities in power and in freedom of action, they are generally unjust and need to be redressed by governmental action; thirdly, that democratically elected governments ought to ensure that primary and basic human needs are given priority within the economic system, even if this involves some loss in the aggregate of goods and services which would otherwise be available. (p. 249)

Accordingly, a Marxist critique of the Piagetian/Kohlbergian scheme of moral development and its postconventional conception of justice as principled reasoning based on skillful and compassionate perspective-taking (reversibility) would not, it would seem, oppose moral theorizing per se, since moral theorizing lies at the heart of Marx's work as well. But, according to many in the school we might call "classical" or "scientific" Marxism, such is not the case.

A materialist science of society holds that objective material conditions—social arrangements or structures—account for social and psychological life. In *Capital* (1965), Marx is explicit:

> It is the ultimate aim of this work to lay bare the economic law of motion of modern society. . . . Here individuals are dealt with only in so far as they are personifications of economic categories, embodiments of particular class-relations and class-interests. My standpoint . . . can less than any other make the individual responsible for relations whose creature he socially remains, however much he may subjectively raise himself above them. (p. 10)

This is no denigration of the value of individuals, only a description of how they come to be. Marx asserted matter-of-factly that individuals' minds are organized and furnished by the objective class conditions of their lives and that to know those conditions—the underlying social structures— is to know the people who live within them and are their embodiments. Subjectivity, then, can be inferred from material conditions. Know my material conditions, and you will know my state of mind. Individuals, in this view, are *epiphenomena*—the tip of the iceberg, skin-deep expressions of underlying socioeconomic causes. Studying epiphenomena as though they were the source, while ignoring the source (material structures), is the very sort of illusory activity of which materialist critics, including but not limited to Marx, charge modern social scientists (see also Freire, 1970; Habermas, 1971; and Jacoby, 1975).

Here is the point: Moralities—codes of right and wrong conduct, conceptions of justice—are in this view epiphenomenal. Conceptions of justice and the whole of moral theorizing are aspects of subjectivity, and *subjectivity itself is an effect of underlying socioeconomic causes*. We think otherwise, that morality is fundamental to personal and social transformation, only because *ideology* (the false beliefs that legitimize current inequalities as sensible and acceptable [Cormack, 1992]) requires that we think otherwise. That is, the preservation and legitimacy of the way society is organized now— the status quo—requires people to believe that individual moral judgment matters. This is the base/superstructure model at the heart of the Marxist critique of the status quo. The socioeconomic system is the base, and everything else—the superstructure of education, the political and legal system, people's beliefs, norms, and values—is built atop this foundation.

Marx has been widely accused in the West as having spoken against the individual and against morality when we could say instead that he wrote as a social scientist endeavoring to describe and explain the causes and conditions for both. In his view, impoverished human relations, including today's prejudices against women, people who identify as LGBTQ, and people of color, and the huge imbalance between haves and have-nots—all of these exist as logical extensions of a socioeconomic structure and are not, then, moral problems to be overcome through individual "development." Similarly, in Plato's (1992b) famous cave allegory, the way out of the cave is not to be found in scrutinizing ever more closely, let alone striving to change, the shadows on the cave wall. What is needed instead is close analysis of the way ideology functions to make the shadows appear real and reasonable, lodging them in common sense, where they are taken for granted. Marx accused fellow social scientists of being preoccupied with justice and, in particular, with the just distribution of resources when they ought instead to have been concerned with the causes of these effects in underlying conditions of production. This materialist science, then, is amoral. It needs no moral theory, since its purpose is to reveal and explain social structures and their effects, one of which is moral theorizing.

Let me take this one step further. If the first scientific-socialist criticism of moral theorizing is that it is epiphenomenal, the second is that it is dangerous. Why? Moral hierarchies carry with them the potential for the repression of those who fall short of the hierarchy's moral ideal. Stalinism is a case in point, argues Andrew Collier (1981). Stalin was morally indignant at social conditions that impeded the rise of a just society. The carnage justified on behalf of that moral righteousness is well known. Other examples can be cited, from the Christian Crusades to Mao's Cultural Revolution, the Terror of the French Revolution, the Holocaust, and the contemporary campaigns of the Christian right and the Islamic right against pluralism. Pol Pot's Khmer Rouge in Cambodia exterminated countless numbers of so-called corrupt individuals who failed to exemplify in one way or another the moral ideals of that revolution. Even the Klan in America justified its virulent White supremacy, its racial terror lynchings and church bombings, on *moral* grounds.

Scientific socialism, then, takes morality to task not only for being epiphenomenal but for opening the door to Red terror, then White terror, to terrorists of the left and right, to fascists and communists, to the Khmer Rouge and the Klan, to religious fanatics, and to impassioned zealots around the world who justify killing children on behalf of some "great mission" to "purify the world."

Further developing this basic amoral position, others have argued that while it is true that Marx roundly condemned capitalist structures for being inherently exploitive of labor, he did not condemn them on moral grounds (Tucker, 1969; Wood, 1972–73). Marx did not call them unjust or unfair nor did he criticize them for abrogating workers' rights. This apparent paradox can be understood by seeing that Marx did have a theory of justice, but one that was radically historical. That is, justice is always to be understood as an appendage of a particular historical era and accompanying social arrangements and, more specifically, relations of production. Justice under feudalism is feudalist justice, justice under capitalism is capitalist justice, justice under socialism is socialist justice, and so on. Marx thought slavery was unjust in capitalist societies because it violated capitalism's own standards, but that the exploitation of labor was not unjust, since that is the essence of capitalism. Using one social arrangement's moral principles to judge another's is a mistake, for doing so fails to grasp the materialist underpinning of justice.

What we have here is a cogent line of critique that would reject the moral theorizing of Kohlberg and Rawls not by contesting its particular conception of justice, as some have done (e.g., Gibbs, 1979, Gilligan, 1982), but by drawing a line around the whole concern and calling it false consciousness:

much ado that serves mainly to mystify us into thinking that individuals make a difference when, in fact, individualism is a shadow on the wall. The activity of civic virtue, of knowing and doing the common good, is fine as far as it goes, but it doesn't go very far because it is actually an effect of something much more powerful. As a cause or force, it is impotent. To summarize, justice is at best a trivial concern and at worst dangerous ideology that obscures rather than discloses real injustice. It fails to inform us that the market economy has stolen the common good and, with it, our minds and, therefore, the sense of vision and capacity for critical thinking needed to reinvent society.

CUTTING THROUGH CONVENTIONAL WISDOM

Considering cognitive-moral developmentalism and historical materialism together, bringing them both to the table, ought to help us enlarge and rethink our understanding of what it means to be teaching for justice. That is my hope. The ideal of civic virtue, defined as knowing and doing the common good, and with it justice defined as fairness, require that we distinguish the common good from the common bad, that we distinguish fair from unfair laws, that we tell right from wrong, that we not only refrain from acting unjustly ourselves but take action against injustice wherever we find it. None of this is easy. But is it mainly a matter of cognitive-moral growth? Is it mainly a matter of developing the capacity for principled reasoning, including reversibility—the ability to imaginatively take the perspective of others? In this view, "puberty" marks the evolution from "me-centered" to "we-centered" consciousness. At last, one can be a law-abiding citizen. And what follows that, if development is not arrested, is postconventional or principled reasoning when, at last, one can make and change laws as justice requires. King (1958) supports this developmental view, at least in part, when he tells the story of his own "intellectual pilgrimage to nonviolence."

> I had grown up abhorring not only segregation but also the oppressive and barbarous acts that grew out of it. I had passed spots where Negroes had been savagely lynched, and had watched the Ku Klux Klan on its rides at night. I had seen police brutality with my own eyes, and watched Negroes receive the most tragic injustice in the courts. All of these things had done something to my growing personality. I had grown perilously close to resenting all white people. (p. 90)

Yet he supports the material view as well, at least in part. "I had learned that the inseparable twin of racial injustice was economic injustice," he wrote in the very next sentence. He tells us that he worked for two summers in a factory that hired both Blacks and Whites. His father was against it ("he never wanted my brother and me to work around white people because of the

oppressive conditions"), but doing it allowed King to see firsthand that economic injustice cast a wide net: "I . . . realized that the poor white was exploited just as much as the Negro" (1958, p. 90). He appreciated Marxism's
"protest against the hardships of the underprivileged" and its "concern for
social justice" (p. 93). But he rejected Marxism's secular materialism, which
"has no place for God. This I could never accept. . . . History is ultimately
guided by spirit, not matter" (p. 92). He also rejected its deprecation of individual freedom: "I am convinced now, as I was then, that man is an end
(not a means) because he is a child of God. Man is not made for the state:
the state is made for man. To deprive man of freedom is to relegate him to
the status of a thing" (p. 93).

Still, King (1958) credited Marx with making him "ever more conscious of the gulf between superfluous wealth and abject poverty" and ever
more committed to "a better distribution of wealth" (p. 94). Ultimately,
he expressed profound disappointment with both capitalism and communism, mainly because of the unacceptable societies and states of mind both
produce:

> Capitalism is always in danger of inspiring men to be more concerned about mak-
> ing a living than making a life. We are prone to judge success by the index of our
> salaries or the size of our automobiles, rather than by the quality of our service
> and relationship to humanity—thus capitalism can lead to a practical material-
> ism that is as pernicious as the materialism taught by communism. (pp. 94–95)

King's commitment to a fairer distribution of wealth made him many
enemies, Black and White. It was one thing to struggle against racism, quite
another to struggle against capitalism. But he found both unjust. Race segregation was bad enough; class segregation went hand-in-hand with it and
supported it all the way. His were postconventional, principled judgments.
This was moral reasoning, not racial reasoning (West, 1993). Meanwhile,
conventional wisdom—the common sense of the day—supported *both* segregation and capitalism.

Scientific Marxists will claim that King's judgments were superficial aspects of a capitalist ideology whose purpose was to safeguard the capitalist
status quo. This claim makes little sense, however, when we consider that
postconventional wisdom, as King displayed so clearly, has the ability (by
definition) to cut through conventional thinking, to see the situation differently, to disrupt and challenge it. Individuals are not only predetermined
personifications of the economic base; they are also agents who think, who
reflect on their situations, and who act. Of course, this thought, reflection,
and action are in some measure determined by social circumstances, and
people's choices are confined in some measure to predetermined options,
but they do think, they do reflect, they do act. Indeed, *only* subjects can do
these things. Maxine Greene (1995) writes, "Only a *subject*, after all, can

choose—can decide to break from anchorage and insert himself or herself into the world with a particular kind of identity and responsibility, a particular mode of valuing what lies around and straining toward what ought to be" (pp. 70–71). To fail to see this is to misconstrue causes as effects. In fact, we are cause *and* effect, both subjects *and* objects. This was Beauvoir's (1948) point, the "tragic ambiguity."

The truth of the matter of individuation, development, and choice, on the one hand, and socioeconomic conditions, on the other, appears to me to lie somewhere in combining the two. By this I mean to intersect the two (subjectivity/socioeconomic structure; individual/ environment; psychology/ sociology) in such a way that their interdependence becomes clear.

Iris Marion Young (1997) captures this combination. She invokes the work of the French existentialist, and Beauvoir's friend, Jean-Paul Sartre (e.g., 1948). Interpreting Sartre, Young writes that "agents are always free insofar as they choose to make of themselves what they are, but they always must do so within an unchosen historical and social situation" (p. 405). "Thrownness" is a term often used in existential writing for the unchosenness of the situation one is born into or in which one finds oneself. Writes Young, "We find ourselves positioned, *thrown*, into the structured field of class, gender, race, nationality, religion, and so on, and in our daily lives we have no choice but to deal with this situation" (p. 391). We are positioned. We find ourselves at the intersection of a number of social conditions (White, male, straight, middle-class, college professor, husband, brother, Buddhist, Democrat, urban dweller—these are some of my own social positions), and this positioning conditions who we are. Yet this positioning does not determine or define subjectivity—one's identity—as the scientific Marxists insist. Young writes:

> Individuals are agents: we constitute our own identities, and each person's identity is unique. We do not choose the conditions under which we form our identities, and we have no choice but to become ourselves under the conditions that position us in determinate relation to others. We act in situation, in relation to the structural conditions and their interaction into which we are thrown. Individuals can and do respond to and take up their positioning in many possible ways, however, and these actions-in-situation constitute individual identity. (1997, p. 392)

Even Louis Althusser (1984), one of the most trenchant historical materialists, suggested that actions-in-situation are not only possible but frequent. He argued that the superstructure has a "relative autonomy" (p. 67), meaning that what sits atop the basic economic system of production and distribution has some amount of independence. This allows elements of the superstructure actually to challenge and cause changes in the base rather than always doing its bidding. Accordingly, economic structures and human agency "should be seen as intertwined frameworks of social action. Changes in one result in changes in the other. Economic change results in ideological change, but this latter change can itself lead to further economic change" (Cormack, 1992, p. 14). Together, they form a complex social totality—a whole that is incomplete when one is missing.

In sum, individuals can and do act on history. But to do so in ways that advance justice, they must not only understand the present situation but be able to evaluate it in such a way that they can choose whether and how to act for transformation.

An analogy may help to convey this interdependence. The analogy concerns setting a clock to display the correct time. The fact that you have learned to tell time and have determined what the correct time is, obviously, will help you know where to set the hands on the clock. So say the individualists. The same knowledge and ability is not pertinent, however, if the clock is broken. So say the socialists. You could set the clock, but it wouldn't do any good; first, you should fix it. Still, "you can't know if you have fixed the clock if you don't know the correct time" (Reiman, 1981, p. 310). This is the point the scientific Marxists seem to have missed. Neither Stalin, Hitler, the Klan, nor the Khmer Rouge knew the correct time.

CONCLUSION

The task of educating just citizens—citizens who are principled and compassionate and who can, therefore, tell the difference between just and unjust laws and, more broadly, between decent and cruel ways of treating one another and who are, therefore, capable of enlightened political engagement—requires a conception of justice that is capable of discerning injustice not merely at the surface of social life but in the underlying, structural modes of relating. In short, a conception of justice must be thoroughgoing and critical. This requires that it see through the spells cast by ideology so that injustices that are legitimized by it might be revealed. Otherwise, tragically, individuals develop out of preconventional hedonism into conventional puberty, developing further, perhaps, the ability to see around and through common sense, only then to limit the power and reach of that achievement to trivial concerns and issues floating on the surface of social life. A developed sense of justice should not be wasted on choosing between Tweedledum and Tweedledee; rather, returning to Beauvoir (1948), it ought to promote efforts to "surpass the given towards an open future" (p. 91). Justice so conceived is necessary to the broader quest for the virtuous citizen and the good society. Its particular contribution to this quest is its capacity for recognizing patterns of domination and unfairness that may be lodged comfortably in everyday life and for working toward alternative ways of living together.

In my judgment, the developmental model of a sense of justice—a justice that matures, given the proper social interactions, from the concrete, egotistic, preconventional level to the abstract, compassionate, postconventional level—makes good sense. Here we have a compelling explanation of the role of intelligence in moral reasoning, and it is supported by an empirical base of considerable depth and breadth. Further, the conception of justice as reversibility describes a democratic, equitable form of discussion—deliberation—which not only helps resolve interpersonal dilemmas fairly but also contributes to the larger task of cutting through conventional wisdom and interrogating the fairness of present and proposed social policies.

Aside from making good sense as a theory about how just individuals evolve, this theory has desirable consequences in educational settings: Educators are more likely to orchestrate classroom and school environments in ways that bring diverse students into meaningful dialogue about the real problems of schooling/living together. These ways or conditions, to review, are as follows:

- Students are engaged in discussions of genuine value conflicts that arise in the course of relating to one another at school.
- Discussion groups are heterogeneous, so that students have the benefit of exposure to reasoning and social perspectives different from their own.
- The discussion leader is skilled at comprehending and presenting reasons and perspectives that are missing—countering preconventional ideas with conventional ideas, conventional with postconventional, and advocating for positions that are being drummed out of consideration.
- The discussion group is free of domination, gross and subtle, because perspective-taking requires the social conditions of genuine exchange.
- Because justice is "drawn out" rather than "driven in," discussions are dialogic. Discussants are engaged in conversation about their reasoning, not alternating monologues.

What the materialist analysis makes clear, however, is that both the theory of development and its conception of justice, along with its pedagogical applications, are hollow when history and the crushing weight of social conditions are ignored and when a developed sense of justice is not applied to a critique of the status quo. Without these connections, even a developed sense of justice is destined, under the weight of present conditions, to be reserved for the relatively trivial dilemmas of our private lives while the public sphere, in which those lives are nested and on which they depend, continues justice's demise.

Our challenge, then, is to comprehend individuation in its social context. On the one hand, there is individual cognition, which appears to evolve toward the more complex operations needed for principled thinking and the capacity for taking others' perspectives in dialogues about mutual problems.

On the other, are social institutions—the structures of relating within which individuals become individuals and of which subjectivity is a distillation. This subjectivity/structure tension cannot be eased without peril. The classical Marxist argument considers subjectivity—the psyche and, with it, one's sense of justice—epiphenomenal. While not entirely untrue, this structuralist argument is partial and reductionistic. It denies the subjectivity/structure tension and, consequently, contributes little to an understanding of how humans might judge one social formation against another. It fails to account for the variation in individuals' responses to the circumstances into which they are thrown and their varying ability, returning to the broken clock analogy, to tell the correct time. On the other hand, the subjectivist position, also not untrue, is also partial. Today it enjoys free reign in a sweeping societal craze Russell Jacoby calls a "cult of subjectivity" (1975, p. 119): a world of choices, will, luck, and merit, or their lack; a world that believes all you need to do to get ahead is work hard or get lucky; a world that is fixated on money and approval and how to get them; a world that tolerates and condones greed and a wealth gap of unspeakable proportions. This is just the sort of ideology needed and generated by market economies.

Rather than easing the tension between the two, the prudent course seems to me to be one that synthesizes them into one whole. The list of ills that we face, from the hedonism of consumerism to terrorism and myriad dominations of class, gender, race, religion, sexual orientation, and ethnicity, cannot be understood exclusively as a crisis in individual moral development or an expression of a flawed social order. The either/or approach can do little more than advocate one side of the tension as an antidote for the other. To reject this approach is to reject the passivity of classifying for the activity of critical thinking, which can hold the subject-structure tension dialectically. To seek virtue and social justice is to understand that the individual and the community must be known simultaneously. While not an easy task, and steeped in ambiguity, it seems the only reasonable alternative to the blind spots of either pole.

Months before his assassination, Dr. King gave his own account of this synthesis in a speech delivered in Atlanta on August 16, 1967, "Where Do We Go from Here?"

> We must honestly face the fact that the movement must address itself to the question of restructuring the whole of American society. (*Yes*) There are forty million poor people here, and one day we must ask the question, "Why are there forty million poor people in America?" And when you begin to ask that question, you are raising a question about the economic system, about a broader distribution of wealth. When you ask that question, you begin to question the capitalistic economy. (*Yes*) And I'm simply saying that more and more, we've got to begin to ask questions about the whole society. We are called upon to help the discouraged beggars in life's marketplace. (*Yes*) But one day we must

come to see that an edifice which produces beggars needs restructuring. (*All right*) It means that questions must be raised. And you see, my friends, when you deal with this you begin to ask the question, "Who owns the oil?" (*Yes*) You begin to ask the question, "Who owns the iron ore?" (*Yes*) Now, don't think you have me in a bind today. I'm not talking about communism. What I'm talking about is far beyond communism. . . . (*Yeah*) What I'm saying to you this morning is communism forgets that life is individual. (*Yes*) Capitalism forgets that life is social. (*Yes, go ahead*) And the kingdom of brotherhood is found neither in the thesis of communism nor the antithesis of capitalism, but in a higher synthesis. (*Speak*) [*applause*] It is found in a higher synthesis that combines the truths of both. (*Yes*) (1967, pp. 8–9)

Part III

GLOBAL CIVIC EDUCATION

In Part III of the book, I turn to civic education on the global stage. Here, the scene changes from the interior life of the nation to relations among nations, from nationalistic *civil* rights to cosmopolitan *human* rights, and from a focus on citizens' rights and responsibilities to controversies over who gets to be a citizen. The interior life of the political community, for citizens, is important, of course. But a narrow focus on the internal life of the political community ignores who is excluded from the community and why. Chapter 8 focuses on what students learn about the world and its peoples, Chapter 9 on human rights education, and Chapter 10 on citizenship boundaries and law.

The United Nations's (1948) *Universal Declaration of Human Rights* states that "recognition of the inherent dignity and of the equal and inalienable rights of all members of the human family is the foundation of freedom, justice, and peace in the world." These are the rights that every human has already (because they are inherent in the person), and these are the rights that liberal-democratic governments are created to protect. But liberal democracies are built atop territorial states: sovereign nations. "World citizen" is a nice idea, but there are no world citizens, actually, for there is no world state of which they could be citizens. Citizens are members of nation-states. To be stateless is, in effect, to have no rights.

I begin Part III with a study of the competing meanings of global education. One available meaning is that students will develop a global perspective and, with it, "perspective consciousness." This is an understanding that one's view of the world is not universally shared. It means also that students will understand that their perspective is shaped to some degree by forces that escape conscious detection—the implicit biases discussed in Chapter 1. At the very least, perspective consciousness means that students learn that others have views of the world that are profoundly different from their own. George Bernard Shaw (1985) featured this insight in his play *Caesar and Cleopatra*. We are in Egypt. Theodotus is Cleopatra's advisor, Britannus is Caesar's. Theodotus is explaining a local custom to the Roman visitors:

> *Theodotus:* Caesar, you are a stranger here, and not conversant with our laws. The kings and queens of Egypt may not marry except with their own royal blood. Ptolemy and Cleopatra are born king and consort just as they are born brother and sister.
> *Britannus:* (Shocked) Caesar, this is not proper!
> *Theodotus:* (Outraged) How?!
> *Caesar:* (Intervening) Pardon him, Theodotus. He is a barbarian and thinks that the customs of his tribe and island are the laws of nature.

CHAPTER 8

Educating World Citizens

International education has concerned educators and government officials for as long as there have been nations and their schools. Shortly after 9/11 there began a new push toward it in the United States. Some public schools went so far as to rename themselves "international" schools. Peering into this trend allows us to see how nationalism and cosmopolitanism compete to define civic education. The nationalistic impulse puts love of the nation first, the cosmopolitan impulse broadens to love of humanity. Imagine a cosmopolitan civic education in which students are taught not that they are, above all, citizens of the nation and stewards of its interests but, above all, citizens of the world and stewards of the planet and its inhabitants. I ask in this study how the new "international" schools are treating this question, and I clarify a set of alternatives that educators can consider when planning civic education.

Not far from my home is a public elementary school that closed for a thorough remodeling and reopened amid fanfare with "international" in its new name and dual-language immersion as its focus. Several years later, the middle school nearby added "international" to its name, too, with "global perspective" as its focus. Across town, a distressed high school was divided into small schools, and one of them became the "global studies academy." Two other city high schools have added the International Baccalaureate program.

These are not unusual events. A new "international education" movement—actually a new wave of an old movement—is under way across the country. It consists of newly internationalized public schools along with state coalitions for international education, an annual International Education Week cosponsored by the U.S. Departments of State and Education, an array of language initiatives, the Goldman Sachs Foundation's awards for exemplary "international" schools, and more. Phrases like "the global economy," "our increasingly interconnected world," and "global citizens" roll off many tongues. Audiences nod their heads knowingly. Indeed, "international education" is the new common sense in education.

But what does it mean? What forms is it taking, and what work is it doing? I have peered into the current wave from three angles: observing a handful of public schools that have transformed themselves into "international" schools, interviewing movement activists who are helping to shape them, and examining government and foundation initiatives.

NATIONAL SECURITY

National security appears to be the main engine of today's international education movement. To those who assumed that world-mindedness, global citizenship, intercultural understanding, or something of that sort was driving the movement, this may come as a surprise. Today's wave is dominated by nationalism. International education as a national security initiative has two key dimensions: economic and military. The economic way to secure the nation is to improve the nation's economic competitiveness with other nations—maintaining it or regaining it if it already has been lost. The military way is to strengthen the nation's armed forces, including its intelligence communities.

Economic Security

U.S. Secretary of Education Margaret Spellings (2005) made the economic argument for international education: "Through the No Child Left Behind Act, we are committed to having every child in the United States learn and succeed in our global economy." She linked school reform directly to success in today's world and defines that success in economic terms; school reform is a technology for accomplishing that goal.

The link is also expressed in a burgeoning number of state reports. For example, according to *North Carolina in the World: Increasing Student Knowledge and Skills About the World* (Center for International Understanding, 2005), "Improving international education is about providing students the best opportunity for success in the emerging workforce." Similarly, the Asia Society's (2005) annual conference "brings together high-level delegates from two dozen states . . . to address a significant problem in American education: the wide gap between the growing economic and strategic importance of Asia and other world regions to the United States, and U.S. students' limited knowledge about the world outside our borders."

In each of these, international education is positioned to address a key problem posed by globalization: the defense of the nation's competitive edge in the new worldwide economy of the 21st century. Schools are seen as *the* solution. Only they can produce the "enterprising individuals" (Caldwell, 2005) who will be successful in this flat new world. This is the calculus of neoliberalism (free-market fundamentalism), with its strategies of privatization, entrepreneurship, and free-trade agreements. Without it

America will lose its edge to Dublin, Beijing, or Bangalore; or if lost already, never regain it.

This is plainly put in the influential report from the National Academies of Science, Engineering, and Medicine (2007), urgently titled *Rising Above the Gathering Storm: Energizing and Employing America for a Brighter Economic Future*. This excerpt frames the problem (competition in a flat world) and the urgency (impending loss of leadership) of finding a solution:

> Thanks to globalization, driven by modern communications and other advances, workers in virtually every sector must now face competitors who live just a mouse-click away in Ireland, Finland, China, India, or dozens of other nations whose economies are growing. This has been aptly referred to as "the Death of Distance." . . . The committee is deeply concerned that the scientific and technological building blocks critical to our economic leadership are eroding at a time when many other nations are gathering strength. . . . Although many people assume that the United States will always be a world leader in science and technology, this may not continue to be the case inasmuch as great minds and ideas exist throughout the world. We fear the abruptness with which a lead in science and technology can be lost—and the difficulty of recovering a lead once lost, if indeed it can be regained at all. (p. 1)

Rising Above the Gathering Storm then moves to solutions. The first among four is K–12 education: "Enlarge the pipeline of students who are prepared to enter college and graduate with a degree in science, engineering, or mathematics by increasing the number of students who pass AP (Advanced Placement) and IB (International Baccalaureate) science and mathematics courses" (p. 6).

Military Security

The military dimension to the national security argument is framed as a communication problem: We don't know our new enemies' languages. In 2003, Rep. Rush Holt (D-New Jersey) expressed this view in the National Security Language Act: "We need to do more to make sure that America has the language professionals necessary to defend our national security. . . . Changing our [armed forces] recruiting methods alone will not solve the problem. To meet new security needs, we need to create a new domestic pool of foreign language experts and we can only do that by investing in the classroom . . . in foreign languages of critical need, such as Arabic, Persian, Korean, Pashto, and Chinese." Later came Congressional Resolution No. 100 of 2005, which urged the United States to "establish an international education policy" that would "promote a world free of terrorism, further United States foreign policy and national security, and enhance [U.S.] leadership in the world."

In 2006, President George W. Bush himself introduced the National Security Language Initiative, which would provide $114 million for the "teaching of language for national security and global competitiveness." In his speech, the president laid out a combined front for the "war on terror" composed of a language-proficient military, language-proficient intelligence network, and language-proficient diplomatic corps who are able to "convince governments" in their own language, and a language-proficient American people who, all together, can participate with greater effect in "spreading freedom."

So at least two national security arguments are at play in the current international education movement. Both are urgent—one with economic threat, one with military threat—and they overlap.

"Schools Are Broken"

The popular belief that the school system is broken also fuels the international education movement. This is a discourse of derision that tirelessly broadcasts the claim that public schools are failing to educate students for life in the new flat world.

The national security and school failure discourses are connected. Consider this statement from Operation Public Education, a reform project geared to "transforming America's schools" so as to respond to "the challenge of human capital development" in the intensely competitive "level playing field of the global economy" (Hershberg, 2005):

> Terrorism and the war in Iraq are high on the list of the nation's concerns, but the greatest danger facing America is, as [former IBM chairman] Louis Gerstner recognized, the challenge of human capital development. Our nation's public schools, the foundation for this effort, are still failing far too many of our children despite an investment of some $500 billion. (p. 276)

The author, an advisor to the Secretary of Education, continues by reminding readers that "sadly, we've known about this threat for quite some time." His reference point is the 1983 report *A Nation at Risk* (National Commission on Excellence in Education), which claimed that the "mediocrity" of our schools was so profound that had it been imposed by "an unfriendly foreign power, we might well have viewed it as an act of war." This is an urgent crisis-and-salvation narrative. The crisis story is that schools are failing miserably to educate students for the new world order. The salvation story is that only schools can rescue the nation. It is a simple formula: Schools caused the crisis and schools can solve it.

There is no small amount of magical thinking in the claim that schools can save society, since schools themselves are embedded in society. Schools are not autonomous agents outside the fray, steering society in this or that direction. They are more its caboose than its engine. Lawrence Cremin (1990), the historian of American education, observed that this formula—he called it a "device"—has been used repeatedly across the nearly 2 centuries of our education system. It was used by proponents of vocational education in the early years of the 20th century, by the post-Sputnik proponents of math and science education in the 1950s, in the 1980s by *A Nation at Risk*, and now, apparently, by the international education movement. "To contend that problems of international competitiveness can be solved by educational reform," Cremin wrote, "especially educational reform defined solely as *school* reform, is not merely utopian and millennialist, it is at best a foolish and at worst a crass effort to direct attention away from those truly responsible for doing something about competitiveness" (p. 103).

MARGINAL VOICES

While the strong discourses of national security and school failure may together dominate the movement, they don't push other meanings and programs entirely off the curriculum planning table. Percolating at the edges, and closer to the ground of school practice, are other interpretations of both the problem and the solution. I found three. One, *global perspective*, gives international education a transnational cultural meaning; another, *cosmopolitanism*, gives it a transnational political meaning; a third, *student body*, gives it a cultural meaning again, but in a decidedly local, student-centered way.

Global Perspective

The first of these marginal discourses emerged in the 1960s during an earlier wave of excitement about international education. In 1965, Congress passed the International Education Act. In 1969, the U.S. Department of Health, Education, and Welfare published an influential report that called for developing the capacity of students "to view the world system as a whole," to comprehend "the interrelatedness of the human species *qua* species," and to think in ways that are "free from the influence of ethnocentric perceptions" (Becker, 1969, pp. 268, 271).

The wave's high-water mark came in 1978 with the publication of Robert Hanvey's *An Attainable Global Perspective*, which argued for a transition from "pre-global" to "global consciousness." That meant understanding that we live in an interconnected world and developing what Hanvey called "perspective consciousness." Hanvey suggested that students needed to learn about political, ecological, economic, and cultural connections by studying problems that cut across national boundaries. "Perspective consciousness" was "the awareness on the part of the individual that he or she has a view of the world that is not universally shared, that this view of the world has been and continues to be shaped by influences that often escape conscious detection, and that others have views of the world that are profoundly different from one's own" (p. 5).

The Reagan administration dealt a direct blow to this era of international education in the 1980s, a decade that saw fierce contests over the meaning of "international" and "global" in schools. A 1986 U.S. Department of Education report, "Blowing the Whistle on Global Education" (Cunningham, 1986), accused the movement of pacifism, anticapitalism, and capitulation to foreign enemies.

The discourse of global perspective has resurfaced into today's movement as a rescaling of "multicultural education" from the nation to the globe. Knowledge, recognition, and respect for diverse cultures are taken out of the national container and extended to peoples everywhere. This approach wants to tackle the cultural provincialism and exceptionalism of American society, along with high school graduates' slim knowledge of the world.

Here's an example of how this discourse shows up in today's movement. Teachers at one new public "international" middle school embrace "global perspective" as the school mission. On the school's website, they display their objectives. Both perspective consciousness and the interconnectedness of the world system are evident:

1. *Global Challenges*: Examine and evaluate global issues, problems, and challenges (e.g., students understand that global issues and challenges are interrelated, complex, and changing, and that most issues have a global dimension).
2. *Culture and World Areas*: Study human differences and commonalities (e.g., students understand that members of different cultures view the world in different ways).
3. *Global Connections*: Analyze the connections between the United States and the world (e.g., students can describe how they are connected with the world historically, politically, economically, technologically, socially, linguistically, and ecologically).

Cosmopolitanism

Another marginal discourse for international education boldly shifts territory to world citizenship and, in so doing, raises questions about allegiance, patriotism, and identity. In contrast to putting the nation first, cosmopolitanism puts humanity and Earth first. In a brief essay that has drawn wide attention, University of Chicago ethicist Martha Nussbaum (2002) proposes a cosmopolitan education for students in American schools. She wants to transform civic education so that children are taught not that they are, above all, citizens of the United States and stewards of its interests, but that "they are, above all, citizens of a world of human beings" (p. 6). To identify oneself as a citizen of the world breaks the old habit of loyalty to a nation and being defined primarily or solely by local origins and membership. That frees us, she argues, to dwell instead "in two communities—the local community of our birth and the community of human argument and aspiration that (quoting Seneca) 'is truly great and truly common, in which we look neither to this corner nor to that, but measure the boundaries of our nation by the sun'" (p. 7).

If the global perspective approach to international education takes *cultural* education beyond the national container, cosmopolitanism does the same for *political* education. It tackles not only the problems of American provincialism and exceptionalism, but also *nationalism*. World citizenship, after all, is more a political than a cultural concept. In most states, students are required to recite the Pledge of Allegiance (to the nation, of course). The cosmopolitan school board member will ask why students aren't pledging allegiance to the larger civic community: the human family. One school may express this by quietly dropping the morning pledge ritual; another by adding a second, cosmopolitan pledge; another by adding stronger forms of environmental education, teaching a course on the United Nations's (1948) *Universal Declaration of Human Rights*, or introducing students to the International Committee of the Red Cross's (2009) curriculum *Exploring Humanitarian Law.*

International Student Body

A third marginal approach returns the meaning of international education to culture but, in contrast to the global perspective, focuses squarely on the cultural composition of the school's student body. Some public "international" high schools serving high-need students in resource-starved urban areas have created a form of international education built on the demographic composition of the student body. Immigrant students, some of them refugees, add a new kind of diversity to the schools' already diverse populations. School leaders creatively seize the opportunity and claim theirs are international schools because they have an international student body. Culture fairs showcase students' home cultures. English language learning is advanced as a central mission of the school and is, in effect, reframed as international education. The stresses on such schools—financial, the discourse of school failure, institutional racism—contribute to this reframing. "International education" can be deployed to mobilize new resources and media attention and, as one parent activist told me, "to attract market share back to the public schools."

The main emphasis of this approach, as a school district superintendent said, "is making students and teachers aware of the diversity within their midst and finding ways to help them value that and trace that to wherever it originated." He continued:

Being a magnet for so many different kids to come together seems to me to be an advantage. . . . You can't avoid it. The kids are going to experience it on the playground, they're going to experience it in the classroom, in the lunchroom, on the bus. They're going to see kids who are different from them. It becomes almost a way of living. Even though kids may never leave this city, the world has come to them.

A SOLUTION ON THE LOOSE

International education today is a broad movement containing, even in my limited study, a disparate mix of meanings and motives. It is being deployed to bolster the nation's economic and military defenses, to liberate multiculturalism from its national container, to promote world citizenship, and, in some urban schools, to take advantage of a vibrant immigrant population. These are a handful of the alternatives curriculum planners will encounter when they consider how to "internationalize" school programs. The first two add up to a national security discourse, which is backed by no less than the federal government, major foundations, the National Academies, and the popular belief that the school system is broken. The other three aim in different directions and are peripheral by virtue of lacking this kind of institutional power to advance their goals. I have painted these five in the broadest strokes, and no doubt there are more.

The multiple discourses at play under the name "international education," some strong, some weak, provide educators with a golden opportunity: to decide state by state and locale by locale how best to prepare children and youth for a changing world. Educators can spread out the alternatives, weigh them against one another, and determine which one or two, or some hybrid, shall stand as "international education."

Deeply held values are woven into each of the alternatives, including conflicting understandings of patriotism and competing visions of what schools are for. Disagreement is inevitable. Voting against House Bill 266 in Utah, which would have provided more funding for the IB program in Utah's schools, Sen. Margaret Dayton said she is "opposed to the anti-American philosophy that's somehow woven into all the [IB] classes as they promote the U.N. agenda" (quoted in Fulton, 2008, pp. A1). Aligning herself with the first of the two national security discourses and clearly against cosmopolitanism, she clarified: "I would like to have *American citizens* who know how to function in a global economy, not *global citizens*" (p. A6, emphasis added). Senator Dayton's antipathy to IB is in stark contrast to the National Academies' support for it, but *both* operate within the strong discourse of economic competitiveness.

Is "international education" anchored somewhere? The short answer, looking through the window opened in this chapter, is "no." It would be an oversimplification to assert that international education today is nothing but a continuation of national defense education under a misleading name. It is partly and strongly that, to be sure, but it is more accurate to portray the movement as plural and discordant. There are multiple meanings and practices underwritten by multiple ideologies, and there is plenty of hype. International education in U.S. schools today is a solution on the loose; it solves a variety of problems, serves an array of masters, and expresses diverse and often conflicting values. There is no coherence to the movement, only an illusion conjured by the common use of a name.

That nationalism plays a starring role really shouldn't surprise readers who, like me, were expecting the movement's centerpiece to be something different. As historians have made abundantly clear, public schools everywhere routinely serve national purposes (e.g., Green, 1990). In a nation's early years, the school system typically is devoted to developing a national community unified by common beliefs and customs. Later, the system turns to reproducing these in subsequent generations and making adjustments that are deemed necessary. International education is caught up in this pattern. As economist Kenneth Boulding (1968) observed during the 1960s wave, the challenge is to

> develop an image of the world system which is at the same time realistic and also not threatening to the folk cultures within which the school systems are embedded; for if educators do not find a palatable formula, the "folk" will revolt and seek to divert formal education once again into traditional channels. (p. 650)

Only with clarity about the various and sometimes contradictory aims of so-called "international education" can educators hope to make wise curriculum decisions. Examining these alternatives should provide a starting point.

CHAPTER 9

Human Rights Education's Curriculum Problem

Human rights education (HRE) has a small presence in the curriculum of U.S. schools. One reason is the rather widespread anti-United Nations sentiment in U.S. political culture. (Presidential campaigns in the United States often feature some amount of resentment toward it.) But there is also contention among supporters of HRE over its meaning and aim. HRE in the United States is situated mostly within the social studies curriculum, which already relies on a civil rights discourse. This is a rights discourse, certainly, but it is nationalistic rather than cosmopolitan. This chapter drills down on the need for disciplinary knowledge about (cosmopolitan) human rights alongside (national) civil rights. Readers will notice that the chapter's conceptual framework is the sociology of knowledge stemming from two of that field's leading scholars: Emile Durkheim and Basil Bernstein.

While evidence suggests that human rights education (HRE) in some respects "has expanded dramatically over the last few decades" (Russell & Suárez, 2017, p. 39), its curriculum remains at best opaque and at worst so underdeveloped as to include only "mentions" of something called "human rights." A deep conceptual understanding of subject matter goes well beyond this, of course, as does the kind of curriculum development that facilitates it. The World Programme for Human Rights Education (United Nations High Commissioner for Human Rights, 2005), to take one prominent example,[1] calls for a curriculum of knowledge, skills, values, and action, but does not develop one. Stopping short of curriculum development may be a wise strategy, as curricula need to be developed locally, where they must make sense, enjoy legitimacy, and get enacted. However, the result is that the HRE curriculum remains scattered, ill-defined, and too variable to be robust. This problem becomes apparent when HRE is compared to curricula that are coherent and well-established—school curricula for algebra and biology, for example, or national history. Such a comparison may strike readers as unfair, like comparing an infant to adults, or novices to experts, but doing so points to factors that can help HRE succeed in schools.

Curriculum development is what HRE requires now if it is to move forward to institutional stability in schools. School courses are notoriously difficult to establish, and once established they become entrenched as part of the "routine delivery of services to local constituencies" (Westbury, 2008, p. 2). Curriculum reform initiatives come and go, and then come and go again (Cuban, 1990). Advocates strain to enact change but face an uphill battle against the inertia of the curriculum already in place. My objective is threefold: to indicate why curriculum development and implementation are difficult; to clarify HRE's curriculum problem; and to suggest particular forms of curriculum development that should strengthen HRE in schools. I will show how countervailing forces to the effort to strengthen HRE come not only from the ethnonationalist-conservative right, as might be expected,[2] but also from the cosmopolitan-progressive left, where we would expect to find a lot of interest in developing the HRE curriculum. A key part of the problem is that curriculum scholars on the left have renounced curriculum development—a trend that began nearly 50 years ago (e.g., Pinar, 1975; Young, 1971). Dismissing curriculum development as technocratic, atheoretical, instrumental, uncritical, and so forth, these scholars disengaged themselves from school improvement, especially curriculum development. This robbed HRE of what could be a useful source of expertise today: curriculum scholarship that is focused squarely on the curriculum and on curriculum initiatives such as HRE.

This chapter focuses mainly on the United States, where the federal system of government decentralizes education policy. Public school curriculum development is a matter for the 50 state governments, most of which further devolve authority to local school districts, thereby making some 14,000 ministries of education nationwide, each with a locally elected board of directors.[3] My own interventions are curriculum research-and-development studies, or design experiments, in secondary schools in several states. As we shall see later in this chapter, these studies involve collaborative curriculum decision-making for college-preparatory courses. These courses have vast amounts of material to "cover," and student learning is often superficial—just enough to pass a high-stakes summative exam. My colleagues and I endeavor to organize this subject matter so that core, driving concepts and skills might be learned more deeply without sacrificing the breadth of knowledge needed for exam success.

The theoretical perspective at work in this chapter is sociological, epistemological, and critical. However, it does not stem from the two prominent sociological paradigms in education—neither the "old" sociology of education that was anchored in structural functionalism and concerned mainly with system stability and efficiency (e.g., Parsons, 1951), nor the "new" sociology of education (NSOE) that was critical in its intentions and approaches and concerned mainly with inequality, class interests, social control, and reproduction (e.g., Apple, 1979; Young, 1971). Each of these two traditions, one conservative and purportedly neutral, and one radical and purportedly emancipatory, has a disabling knowledge—and therefore curriculum—problem as we shall see. Instead, I draw on a more recent development in the sociology of education, one that is called social or critical realism. Contemporary exemplars are collected in the volumes *Knowledge, Curriculum and Equity: Social Realist Perspectives* (Barrett et al., 2018) and *Knowledge and the Future School: Curriculum and Social Justice* (Young & Lambert, 2014). These scholars are intellectual descendants of Emile Durkheim and Basil Bernstein. They are sober about what the education sector of society can and cannot do to ameliorate social inequalities originating in the surrounding political economy, but they have produced discerning scholarship focusing on what education *can* do. They are able to focus on the social justice potential of the school curriculum without committing either of two common, albeit contradictory, errors made by the left: exaggerating education's ability to change society (e.g., Dewey, 1956), and dismissing education as merely epiphenomenal (e.g., Bowles & Gintis, 1976). The relevance of this scholarship to HRE is straightforward. If the reaction to the structural functionalists was to abandon the rough-and-tumble of school improvement for the rarified chambers of radical theory and critique, then the current requirement for curricula, in general, and HRE, in particular, is a synthetic praxis: a form of critical educational scholarship that is engaged unabashedly in school improvement, especially curriculum development.

My method is interpretive, except for a brief section of empirical research that I include to illustrate a content selection strategy. I have organized this chapter with the assistance of a problem–solution frame drawn from social movement theory (Gamson & Meyer, 1996). Nothing as firm as a solution is actually offered, however; rather, solution strategies are tendered. I begin with a brief examination of the general lack of HRE in U.S. schools and then move to a broader treatment of the main task before us: developing and institutionalizing an HRE curriculum in schools.

PROBLEM: ACCESS TO *WHAT*?

HRE has a small presence in U.S. schools. The reason, in part, is rather widespread anti–United Nations sentiment and political opposition to cosmopolitan discourses in U.S. political culture (see analyses by Caporaso & Mittelman, 1988; Parker, 2011). For example, when a Utah legislator voted against additional funding for the International Baccalaureate (IB) program in that state's schools, she explained that she was "opposed to the anti-American philosophy that's somehow woven into all the classes (IB courses) as they promote the U.N. agenda" (Fulton, 2008, ¶ 10). She did not feel the need to explain further, confident that this brief rationale would be understood. And presidential campaigns in the United States typically feature some amount of resentment toward the United Nations, at least by the more conservative candidates, blaming it for undermining American sovereignty and for taking a disproportionate share of U.S. dollars without producing commensurate results or acquiescence to U.S. geopolitical positions. Recently, President Trump's "America first" campaign is indicative, as is his bellicose criticism of the United Nations.

Equally consequential, however, is that there has been much contention over the meaning and aim of human rights education among its enthusiastic advocates. This constitutes a significant signal-noise problem that hampers HRE curriculum development. Starkey (2012), for example, advocates HRE as an intervention that will enable "people whose value systems are diverse and apparently incompatible nonetheless to recognize and accept common standards and principles that make living in society possible" (p. 22); meanwhile, Matua (2011) suggests that the whole U.N.-based human rights initiative, while not exactly "a Western conspiracy to deepen its cultural stranglehold over the globe" (p. 3), is nonetheless delaying an open debate about the "reformation, reconstruction, and multiculturalization of human rights."[4] This is only one example of the tension Barton (2015) has identified "between widespread recognition of its importance and lack of consensus over its meaning" (p. 50). Conflict over definitions and goals, and, for some at least, a sort of existential crisis about the regional (European) origins of a putatively "universal" initiative, rumble on unresolved alongside passionate support for the project.

The United States is not the only country facing this second obstacle to HRE being taken more seriously (see examples in Bajaj, 2017, and Banks, 2017). But there is a third obstacle that is more specifically American: HRE in the United States is situated mostly within the social studies curriculum, when it is found at all; and the social studies curriculum already relies on an alternative rights discourse: *civil* rights. The civil rights idiom in the United States is a rights discourse, to be sure, but it is nationalistic rather than cosmopolitan. It is based on a 3-century historical narrative that runs from the Declaration of Independence of 1776 and the Bill of Rights of 1789, neither of them rejecting slavery or patriarchy, to the Declaration of Rights and Sentiments of Women in 1848, the Civil War and Emancipation Proclamation soon thereafter, Amendments 13–15 to the U.S. Constitution, and then the Civil Rights Movement of the 1950s and 1960s. These benchmarks of the American "civil rights" struggle show that the story begins with a human rights promise ("We hold these truths to be self-evident: that all men are created equal"), moves quickly to a codification of those rights (for some), proceeds to a struggle for the extension of rights to women (". . . that all men and women are created equal"), and then goes on to secure racial equality. Here is Martin Luther King Jr. using the civil rights idiom in his "I Have A Dream" address at the March on Washington in 1963. Note his reference to the earlier promise:

> We have come to our nation's capital to cash a check. When the architects of our republic wrote the magnificent words of the Constitution and the Declaration of Independence, they were signing a promissory note to which every American was to fall heir. . . . We have come to cash this check, a check that will give us upon demand the riches of freedom and the security of justice. (King, 2001, pp. 81–82).

My point is that a rather widely accepted *civil* rights discourse in U.S. schools—a discourse that is mainly national and political—may be precluding more attention to a *human* rights discourse that is cosmopolitan in reach and, further, that adds social and economic rights to political rights. (Granted, King made this transition later in his campaign, as did Malcolm X, but public opinion generally did not.[5]) A *human* rights approach would decenter the national narrative for a global narrative and, of course, include the study of an additional set of texts, such as the *Universal Declaration of Human Rights* (United Nations, 1948) and the *Convention on the Rights of the Child* (United Nations, 1989). In a number of countries where civil and cosmopolitan rights discourses compete for curricular space, we find similarities to the situation in the United States (e.g., see Bozec, 2017, on France; Ho, 2017, on Singapore; Osler, 2016, on Norway). However, it would seem that a United Nations–based, cosmopolitan, human rights discourse is more common in much of the rest of the world.[6]

A fourth reason for HRE's small footprint in the U.S. school curriculum is epistemological. This is the problem that I will explore in greater depth, before turning to some ways forward—solution strategies—that are aligned with this problem. The problem itself can be called "knowledge blindness" (Maton, 2014, p. 3), and its crux is the curriculum field's lack of attention to the curriculum. I am referring to the fact that curriculum scholars have abandoned curriculum planning, implementation, and evaluation. These very experts with the pertinent knowledge (historical, theoretical, comparative, and practical) are interested in other things, and largely ignore questions about the selection of knowledge and skills for teaching and learning in schools (the curriculum). This is ironic on several fronts. We live in a historical period that is branded as the "Information Age," and many people are said to work in a "knowledge economy." The very thing that is trumpeted as central to nearly every aspect of our lives today is itself undertheorized, and this negligence extends to the one field where everyone needs it to be addressed deliberately and explicitly: education and, especially, the curriculum field.

What explains the lack of interest in school knowledge-formation—the curriculum—in the scholarly community? It is here we would expect to find the most nuanced and robust attention. A good part of the explanation lies in the rise of competing discourses in the education field.[7] Curricularists have turned their attention elsewhere, mainly to ideology critique (skepticism, debunking, unmasking covert interests). Unfortunately, the curricular baby was thrown out with the structural-functionalist bathwater. Additionally, curricularists have turned their attention to a *learner* discourse and a *learning* discourse. Each is important, but attention needs to be paid to both of them. Schooling is not about one thing only; it is an interdependent mix of things.

The first of these competing discourses is a 50-year-old sociological program of educational criticism that debunks schools' pretenses to ideological neutrality. This critique reveals how the school curriculum reinforces rather than challenges the status quo and reproduces the inequalities of the surrounding society. This discourse has identified and analyzed educational inequality. It has also passionately advocated equal access to schools and, within them, to knowledge. This project is obviously very important insofar as it goes, but it does not go far enough. It is incomplete, for it does not attend to the forms of knowledge thus distributed nor to curriculum decision-making about which forms *ought* to be distributed. The question left unasked in this discourse is, "Access to what?" To what knowledge in particular?

This critical discourse has become mainstream in educational scholarship, despite its radical origins, and is often today's default setting in the academy—at least in education and the social sciences. The original works in England were by Bernstein (1971) and Young (1971) and then a bit later, in France, by Bourdieu and Passeron (1977) and the United States by Bowles and Gintis (1976), Apple (1979), and Giroux (1979). Mostly neo-Marxist, but not exclusively (e.g., Pinar, 1975), this critical discourse focuses on political-economic factors that are external to the education sector of society but structure what goes on there, reproducing relations of domination and subordination. Moore and Muller (1999) summarize: "Knowledge relations were transcribed as class relations" (p. 190) and soon thereafter as gender relations and then race relations.[8] Once transcribed in this way, such that knowledge is conflated with knowers, the category of knowledge becomes, as Moore (2007) writes, "exhausted in standpoints and interests that it is held to represent. Once knowledge is 'named' in this manner there is nothing else than can be said about it—the job has been done" (pp. 32–33). Instead, we say things about the learner and learning.

The contemporary discourse on the *learner* is child-centered and progressive. It places the learner in familial, ethnic, and other primary cultural contexts and identifications, and uses these referents to help students recognize themselves in the curriculum and to help them learn the curriculum, whatever it may be. Learners are individuals embedded in cultures; they have funds of relevant and usable knowledge—assets, not deficits. There is a touch of Rousseauian romanticism in this discourse: The child's purity is assumed and is not to be corrupted. The curriculum should be guided by the intention to draw out and nurture the child's true self. The child's culture, too, is to be drawn out, recognized, and sustained. Contemporary exemplars of this literature in the United States are Ladson-Billings (1995), Moll et al. (1992), and Paris (2012). This discourse may now be even more popular than the critical discourse, particularly in the wide-ranging discussions of culturally relevant pedagogy and differentiated instruction, both now standard fare in many teacher education programs.

The third, a *learning* discourse, draws attention to learning processes and the psychology of learning. It is dominated today by a newer education discipline that calls itself "learning sciences," which is rapidly replacing educational psychology, at least in name. This discourse reached its zenith in the United States with the publication of an influential report, *How People Learn* (Bransford, Brown, & Cocking, 2000). Here, teaching is for and about learning, and learning includes learning processes, learning environments, and learners' sociocultural groups and home life. Biesta (2009) derides this "learnification" (p. 36) of educational discourse. It is

> the redefinition of teaching as the facilitation of learning and of education as the provision of learning opportunities or learning experiences; it can be seen in the use of the word "learner" instead of "student" or "pupil"; it is manifest in the transformation of adult education into adult learning, and in the replacement of "permanent education" by "lifelong learning." (p. 37)

Learning in this discourse is intellectual labor done by the learners themselves—this is constructivism—and it is facilitated and scaffolded, assessed and evaluated by the teacher. Teaching becomes the orchestration of learning. Additionally, learning is enhanced in some (often unspecified) way by new media and information technologies, which are lionized in this discourse. In all of this, knowledge is assumed. McEneaney and Meyer (2000) explain that "research inattention to curricular content arises, not because scholars think the matter unimportant, but because they tend to see it as obvious" (p. 191). Scholars take the curriculum for granted because "the necessary content of modern education . . . is mostly established." Today we accept more or less without question that schools teach math, science, social studies, literature, and language. This is the curriculum—these are the school subjects. The matter is settled, more or less, around the world, and the urgent questions are about other things, especially *access*: achieving equal access to the curriculum (whatever it is), and then achieving equal learning of it (whatever), by better understanding how people learn it (whatever).

There is overlap among the three discourses and variation within them, but each highlights a crucial facet of education: First, the schools' reproduction of unequal power relations and distributive injustices in the surrounding society; second, the child, understood as a cultural being deserving care and recognition at school; and third, processes of learning.

For present purposes, note: None of the three discourses attends to *which* knowledge students should learn and are entitled to learn at school.

None proposes a curriculum, a selection of subject matter. This is a problem; since not everything can be taught, choices have to be made and, inevitably, are made. This subject-matter selection is anything but neutral, as Young (1971) and Apple (1979) established long ago; the curriculum is a social construct (it is located materially in the social and historical practices and conditions of its production) and, as such, relays power relations from the political economy into the school. Much "critical" scholarship reveals how, where, and to whose disadvantage this occurs. Still, and here is the rub, a curriculum is needed if the school is to be a school. It is the asset that anchors and justifies the others: teachers, instruction, students, classrooms, assessment, parent–teacher conferences, administrators, cafeterias, and janitors. Save for its curriculum, there is no need for a school. And at school, some forms of knowledge are more powerful—that is, more empowering to learners and to society—than others. HRE should be focusing on these forms.

Scholarly inattention to this project means that schools generally, and HRE in particular, must proceed without curricular expertise. The curriculum field, having been drawn to adjacent matters (critiques of neoliberalism and reproduction, rapt attention to learners and learning), is of little help to HRE. Whatever may have been its problems when Joseph Schwab (1969) called the curriculum field "moribund" (p. 1), today it has simply renounced its object. The curriculum field is circling inside an old discovery, rearticulating the seminal, critical work of the 1970s. This is important work, to be sure, but the project does not end here. Curriculum-making, implementation, and evaluation are needed. In the postwar years, progressive educators began to associate curriculum development with conservatism, and by the 1970s, the left was abandoning subject-matter concerns altogether.[9] The consequences of this have dealt a serious blow to social justice education. The school curriculum was surrendered to interest groups and market forces whose testing-and-accountability initiatives and social-efficiency imperatives narrowed the curriculum in socioeconomically distressed schools to reading and math, thereby exacerbating inequalities in educational achievement, fueling school privatization and segregation, and opening the door to an instrumental curriculum of so-called "21st-century skills."[10]

SOLUTION: TOWARD AN EPISTEME FOR HRE

The situation is one of "crisis," according to sociologist of education Michael Young (Young, 2013, p. 101). What compels us to listen to him is that he is the same Michael Young whose 1971 book *Knowledge and Control* launched the critical discourse discussed above—the "new" sociology of education that jettisoned knowledge from the curriculum field by transcribing the field as power relations. Young now sees that the critical sociology he initiated was only half correct. Showing how school curricula relayed power relations from outside schools into the schools themselves, creating rather than attenuating achievement gaps and reinforcing rather than reforming the status quo, was enlightening, but the exposé left in its wake no curricula for schools to teach. Curriculum development, then, was left to politicians, corporate wunderkinds, entrepreneurs, and a multitude of state and local committees charged with creating curriculum standards. Furthermore, curriculum theory itself, where we would expect to go for expertise, was left without an epistemology, that is, without a theory of knowledge for content selection. Accordingly, let us turn to Young's newer analytic framework, which is the social realist alternative referenced in the introduction to this chapter and neatly summarized by the title of his book, *Bringing Knowledge Back In* (2008).

Bringing Knowledge Back In

If there is to be HRE in schools, there needs to be an HRE curriculum. The curriculum is the knowledge, the subject matter, the *what* teachers and others choose for instruction and, therefore, *what* students have the opportunity to learn should they be fortunate enough to gain access to good schools and good teachers. The curriculum is the school's defining characteristic, its raison d'être. It is what parents send their children to school to learn. Furthermore, the *what* is not to be confused with the *how*: instruction. Instruction is about how teachers teach the curriculum and how they relate to students.[11] Just as there are different kinds of instruction (didactic, constructivist, teacher-centered, student-centered, etc.), there are different kinds of curricular subject matter. The two main kinds of subject matter are content (information, concepts, principles) and skills, sometimes called know-what and know-how, or in Schwab's (1964) terms, the substantive and syntactical structures of knowledge. Together, they constitute the largest portion of the school's explicit curriculum.[12]

Like any curriculum (e.g., courses in biology, music, or history), a human rights curriculum needs to be based on a theory of knowledge (an idea of what is meant by knowledge). Further, it needs a pedagogical theory about how to organize that knowledge for learning by children and young people of different ages and stages. This will include, among other things, a framework explicating beginning, intermediate, and advanced understandings of human rights. The scheme for the former epistemological theory cannot simply distinguish one subject from another—say, physics from history—for this barely touches the problem. And the latter pedagogical theory cannot rest simply on a quantitative metric of more (for "advanced") and less (for "beginning") knowledge of human rights, as this confuses breadth with depth. Moreover, and importantly for present purposes, both theories, the epistemological and the pedagogical, are, like any theory, social constructs; they are not found in nature or the heavens but in social activity. But this does not obviate the need for both. (Believing it does is the error made too often in the critical discourse described above—this is Young's "crisis.")

Both theories contribute to the classification of the resulting knowledge as "disciplinary." Disciplinary knowledge is undergirded by a theory of what knowledge is, as well as a theory of how to organize it for teaching and learning. But more central to defining disciplinary knowledge is Young's reintroduction of Durkheim's (2001) insight that there are two kinds of knowledge, abstract and concrete; that is, theoretical (disciplinary, scientific, academic) and experiential (everyday, sociocultural, local). The two overlap to some extent in pedagogical practice, but the distinction is useful and has profound implications for deciding on the school curriculum.

Disciplinary knowledge transcends the everyday, context-dependent, experiential knowledge of students; it is not common sense. It is generative, not static, because its central ideas stimulate additional inquiry; one discovery prompts another. Consequently, it is the most powerful knowledge students can be taught at school. It enables them to think outside the boxes of their upbringing. Students deserve to be taught this knowledge—and need to be taught this knowledge—precisely because it is not available in their experience. This is its window-opening, emancipatory promise. McPhail and Rata (2018) capture it well:

> By having access to disciplinary knowledge, with its counter-intuitive character (i.e., it does not correspond to the everyday world of appearances), students can think about the world in abstract or context-independent ways. This takes students beyond the common-sense understandings acquired from their socio-cultural location, enabling them to develop a critical awareness of the forces structuring their lives and to imagine alternatives beyond their everyday experiences. . . . It is this liberating potential of disciplinary knowledge that makes it a political, as well as an epistemological, resource, one that all students should have access to. (p. 70)

The concepts that we expect to see at the core of a curriculum on human rights education are disciplinary concepts. These include, inter alia, *universal rights, universal respect, human dignity, peaceful coexistence, justice, dissent,* and *activism.* These are abstract ideas that are exemplified in and animated by an array of day-to-day cases and struggles (see Chapter 4, this volume). The ideas transcend the particulars, but they arise from them and are applicable to them. We use the concepts to recognize and analyze the cases, clarifying and defining them. We use them also to identify and define violations of human rights and to protect rights and prevent violations. Imbued with such concepts, students have the intellectual power to take intelligent action because they understand the world in new ways. In the United Nations's (2011) *Declaration on Human Rights Education and Training,* concepts like these fall into the category of "education *about* human rights." This category "includes providing knowledge and understanding of human rights." Here are the norms and principles of human rights, the values that underpin them, their histories, the mechanisms for their protection, and methods and stories of political activism to hold governments accountable for protecting human rights and to protest and prevent violations.

The authority for these concepts is found in intellectual fields: the HRE specialist communities that create them. This is true across disciplines: the physicists, biologists, and historians who argue over the core concepts, values, and procedures of those intellectual fields are the specialists who define those fields. "Such fields have structures, principles, and logics of their own," writes Moore (2007, p. 36), which is what make their output "disciplinary." Similarly, the HRE specialists who argue over the goals of HRE and the meaning of core categories such as rights, respect, and peaceful coexistence are the actors who define human rights education. But more pertinent to the *E* in HRE are those specialists who focus on *education* for human rights. Human rights is a scholarly field within law, sociology, political science, and other academic fields as well as in interdisciplinary centers. Human rights *education* is a related scholarly field, but the two are not identical. It is one thing to identify a field or discipline and another to select the subject matter and pedagogies for teaching and learning it in school. Making the move from one to the other—"recontextualization" is Bernstein's term (2000, p. 41)—requires a consideration of subjects (these are young people, not adults; students, not experts), setting (schools, not workplaces or ballfields), and purpose (general education, not vocational or higher education).[13] The point is that a specialist community is at the social heart of any discipline and that the disciplinary knowledge it produces is provisional, by definition, and subjected to ongoing criticism and revision within the community. The specialist community argues over the field's truth claims and interventions, constructs its parameters and the rules and procedures by which claims are legitimated, and, in the process, defines its substance and syntax. Knowledge is both social and real—both the knowledge claims *and the conditions of their production* are available for examination. The specialists' arguments are transparent thanks to their communities' conferences and peer-reviewed journals.[14] This is not the case for everyday, sociocultural knowledge. One is not better than the other, but they are different; and to acquire the one, but not the other, is why children are sent to school.

We can further specify three conditions needed for a powerful human rights curriculum in schools. First, as we have seen, its knowledge is abstract and therefore applicable to and anchored in numerous on-the-ground examples and contexts. Second, this knowledge is generated socially in specialist communities that are more or less autonomous collectives. Historically, this has meant that these communities are relatively independent of religious dogma and government intimidation. Galileo, recall, was forced to recant his observations of the Moon when he was called to the Inquisition in Rome. However, he was not working alone but sharing his observations with other specialists who were also observing nature. So, in the end, while disciplinary knowledge lost a battle in Rome in 1633, it began to win the war that became the scientific revolution. Today, the membership of the International Astronomical Union, not the Pope, decides whether Pluto is a planet. Similarly, content selection for schools draws largely on the specialist communities known as the academic disciplines rather than on the clergy, the party, or the military police. The proceedings of these scholarly collectives are transparent, and their truth claims are subjected to ongoing criticism and revision via conferences and peer-review journals. Fallibilism (belief in the provisional nature of truth claims) anchors the value system. Therefore, the knowledge selected for instruction in schools is warranted by the procedures used to generate that knowledge.

Third, a powerful human rights curriculum is powerful because it is organized into a coherent symbolic order, as are the established curricula in physics, history, and biology. This includes logical conceptual progression from incipient understandings to complex and integrated ones—to "advanced" knowledge of human rights. It is in this third condition that HRE's curriculum problem mainly resides and where curriculum development initiatives can be most fruitful. As we saw at the outset of this chapter, the minuscule attention paid to HRE in U.S. schools can be attributed in part to opposition to cosmopolitan discourses in schools and in part to a national civil rights discourse that already occupies the space that might be given to an international human rights approach. But the two additional problems discussed at the outset especially affect this third condition: one is the tension caused by HRE advocates who disagree with one another about goals and meanings; the other is the abandonment of curriculum development and evaluation by its primary specialist community—curriculum scholars. These two problems produce the epistemic incoherence of HRE—its "weak grammar" (Bernstein, 1999, p. 168). The solution is to work toward greater epistemic strength. The school subjects of physics (with a hierarchical knowledge structure) and history (with a horizontal knowledge structure)[15] can serve as models, for they have successfully achieved, despite their epistemic differences, institutionalization in schools. They have stable, large footprints. We see the feeble school presence of HRE when we contrast it with these relatively successful school subjects.

Conceptual progression (Rata, 2016) means that a school subject has an epistemic framework—an organized system of meaning—which includes a scheme for sequential teaching and learning. This requires in turn that educators possess a shared understanding of what constitutes a preliminary grasp of the subject and a more advanced grasp, and an understanding of the difference between superficial and deep knowledge of the subject. These understandings allow educators to plan instruction (lessons 1, 2, 3; courses 1, 2, 3; etc.) that systematically deepens students' understanding of the subject.

But to do this, and here is my point, HRE has to be organized and coherent within itself, internally. This is its *episteme*.

Strategies

HRE lacks this basic structure, this disciplinary integrity. The first step to achieving it, as we have seen, is to identify HRE's knowledge base: its disciplinary concepts, cases, history, literature, and skills. This involves organizing its knowledge into at least two sets: a smaller one judged to be core and a larger, broader one judged to be marginal. The two sets are interdependent and related center-to-periphery, like a sun with its orbiting planets and moons. This strategy (if not the solar metaphor) was made popular by the mid-20th-century "structure of the disciplines" movement led in the United States by Bruner (1960) and Schwab (1964). As they saw it, nearly any curriculum will contain too many topics to be internally coherent, let alone teachable and learnable, if it is not organized in such a way that some topics—let us call them core topics—anchor the others.[16] Hilda Taba (1945) had written earlier that the overcrowding of a curriculum "is such a time-worn criticism as to appear trite. The content in many subject areas . . . has been expanded to the point where only superficial knowledge is possible, and little or no time is available for thoughtful reflection and generalization" (p. 93). This is precisely the problem that requires content selection and core–periphery organization. As Bruner argued, to learn any meaning system—any conceptual framework—is to grasp how its parts are related. This insight requires HRE specialists to do the intellectual work of selecting and articulating core and peripheral knowledge in such a way that the gravitational pull of the suns carries the planets and moons along with them. An illustration of this strategy from a recent empirical study may be helpful.

My research team was attempting to select and organize knowledge for a college preparatory course that hundreds of thousands of American high school students take in upper secondary school. The course is called Advanced Placement U.S. Government and Politics. Our goal was that students would perform as well or better on the summative, breadth-oriented exam as students in traditional versions of the course, but they would learn the subject matter more deeply. This meant that students would need to learn both the core content deeply and the peripheral content at least superficially. Our task was not to replace breadth with depth but to articulate the two, and our procedure was a practice we called deliberative content selection. This practice entails deciding collaboratively and iteratively, in face-to-face meetings, on the substantive and syntactical structure of the course.[17] The concepts *federalism, limited government,* and *separation of powers* were eventually selected as the substantive suns of the course and *constitutional reasoning* and *perspective-taking* as the syntactical suns.

Once these core concepts and skills were selected, they could be spiraled through the course, thereby affording recursive, cyclical instruction on them, deepening students' understanding while drawing in the peripheral knowledge along the way. Details and results of the study can be found elsewhere (Chapter 5 of this book plus Parker et al., 2011, 2013, 2018; Parker & Lo, 2016b). Generally, students in the course did as well or better on the exam as students in traditional courses. However, they learned the core knowledge more deeply. The point to be made for present purposes concerns the essence of this strategy: selecting and organizing the curriculum so that instruction has a clear object.

A second strategy is needed, too, although this one is instructional rather than curricular. Beyond selecting and arranging knowledge into a center–periphery scheme, teachers need to articulate this disciplinary knowledge with students' everyday, sociocultural knowledge. These two are also related and interdependent, for as Moll (1990) wrote, after Vygotsky, "Everyday concepts mediate the acquisition of scientific concepts" (p. 10).[18] Children's home knowledge mediates their learning of disciplinary knowledge at school. This second strategy has enjoyed renewed attention in the past 20 years as part of the rise of the "learner" discourse sketched above and is a familiar theme in the HRE literature (e.g., Bajaj, 2017; Lundy, 2007; Osler, 2016). It represents a traditional, one could say classic, tension in education. It appears in Plato's dialogue "Meno" (1956) and is summarized in the title of John Dewey's 1902 essay *The Child and the Curriculum*. Dewey wrote,

> Abandon the notion of subject matter as something fixed and ready-made in itself, outside the child's experience; cease thinking of the child's experience as also something hard and fast; see it as something fluent, embryonic, vital; and [then] we realize that the child and the curriculum are simply two limits which define a single process, just as two points define a straight line. (Dewey, 1956, p.11)

The two strategies—the articulation of core and peripheral disciplinary knowledge and the articulation of disciplinary knowledge with students' everyday knowledge—will go a long way toward organizing a curriculum and helping students learn it. The second without the first, however, is meaningless because instruction is adrift without a curricular object. A human rights education designed with both strategies in tandem, whether for a single course or spiraled systematically across the years of compulsory schooling, would be an achievement.

CONCLUSION

Knowledge is the central category of education. It is education's activity (transmitting knowledge) and goal (achieving knowledge and, in the name of justice, closing achievement gaps between groups of students). HRE can be strengthened in schools if concerted attention is paid to its knowledge base—its curriculum. School subjects like physics and history have been successfully institutionalized around the world, not without argument and variation, of course, but they are relatively stable and routine nevertheless. They have strong grammars—epistemic coherence—constructed through decades of theoretical debate, research, practice, and revision in more or less autonomous specialist communities. HRE does not have this advantage, this path to institutionalization. Far from it; HRE is young and fractious and anything but a school staple. In the United States, it is a curricular wannabe. Its prospects for institutionalization are limited, and progress will be slow and episodic. Furthermore, the abandonment of curriculum development by curriculum scholars has not helped. The shift of attention to ideology critique, learners, and learning has resulted in the lacunae at the core of HRE: content selection and organization.

My argument has been that knowledge matters in HRE, and that we must pay concerted attention to it. I have critiqued the trends that have pushed it so far into the background that knowledge blindness affects the very field we rely on for advice on the knowledge dimension of schooling: curriculum studies. I do not suggest that ideology critique and attention to learners and learning should be pushed to the background to make room for curriculum in the foreground; rather, I suggest that all four concerns be kept in the foreground at once, rather like a juggler keeping multiple balls in the air. Schooling is not about one thing only, but an interdependent mix of things; and if epistemology and curriculum decision-making are missing from the action, it is difficult to claim that the action is educational or that it has a social justice mission. Wanting to learn important content and skills is, after all, the reason why marginalized groups struggle to gain access to schools. Similarly, it is why already advantaged groups scramble to get into ever-better schools (Labaree, 2010). If school-access and school-inclusion initiatives are to be meaningful, then the school curriculum itself must be meaningful; and this requires that it be deliberated, selected, and organized rather than presumed.

HRE's curriculum problem is twofold: the flight of expertise from the field of curriculum practice, redefining it away from subject matter to students, their lives, and their learning processes, and HRE's lack of a coherent knowledge structure—an episteme. A more robust HRE requires not only advocates and arguments but a reasonably stable curriculum that its advocates—teachers, policymakers, and HRE specialists—can adapt to local needs and circumstances. It will be particularly interesting in the United States to see how HRE curriculum-makers articulate its core concepts, cases, history, and skills with those already at the center of the more successfully institutionalized *civil* rights curriculum. There are, no doubt, parallels in other nation-states where local norms, desires, and understandings encounter abstract, cosmopolitan ideals.

CHAPTER 10

The Right to Have Rights

Citizenship matters. It designates who is and isn't an authorized member of a po-litical community. Being a member of a nation, in particular a liberal democracy, is what gives a person access to rights. Criteria for membership are the subject of fierce debates. Can you belong simply by living in the country for a long time? Or must you be born here? Do you need additional qualifications concerning race, language, religion, or skills? Must you be literate? Civic education often ignores these questions because it focuses on life inside the political community. The interior life, for citizen-members, is important, of course—participation in government is at stake, for example. But emphasizing the internal life of the politi-cal community ignores issues related to membership boundaries: Who is included, excluded, and why? These are the focus of this chapter as I review an important proposal by legal scholar Angela M. Banks.

Citizenship is a kind of membership—the political kind. And in a society that is trying to sustain a liberal democracy, citizenship entails a way of re-lating to other citizens: resolving conflicts with dialogue, persuasion, elec-tions, and respect, not violence and intimidation. "Speech takes the place of blood, and acts of decision take the place of acts of vengeance" (Pocock, 1998, p. 32).

Citizenship has long been associated with territory as well. One can be-long to other kinds of communities, such as a faith community or a profes-sion, without implying location. Catholics and Buddhists, for example, can be found almost anywhere, their location peripheral to their membership, as can teachers and plumbers. But to be a citizen is to belong lawfully to a political community that is also a territory. Hannah Arendt (1968) wrote that a citizen "is by definition a citizen among citizens of a country among countries." A citizen's "rights and duties must be defined and limited . . . by the boundaries of a territory" (p. 81). *Must be.* Arendt is expressing not a preference but a fact. Membership in a territorial state—a nation—is what gives a person, as she put it, "the right to have rights."

So, citizenship matters. It designates who is and isn't a member of a po-litical community. DREAM activists may be living *in* the United States, and they may feel "at home" here, but while they are, in fact, "at home," they are not, in fact, citizens: They have not been granted the status of lawful membership. This may be wrong or right—it is an ongoing policy controversy about which people have strong feelings. It is but one example, worldwide, of conflict over the boundaries of citizenship.

To think critically and ethically about who can be a citizen of the United States, who ought to be, and on what terms, is the subject of Angela Banks's (2021) timely, erudite, and carefully organized book, *Civic Education in the Age of Mass Migration*. Banks approaches civic education from the field of legal studies, where she is a distinguished professor of law at the Sandra Day O'Connor College of Law at Arizona State University.

A CURRICULUM PROPOSAL

Banks seeks to expand the purpose, scope, and inclusiveness of civic education. She proposes a civics curriculum that not only teaches the knowledge and skills that citizens require but also provides students the opportunity to examine the meanings and boundaries of citizenship itself. "The line between citizen and noncitizen, the criteria for citizenship, the goals achieved by drawing the lines as they are, and the need for a line in the first place are questions addressing the boundaries of citizenship" (p. 1). She proposes that the concepts *migration, membership, citizenship*, and *citizenship status* become regular and explicit subject matters of civic education. And she concentrates on two questions: Who gets to be a citizen? And on what values and laws is that decision based?

Banks observes correctly that conventional civic education (or what traditionally has been called "citizenship education") has ignored these topics. The main reason is that civic education typically has focused on life *inside* the political community. The life inside, for citizens, is important, of course. It includes knowing and caring about many things: the rights and duties of citizens, elections, interest groups, political parties, protests, the separation of government powers into branches, checks and balances, federalism, inequality, incarceration, and struggles for the right to vote, both historical and contemporary. But emphasizing the internal life of the political community, Banks writes, "ignores issues related to the *threshold* of the community" (p. 39). These threshold or admission issues involve member/nonmember boundary lines: Who is included in the political community, who is excluded, and why? Furthermore, what are the procedures and policy shifts needed to admit at least some of those people currently being denied, such as long-term unauthorized residents like DREAM activists?

Across four chapters and an appendix containing primary documents for classroom activities, Banks lays out a curriculum proposal with four objectives. Note the interplay of knowledge and values. Students will

- know the boundaries to membership in the United States and access to citizenship status;
- know the foundational values (shared goals) governing membership in the United States;
- examine the boundaries in light of these values; and
- think creatively about now to narrow the gaps between the boundaries and the values.

RATIONALE

Banks's rationale is twofold. One concerns students, the other, subject matter. First, right there in a school classroom are youth of various membership and citizenship statuses. Unauthorized immigrant youth are likely to be there alongside authorized immigrants, nonimmigrant visitors, and citizens. Some students may be the children of low-wage foreign workers; others, the children of naturalized citizens; others, the children of lawful permanent residents, green card holders, and more. This mixture of statuses is especially relevant in social studies classrooms, where law, immigration, government, history, and economics are the explicit subject matters. Banks cites Dafney Dabach and colleagues' (2015, 2018) groundbreaking research for its attention to this mixture. Dabach and colleagues ask, How do teachers teach about citizenship when they believe that some of their students are unauthorized?

There is a second aspect to Banks's rationale. She believes the topics of membership and citizenship boundaries are important in their own right and deserve space in the civics curriculum. She cites political philosopher Will Kymlicka, who believes that a central task of civic education "is not to evade the distinction between members and nonmembers, but to think in a critical and ethically responsible way about the diversity of people who belong to society" (p. 6). From the array of topics that potentially could be included in a civic education curriculum, concepts and questions of membership and citizenship deserve space. They are important, even urgent, and rich. These concepts and questions are at once practical, legal, empirical, and ethical matters. Race, class, and gender categories are pertinent. And for the students themselves, like the rest of us, the fact of residence—where we live now—is a defining, existential matter.

THE IMMIGRANT LABOR PARADOX

Banks is keen to draw readers' attention to what she calls the "immigrant labor paradox." The paradox is that current law authorizes employers to hire low-wage foreign workers to labor on their farms and in their factories, making long-term residents of many of them, but creates no pathway for them to become citizens with citizenship rights and privileges. She explains:

> Low-wage foreign workers are critical for the economic growth and development of American society, yet they are viewed as a threat to American society and denied consistent access to American citizenship. This is a paradox that prevents the 11 million unauthorized migrants in the United States from accessing the legal status of citizen. (p. 19)

By framing this situation as a paradox—a contradiction or puzzle—Banks leverages the normative principles of democracy against the rapacious forces of capitalism. Owners get their desired workers, yes, "but in a way that requires the workers to remain on the periphery of society without a pathway to *de jure* (legal) membership" (p. 29). Current law and law enforcement cooperate in this scheme by granting temporary work permits or, sometimes, looking the other way.

Justice demands a response to this paradox. In addition to proposing these concepts and questions for teaching and learning in civic education programs, Banks proposes in Chapter 3 a policy shift toward a more inclusive conception of membership. This conception is based on the "social fact of membership," known in legal studies as *jus nexi* principle. According to this conception, citizenship boundaries should be changed to accommodate a person's actual, lived connections to the place rather than drawing them based on bloodline or birthplace. Banks writes:

> Citizenship status does a poor job of accurately identifying members of American society. This approach to membership fails to identify long-term residents who lack citizenship status but who actively participate in American society and have significant connections to American society as members. (p. 48)

Accordingly, long-term residents would be admitted to the political community because they already are, in fact, participants in the society and because they experience themselves that way. On this principle, the identity assertion "I am an American" makes a person an American. DREAM activists provide the clearest example today of this identity-based approach to membership. While lacking legal immigration status, these unauthorized immigrants *feel* that they belong, and they *are* connected to the society in myriad ways. They have been fighting for lawful immigration status and a pathway to citizenship "because they see themselves as Americans" (p. 41).

Banks draws on legal scholar Linda Bosniak (2006) to bolster her argument for a pathway to citizenship for long-term residents. Bosniak, in *The Citizen and the Alien: Dilemmas of Contemporary Membership*, presents a typology of citizenship with four dimensions: identity, legal status, rights, and participation. She brings attention to a particular dilemma: When we redraw the boundaries of membership, allowing greater access to these four dimensions for long-term residents, do we not then undercut the community, the bounded affinity, felt by and with those who already are fellow citizens? Do we not threaten the necessary civic partnership and solidarity and the very idea of community? The warmth and safety of belonging are valued social goods, not dispensable luxuries; humans need to belong if they are to survive and flourish. But, Bosniak asks, is this concern for the feelings and comradery of insiders not merely a form of xenophobia mixed with "selfishness, self-interestedness, or indifference" (p. 206)?

There's the rub: Community belonging and membership are, by definition, both inclusive and exclusive. Like any fence or gate, they have two sides. The inclusionary and exclusionary dimensions of citizenship collide in this value tension, and there is no easy way around it.

Banks does not resolve this dilemma but proposes that students examine it as part of their civic education. This is her curriculum proposal. However, she does take a side. She advocates for greater inclusiveness and, therefore, expanded membership, and she bases her case on the *jus nexi* principle. In her analysis, capably elaborated in her third chapter, the *jus nexi* principle is based on the foundational democratic principle of popular sovereignty. According to this principle, anyone who is affected by a governmental decision has a right to participate in making that decision. (Governments derive their legitimacy, as the Declaration of Independence states, "from the consent of the governed.") Banks then extrapolates: "Popular sovereignty demands, at a minimum, that unauthorized migrants, particularly long-term residents, be viewed as members of the polity and entitled to participate in governance" (p. 51). To base it otherwise, as now, on "racial hierarchy, patriarchy, and capitalism . . . contradicts the stated principles on which the United States was founded" (p. 37).

Banks does not suggest that teachers advocate the *jus nexi* principle. Rather, she wants teachers to give students the opportunity to learn it. She suggests that students consider these questions:

1. Does the *jus nexi* principle do a better job of achieving the purposes and goals of membership within a democratic society?
2. Does application of the *jus nexi* principle create new problems of exclusion that do not exist within the current approach to citizenship?
3. How can the *jus nexi* principle be operationalized?
4. Is it practically possible to utilize the *jus nexi* principle to allocate the legal status of citizens? (p. 56)

CLASSROOM ACTIVITIES

Banks devotes fully half of the book's pages to five classroom activities that explore the boundaries of membership and belonging. Each is tied to a specific case ranging from 1943 to today. In each of the five cases, membership decisions were made that determined access to resources, from jobs and financial assistance to rights themselves. In Table 10.1, I outline the activities that Banks proposes. I highlight the topics, central concepts, the gist of the student activity, and the accompanying primary sources.

The five activities involve both curriculum (the *what* of the lesson) and instruction (the *how*). On the curriculum side are the core concepts, guiding questions, and primary sources. The instructional side includes reading of complex texts, role-playing, and discussion. Additionally, Banks anticipates student discomfort with the material and addresses it. Psychological discomfort is probable, she believes, because the activities are likely to upset students' identities and prior beliefs. The resulting "cognitive dissonance" (p. 59) will arouse students' self-protective strategies, and these will shape how students process the information provided in the documents and how they engage in discussion. Consequently, Banks believes an orientation is needed before each activity—a kind of advanced organizer—in order to mitigate discomfort and defensiveness and prevent them from derailing the lesson. Her strategy is to affirm what she believes students have in common: a shared commitment to the superordinate American creedal values of liberty, equality, and justice. "Reminding students of their identity as individuals who are committed to these values before beginning the [lessons] and then framing the [lessons] as opportunities to explore these values has the potential to minimize students' psychological discomfort" (p. 59).

I appreciate Banks's recognition of the likelihood of student discomfort and her suggestion for addressing it. I know and admire good teachers who teach controversial current issues precisely because they are in the news and debatable and, therefore, generate student interest, which can then be channeled into learning the concepts and questions at hand. Curricular rigor, relevance, and student engagement are thus combined—the serious teacher's holy grail. But I also know and admire teachers who avoid this subject matter because they don't want to make vulnerable students feel uncomfortable. Additionally, they don't want other students to silence themselves on the very concepts and questions that are at the heart of the curriculum. These teachers are aware that microaggressions are likely for some students but that others will stifle their own views, whether to not make other students uncomfortable or to avoid being ridiculed for expressing an unpopular opinion. Immigration and citizenship are, after all, matters of heated policy disputes. Opposing views on these matters are likely to exist in classrooms as they do outside of school. And let us not forget that we have had a president who launched his first candidacy in 2015 with a speech calling immigrants "drug smugglers" and "rapists" and promising to "build a great, great wall." Despite such brazen fearmongering, stereotyping, and xenophobia, *he won the election*. Americans by the millions support this discourse. Our society is polarized on the matter of citizenship boundaries, and

Table 10.1. Banks's Five Lessons on Citizenship and Immigration Status

Topic	Concepts	Activity	Primary Sources
1. Repealing the Chinese Exclusion Act	• race • citizenship and immigration status • naturalization • values and norms	Role-playing members of House Committee on Immigration and Naturalization during WWII, students deliberate, in small groups, the question "Should the repeal bill move to the entire House?" Eight subquestions guide the deliberation.	• Congressional testimony (1943) of Pearl Buck (pro) and James Wilmeth (con)
2. Gender and Citizenship Acquisition	• birthright citizenship • gender and the Equal Protection Clause, 14th Amendment	Role-playing members of Congress, students deliberate, in small groups, how to rewrite the rules governing citizenship acquisition for children born abroad to an unmarried citizen. Eight subquestions guide the deliberation, e.g., What is the purpose of birthright citizenship?	• *Sessions v. Morales-Santana*, SCOTUS (2017)
3. Analyzing Narratives in the Immigrant Rights Movement	• immigration status • narratives of advocacy for unauthorized migrant youth (e.g., DREAMers) • pathways to citizenship • framing • conceptions of membership	Students find and compare narratives of immigrant rights activists that use different "frames," and then respond to five questions, e.g., How is membership conceptualized in this narrative?	• Documents are suggested but not provided.
4. Low-Wage Worker Admissions	• immigrant labor paradox • "W" visa program • guest worker program • permanent & temporary resident status • low-wage noncitizen laborers	Small-group and whole-class analysis of a short excerpt focused on the immigrant labor paradox and conceptions of membership. Six questions guide the reading, e.g., How are the interests of employers and workers addressed with the nonagricultural "W" visa program?	• *American Immigration Council Guide to Senate Bill 744* (2013)
5. Essential Workers	• essential worker • conceptions of membership	Students compare conceptions of membership in two pandemic relief programs, one federal and one state. Six questions guide the reading, e.g., Who is viewed as a member of American society?	• White House press release • CARES Act • *CA Disaster Relief Fund* (2020)

I imagine that most students, not just a few, will have cause to feel discomfort with such activities, and for different reasons.

Banks's introductory orientation may be of some help, but its assumption that students share a set of foundational values is questionable. That cornerstone of democracy, I am sorry to say, may now be cracked (e.g., Mason, 2018), or it may never have existed (Mills, 1999). In any case, and shifting now to a parallel concern, teachers cannot overlook the instructional support students will need as they move from Banks's orientation into the thick of her learning activities. Here, students must work to understand the issue, comprehend the documents, grasp the concepts, exchange interpretations with classmates, and form their own arguments. Getting this work from students, prompting and facilitating it, will require robust instructional practices. Those teachers who do take on teaching controversial issues aren't merely brave and daring; they are buttressed with instructional know-how that is based on a trove of research and practice.[1] So, allow me to conclude this review by suggesting two instructional strategies that should boost student learning in Banks's activities.

INSTRUCTIONAL SUPPORTS

First up is Structured Academic Controversy (SAC). Originally developed as a cooperative learning strategy that takes advantage of the interest generated by intellectual conflict in the classroom (Johnson & Johnson, 1988), SAC is both a discourse structure (it organizes student discussion) and an instructional procedure (there is a sequence of learning tasks). Rather than avoiding controversy, SAC mobilizes it as a learning opportunity, but also controls it and deepens students' understanding of the issue itself. SAC is somewhat similar to debate; however, the entire procedure occurs in a small group of four and there are no winners or losers. I have used it in my own teaching, revised it along the way, and taught novice and experienced teachers to use it in their classrooms. I am routinely impressed by the depth of thinking a SAC provokes and the literacy work it accomplishes. I appreciate its suitability to rigorous curriculum goals, such as Banks's concepts and questions, and its promotion of reasoning with evidence and respect for multiple perspectives. Let me suggest a few ways SAC can be incorporated into Banks's first two activities, and then I will move to Banks's next three activities and focus on a second strategy: the Socratic seminar.

Activities 1–2

The first two of Banks's learning activities (see Table 10.1) require a kind of discussion called *deliberation*. A deliberation is a discussion aimed at deciding on a course of action. Deliberation—with others, in public—is the basic democratic function of juries, legislatures, city councils, and committees of all sorts (Gastil & Levine, 2005). In the first activity, Banks invites students to role-play members of Congress who are deciding, during World War II, whether to advance a bill that would repeal the Chinese Exclusion Act of 1882. China was an ally in the war, but opposition to repeal was widespread on account of racism and fear that Chinese immigrants would take jobs from U.S. citizens. Students' deliberation is informed by reading two congressional testimonies given in 1943, one supporting repeal and the other not. In the second activity, students decide whether and how to rewrite rules on birthright citizenship. Their deliberation is based on reading an excerpt from the 2017 Supreme Court decision *Sessions v. Morales-Santana*. This case focused on children born abroad to U.S. citizens, and it involved a law that favored mothers over fathers. (Justice Ruth Bader Ginsburg wrote the decision overturning that law.)

SAC makes a controversial issue like this one accessible to students by reducing the number of alternatives initially to two,[2] and then structures the deliberation as follows: First, the teacher assigns students to teams of four, which are then subdivided into two pairs. Each pair is assigned to a position on the controversy—one side or the other—and asked to role-play advocates of that position. Next, each pair prepares reasons and evidence to support their position. They get this information from primary documents Banks provides. The partners in each pair will work alone and together to read and interpret the information provided in order to create a presentation, which they will share with the other pair of students on their team. The pairs will take turns making their presentation to each other. Next, the pairs reverse perspectives; that is, each pair presents the other pair's argument to make sure they understood it. The point here, of course, is to grasp the facts and logic used by both sides. A general discussion then unfolds, and finally, students are invited to drop their assigned positions and express their own views on the matter: "What do you really think? Feel free to change your mind" (see Chapter 2, this volume).

SAC is an effective *learning* activity. The small-group participation structure, the preparation and presentation of evidence and reasons in pairs, and the reciprocity of role assignments are all a boon to student interest and engagement. Most important, however, is that students are supported to learn important and challenging material.

Still, Banks's caution about student discomfort and the risk of further marginalizing already vulnerable students must be taken seriously. Banks's affirming orientation to each activity and SAC's clever sequence of tasks may help, but teacher judgment is (as always) indispensable. No one's humanity or dignity should be put up for discussion, certainly; and students shouldn't be asked to play untenable roles. Teachers will need to judge whether role-playing is acceptable in either case. At any rate, the same documents can be read critically and discussed without the role-playing, which takes us to a different instructional strategy.

Activities 3–5

The next three of Banks's classroom activities require close, interpretive reading of textual material, but without role-playing. Unlike deliberations, these activities do not involve deciding a course of action but, more basic than that, comprehending the texts. They focus squarely on understanding the concepts and information in the primary documents that Banks provides. Students read and analyze them with the aid of the guiding questions Banks provides, along with interpretive dialogue with other students.

In Banks's third activity, students compare arguments that advocate membership for unauthorized migrants. What meanings and assumptions do they stand on? This activity centers on the sociological concept *framing* (Goffman, 1974) and is perhaps the most difficult of the five activities because students will need to develop the concept in order to identify it in various texts. This is a tall order. Furthermore, students (or their teacher) will need to locate the texts they will examine, since they are not provided in the book's appendix (as are the documents for the other four activities). Still, the activity is compelling. The concept is useful to understanding not only rhetoric used in the DREAM movement, but in any social movement or campaign. *Framing* is the way a speaker presents a message to an audience by locating it in a particular field of meaning, thereby shaping the sense the audience will make of it. While Trump and his media resonators framed Mexican immigrants as criminals, DREAM activists often frame themselves as ideal Americans: hard-working, law-abiding, dedicated to their studies and their families, budding professionals and civil servants, patriotic to the core. They express this narrative in hopes of gaining access to citizenship status. But, as Banks notes, and this is the comparison at the heart of this third activity, there is disagreement among DREAM activists themselves as to the ethics of this frame. Some oppose it on the grounds that it has the unintended consequence of blaming DREAMers' parents. Likewise, it marginalizes other immigrants who are older and less educated and cannot compete well with the young activists.

Banks's fourth and fifth activities also rely on close reading of primary documents, and these are provided in the book. In both activities students grapple with conceptions of membership and belonging as applied to low-wage workers, a significant number of whom are unauthorized immigrants. The fourth activity focuses on the immigrant labor paradox. Students read and discuss a description of the unsuccessful U.S. Senate Bill 744, developed by the bipartisan "Gang of Eight," that would have reformed the immigration system. (The bill died in the House.) The fifth activity concentrates on "essential workers" during the COVID-19 pandemic, many of whom are long-term residents without citizenship status. Students compare two relief acts of government in 2020: the federal government's CARES Act and California's Disaster Relief Fund. The latter provided financial assistance to a broad group, including unauthorized migrants; the CARES Act did not include them.

A suitable instructional strategy is needed in these three activities where the goal is for students to read and then analyze together the information contained in primary documents. I believe the Socratic seminar is a good candidate because it is structured to support close reading of Banks's documents and productive discussion of their meanings. In a Socratic seminar, students learn with and from one another while interpreting one or more such texts (Kohlmeier, 2022). Additionally, the Socratic seminar invites students' values into the discussion. For a seminar, the teacher plans two kinds of questions: interpretive questions, which prompt close reading and analytic discussion of portions of the text, and then evaluative questions, which ask students to make judgments based on their values. There is an art to asking the right kind of question at the right time, of course.

Finally, because close reading is necessary in all five of Banks's activities, the provision of reading supports cannot be overlooked. Reading skill varies widely in classrooms, and complex texts anchor each of Banks's activities. Fortunately, both SAC and the Socratic seminar scaffold the hard work of reading for understanding (e.g., Greenleaf & Valencia, 2017). Such supports are essential if the concepts and questions at the center of Banks's proposal are to be accessible to all students.

CONCLUSION

Angela Banks has written a book that proposes powerful concepts and questions for the civic education curriculum. These subject matters are long overdue. *Migration, membership, citizenship*, and *citizenship status* need to be integrated with the conventional curriculum of civic education so that the thresholds of membership—the inclusionary and exclusionary boundaries of citizenship—are examined alongside the rights and responsibilities of those already included. Long-term residents, especially low-wage essential workers, need pathways to membership, and the injustice of the immigrant labor paradox demands repair immediately.

For any curriculum to be powerful and worthy of its teachers and students, its central aims, concepts, and questions need to be identified and then made squarely the focus of instruction. An obvious point, perhaps, but rare in practice. Curriculum committees and textbook publishers routinely take refuge in curricular breadth so as to offend no one, and they shy away from singling out topics for in-depth study. Banks's proposal, by contrast, is bold and focused. Its objectives, concepts, and questions are explicit and limited, and together make a coherent unit of study. Additionally, Banks devotes half the book to pedagogy, making it a practical resource for teachers, especially those who teach the ubiquitous high school U.S. government course and the even more common U.S. history course. In this review, I offered instructional strategies that take strategic advantage of controversy and viewpoint diversity and feature structured reading and discussion. These strategies should enlarge students' opportunity to learn the proposed subject matter, deepen their understanding of the core concepts and questions, and teach them to dialogue across differences. The strategies are already familiar to many teachers, and ample guidance is available for teachers (and professors) who want to learn more (see note 1).

This book appears in the Multicultural Education Series at Teachers College Press, which is so capably edited by Banks's father, James A. Banks.[3] The senior Banks writes in his foreword that the book "fills an important gap in the civic education literature" (p. x). Nothing could be truer. Angela Banks has herself crossed a threshold, from law to education, in order to address a lacuna in our field. As a longtime member of this field, I am grateful. Most of all, I am enthused. These concepts and questions are ripe for study and discussion, for instruction, and for policy action. For people who think about civic education, Angela Banks's book will be provocative and energizing.

CHAPTER 11

Afterword
Cultivating Judgment

In the three sections of this concluding chapter, I summarize the two basic forms of classroom discussion—seminar and deliberation—and then return to what a centrist approach to civic education means for students and their teachers. Should teachers indulge their passions and disclose their own opinions about the questions under study? Finally, I argue that the social studies curriculum is the logical epicenter of civic education in K–12 schooling and, consequently, that a robust social studies curriculum needs to be restored to the elementary grades, where it can lay the needed foundation for civic learning in middle and high school.

The context for this book is the civic chaos of the present, particularly the twofold crisis in which our political culture is mired today. Trust in institutions of governance has been riven. This is a legitimacy crisis. And an epistemic crisis leaves us without a shared standard of truth for distinguishing facts from falsehoods. Together, these problems are a witch's brew that has thrown "we the people" into a state of disorientation. Our political culture is wracked by enmity. Neal Stephenson's shrewd summary bears repeating: "The ability to talk in good faith about a shared reality is a foundational element of civics that we didn't know we had until we suddenly and surprisingly lost it."[1] Subjected to consistent lying, trolling, and infotainment, Peter sober has become Peter drunk (Holmes, 1995). Trust and truth don't lie in ruins just yet, but they are at a critical juncture. This is why observers warn of a civil war or, at the least, more political violence (e.g., Marche, 2022).

Can civic education in K–12 schools help? As the foregoing chapters demonstrate, I believe it can. Of course, there are other institutions (e.g., family, capitalism) and forces (e.g., populist authoritarianism, fear) with much greater reach, but there is still room for action. Civic educators need to seize the opportunity. They can do so by sharpening the aim of civic education to preparing young people to participate in liberal democracy—that hybrid of popular sovereignty and legally guaranteed individual rights.

In this final chapter, I return to two of the book's central themes, classroom discussion and student voice, and then I locate civic education in its disciplinary home base: the social studies curriculum and, therein, courses in history and government.[2]

CLASSROOM DISCUSSION

The novel *1984* gives us a nightmarish account of the impoverishment of civic discourse. Citizens in George Orwell's dystopia have been bamboozled to the point where they are no longer able to express themselves to one another. They atrophy. Their knowledge and voices shrivel up. Today, as we struggle to keep our heads above Orwellian waves of information, disinformation, misinformation, scrolling, trolling, and gun violence, the public has become both numb and enraged. We have taken our discourse to the inner chambers of family and friends and the echo chambers and algorithms of social media. The fracturing of the public into tribes of like-minded partisans has intensified and, as Cass Sunstein (2002) showed in "The Law of Group Polarization," the pod members become more extreme.

It is no wonder, then, that teachers want to mobilize the diversity of viewpoint, culture, and status in their classrooms to engage students in speaking and listening to one another in productive discussions. Both democracy and academic achievement rely on it: democracy because forging public policy together is the basic labor of popular sovereignty, and academic achievement because dialogue is the basis of thinking. Well-facilitated academic discussions build both knowledge and voice. With the appropriate planning and facilitation, these discussions foster the formation of opinions and claims via deep reading and the exchange of information, perspectives, and reasons.

A caution: Many of us who teach claim that we lead discussions in the classroom. "Today we discussed. . . ." is a common phrase when telling a colleague about a class. But observation reveals that many of our "discussions" are in fact something else, called recitations: Teacher asks a question, a student responds. Teacher evaluates the response and moves to another question and another student. Recitation is an instructional model that is useful for some purposes, like drill and practice. But it is not discussion and cannot achieve what discussion uniquely can. Discussion involves an exchange—a dialogue—among the participants. Returning to Bridges's (1979) masterful definition first presented in Chapter 2: "The distinctive and peculiar contribution which discussion has to play is to set alongside one perception of the matter under discussion the several perceptions of other participants . . . challenging our own view of things with those of others" (p. 50).

Leading discussions well is one of the great difficult things in teaching, as anyone knows who has tried and is honest about the results (Greene,

1954). Capable discussion leaders differ in style and procedure, but those I admire walk essentially the same path: they value discussion for both pedagogical and civic reasons, they have high standards for discussion, and they don't just use it but want students to learn how to do it. They deploy different discussion models to suit different curriculum objectives, and they try to instill in students the same curiosity they themselves feel about the topic and question at hand. This, the intentional propagation of curiosity, is the essence of the Socratic method of dialogue.[3]

A second caution concerns reading. Close reading of texts is essential in each of the two kinds of discussion presented in this book, but students' reading skill (both decoding and comprehension) varies widely in most classrooms, even in so-called "advanced" courses. In seminars and deliberations, reading must not be evaded by the usual work-arounds, such as teachers doing the reading for students and then explaining it to them orally in lectures. Doing so develops neither deep knowledge nor voice, let alone reading ability. Both of the two discussion formats require reading of the texts on which the discussions are based, and these texts need to be open and available for rereading and scrutiny during the discussion. Fortunately, both seminar and deliberation, by virtue of their structures, support the work of reading. This is all the more reason to use them.

Here, then, is a classification tool that will clarify the distinction between seminar and deliberation (see Table 11.1). The typology permits a rough, at-a-glance comparison of seminars and deliberations along four dimensions: (1) aim or purpose, (2) subject matter, (3) opening question, and (4) exemplars. But first, let's briefly consider five of the central terms involved.

Table 11.1. A Typology of Classroom Discussion

Dimensions	Seminar	Deliberation
Purpose	1. Reach an enlarged understanding of a powerful text. 2. Improve discussants' powers of understanding.	1. Reach a decision about what a "we" should do about a shared problem. 2. Improve discussants' powers of understanding.
Subject Matter	Ideas, issues, and values in a document or other text or film selection, artwork, performance, or political cartoon.	Alternative courses of action related to an academic or public policy problem.
Opening Question	What does this mean?	What should we do?
Exemplar	Socratic seminar, aka Shared Inquiry (Great Books Foundation, 2022)	SAC+ (Parker, Chapter 2, this volume)

- *Discussion.* Discussion is a form of group inquiry—a consciously shared form that involves listening and talking. The two forms featured in this book make an ideal couple—a partnership for learning and doing.
- *Deliberation.* A deliberation is a discussion aimed at deciding on a plan of action that will resolve a problem that a group faces. The essence of deliberation is weighing alternatives. (The *liber* in deliberation is Latin for scale.) Deliberating public issues is the key citizen behavior in democracies where, otherwise, citizens exercise power (e.g., voting; direct action) without necessarily having thought together about how to exercise it. The opening question for a deliberation is usually some version of, "What should we do?"
- *Seminar.* A seminar is a discussion aimed at developing, exposing, and exploring meanings. A seminar's purpose is to enlarge participants' understanding of the ideas, issues, and values in a text. The text may be a historical novel, a primary or secondary document, a film or play, a photo, or a painting. A seminar does not involve planning for action as does a deliberation. There may be deliberative moments within seminars, particularly in the social studies classroom where "What should we do?" is never far from consideration. The seminar's primary purpose, however, is not to repair the world so much as to reveal and interpret it with greater clarity. Seminars enrich deliberation, to be sure, and for social studies teachers they go hand-in-hand by widening students' knowledge and deepening their understanding of issues. Seminars and deliberations thus overlap, but their emphases and pedagogical purposes are distinct.
- *Powers of Understanding.* Improving students' capacity to think is a secondary aim of both seminars and deliberations. Other-wise termed "habits of mind" or, simply, "critical thinking" or "reasoning," these are the intellectual arts of interpretation. They are the inquiry skills and dispositions needed to apprehend the world (the purpose of a seminar) and those needed to help us decide what changes should be made (the purpose of a deliberation).
- *Opening Question.* The opening question is aimed at the purpose of a discussion—to reach a decision (deliberation) or to enlarge understanding of a text (seminar). The question gets quickly and simply to the heart of the matter, and it is genuine. A question is genuine when the askers have not made up their mind as to the answer. This facilitates curiosity and close listening.

UNCOERCED DECISIONS

The pedagogy presented in this book turns on three axes that prepare students to participate in liberal democracy. First, curriculum decision-making: choosing from the vast universe of possibilities the core subject matter for civic education. Second, organizing curriculum and instruction to help students achieve deeper understanding rather than superficial, test-prep learning. This requires a curriculum of ideas where instruction is looped or spiraled to elaborate core concepts with well-selected examples and controversies. Third, a kind of instruction that puts young people in the habit of speaking and listening to one another in public: exchanging reasons, taking the perspectives of others while developing their own voice, and making judgments about whether what they are hearing and reading requires them to adjust their own views. This is a knowledge-and-voice curriculum geared to the development of intelligence and the freedom to formulate claims and arguments without coercion.

Without coercion? At the core of many policy disputes in education is disagreement about the relationship between education and society: Should schools serve the status quo, helping students to succeed in it, or work to transform it, making it more just? The responses to this question fall on the political right, left, and center. On both the right and left are rather clear visions of the good society, and schools are technologies for realizing them. In other words, educators on both the right and left have an end in view. For them, education is, to whatever extent, a means to this end. On the right, students are to be taught to thrive in the current social order and respect tradition. On the left, students are to be taught to change the status quo in order to achieve greater equality and a more vibrant democracy, one that would actively combat racism and mitigate rapacious capitalism. In the center is the moderate position of John Dewey (1935): Educators should help students acquire knowledge through "intelligent study of historical and existing forces and conditions" (p. 9), and they should teach students to use their minds well—to think critically, to gather and adjudicate competing accounts and perspectives, and to value and use democratic deliberation and disciplined inquiry to sort them out and reach decisions. In this centrist position, it is best for teachers to cultivate their students' own judgment rather than telling students what they (teachers) believe or what they (students) should believe. In other words, we who teach should respect our students' autonomy enough to cultivate *their* thinking and not use school time to propagate *our* ideology.

A little history will illustrate the difference between these views and how I came to agree with Dewey. The centrist stance was developed in a later phase of the Progressive Era in the period between the two world wars (Fallace, 2016). Educators like George Counts and Charles Beard embraced indoctrination as an inevitable component of social reform and encouraged their fellow educators to get on board. Counts argued that "capitalism could not be reconstructed into a more humane social order unless the conservative indoctrination to which students were subjected was challenged by radical counterindoctrination" (Westbrook, 1991, p. 506). The supposedly neutral or apolitical school curriculum was in fact a vehicle for inculcating a nationalist-capitalist worldview that sanctioned and fueled inequality. Dewey took a more moderate stand:

> Dewey agreed that much of the education in American schools was little more than indoctrination, especially with reference to narrow nationalism under the name of patriotism, and with reference to the dominant economic regime. But these threats to democracy, Dewey argued in 1935, did not justify counterindoctrination as a means to promote democratic ends. (Westbrook, 1991, p. 507)

While critical of the status quo indoctrination that was present in schools already, Dewey scolded Counts and other indoctrination advocates on the left for doubting the power of evidence-based reasoning and liberal democracy in their students' hands when it had been so effective for themselves. "If the method of intelligence has worked in our own case," he asked them, "how can we assume that the method will not work with our students . . . ?" (1935, p. 9). I appreciate Dewey's question, its humility especially, and would add only that illiberalism on the left is hardly a solution to illiberalism on the right.

At any rate, the horrors to come changed the terms of this debate. The rise of the Nazis and the Soviets—both ideologically doctrinaire, both totalitarian, both murderous, both ethnonationalist and intent on making youth, through "education," into good fascists or good communists—spurred a reaction. That reaction was a less partisan movement in education that opposed ideological extremism per se. It has lasted, for the most part, until today. Dewey's middle way prevailed. That it is a "middle" way does not mean that it is neutral; it does have an end in sight—continuation and consolidation of the liberal-democratic experiment. It rests on values, as we have seen, such as liberty and equality, tolerance, pluralism, freedom of conscience and expression, justice, the scientific method (inquiry, evidence, fallibilism), and the rule of law. It does not propagandize students but instead, and here is the key, nurtures their budding autonomy and, with it, their growing capacity to make just decisions on their own. This is Dewey's educational wisdom, and his method, in a nutshell: cultivate in students both freedom and intelligence.

People living in societies that are attempting to create or maintain liberal-democratic ways of living are obliged to weigh evidence and grapple with competing accounts. They are required not to jump to conclusions but to be patient and evenhanded, to sort things out, to listen and read, to think and observe, and to exercise judgment. Everything from jury duty to voting and participating in public policy debates depends on "We, the people" being able to pull this off. It is democratic work and intellectual work all at once. It is not easy and certainly not natural (people are not born this way). Education is needed, for it sponsors the evidence- and logic-based way to apply the mind to problems. It is a values-rich way, too, for it unabashedly values critical thinking and experimentation, regard for multiple perspectives, and an open future. It does not prescribe where students should end up.

So, to fellow teachers, I suggest the following: Strive to sharpen your students' thinking and cultivate their capacity for independent judgment. Give *them* ample opportunity to exercise both. Generally, do not share *your* beliefs about the questions and controversies under examination, but work to develop *theirs*. And when you do share *your* beliefs, do it for a purpose: Share to show; share to model how judgments are made (Talbott, 2006). That is, when teachers disclose their own positions on controversial questions—whether empirical, conceptual, ethical, or policy questions— they can do so for the purpose of making transparent how they reached their judgment, taking care to demonstrate how reflection, perspective consciousness, and argument look and sound, displaying especially the skills of evidence seeking, sourcing, and corroboration alongside a respectful stance. Modeling is a venerated form of instruction, and it can help students' grow their own powers of critical judgment.

THE SOCIAL STUDIES

Finally, let me put knowledge, voice, and civic education in the context of social studies curriculum and instruction at school. "Social studies" is an umbrella term used in K–12 education for history and social science courses, just as "science" is a moniker for courses in disciplines such as biology and physics. It's the same for "math"—arithmetic, algebra, geometry, and so forth. Of these, the social studies curriculum is the logical epicenter of civic education. Recall that most social studies courses are history courses: world history, national history, and state history. History is the discipline where students attempt to understand the human past—a slippery foreign land— by reading and hearing and comparing stories about what has happened but also, and here's where the hard intellectual work is, by making and evaluating evidence-based claims. Keith Barton and Linda Levstik (2015) provide a compelling rationale:

> If students are simply asked to remember a body of information, which they think is true because someone in a position of authority said it was, then they don't actually have any knowledge at all, they just have a memory of baseless assertions. Moreover, they have no way of distinguishing historical claims that are

based on evidence from those that aren't—such as myths, legends, or outright lies. The inability to distinguish between a myth and an evidence-based claim about the past destroys the foundation for participatory democracy, because students will be susceptible to any outrageous story they may be told. (p. 39)

Barton and Levstik's statement deserves a seminar in order to plumb its depths. The first sentence alone, on the distinction between knowledge and memory, is startling in its insight. And then the second and third bring us to the epistemic crisis we face today. But theirs isn't a new interpretation. A National Education Association curriculum committee wrote over a century ago, "History and its allied branches are better adapted than any other studies to promote the invaluable mental power which we call judgment" (1894, p. 168).

In addition to history courses, the established social studies curriculum in the United States typically includes one or two courses in government and, less often now, geography and economics, and less still, psychology and sociology. Fortunately, a government course is a fixture of the American high school. Often, this course occurs in the senior year when students are turning 18—voting age—and follows the final course in U.S. history students will take. This can be a powerful sequence. The U.S. history course teaches the circumstances, debates, and compromises that formed (thanks to the Articles of Confederation) and re-formed (thanks to the Constitution and its amendments) the nation's government, and then the U.S. government course focuses on how and why power is divided (the three branches, federalism) and the rights and responsibilities of citizens. Lest these topics strike readers as boring, old-fashioned, or unnecessary, recall, first, that many adult voters don't know them, making them easier prey for demagogues (e.g., Annenberg Public Policy Center, 2016); and second, that educators have developed highly engaging instructional approaches for this course. Chapter 5 of this book, for example, explained the Knowledge in Action approach, where political simulations and controversial issues are the spine of the course.

But a serious problem now affects the ability of the social studies curriculum to accomplish its objectives. The testing-and-accountability frenzy of recent decades marginalized the social studies curriculum in elementary and middle schools. This made more room in the school day for the now hypertested subjects of reading and math. Alas, the result was what Albert Hirschman (1991) terms "perverse." It made things worse. Not only did it limit students' opportunity to learn basic knowledge in history, government, geography, and economics—the subject matter students were introduced to in elementary schools before the testing madness began—but it didn't improve their reading skills much. Why? Despite the increase in reading instruction, the corresponding reduction in social studies instruction robbed students of the background knowledge needed to comprehend the texts in the reading curriculum (Willingham, 2017).

So, a rich social studies curriculum should be restored to these grades not only for its own sake but so that students are enabled to learn other things via the ability to read information-rich texts. Primary-grade students learn in their social studies units about foods and farms, fisheries and factories, clothing and shelter, forests and islands, goods and services, cities and towns, countries and continents, their own state and neighboring states, presidents and judges, plateaus and peninsulas, firefighters and police officers, cities and suburbs—the world and its peoples, near and far, now and then. *This is essential background knowledge for learning everything else.*[4]

When students are introduced to these subjects in the early and middle grades, what results is a snowball effect: *cumulative* knowledge growth with each passing year. Educational researchers dub this the Matthew Effect (Walberg & Tsai, 1983). The name comes from the book in the Bible where we read that the rich get richer and the poor get poorer. The rich get richer because they can invest what they're not spending to subsist, thereby earning more, which they reinvest, becoming wealthier. The Matthew Effect in education, similarly, is based on the fact that prior knowledge predicts future learning. The vocabulary and skills children *already* possess from earlier learning, their existing funds of knowledge, serve as a seedbed in which additional knowledge can take root and grow. Switching metaphors, knowledgeable students are building a house atop a foundation that already has been laid, which is far easier than building the house at the same time they are struggling to lay its foundation.

The overarching disciplinary aim of social studies curriculum and instruction is the ability to make and evaluate evidence-based claims about the past, present, and future. The implications of this aim for civic education are straightforward and potent. Students must not only learn facts but how to verify them, and then how to adjudicate competing claims. They must learn to scrutinize sources, find and weigh counterarguments, and control their attention online rather than spend it on clickbait. This is freedom and intelligence acting together. As we have seen, it is a content-rich way, because inquiry is nothing without powerful subject matter. It is a values-rich way, too, for it values evidence (the empirical rule), revision in light of new evidence (the fallibilist rule), and an open future (autonomy and choice). It values, in other words, a political culture that favors rationality and the scientific method over folklore or dogma, and it values liberal democracy over tyranny and oppression. Importantly, it respects and fosters students' voice–their growing capacity to make uncoerced decisions.

Debates over *which* and *whose* history should be taught are making news again today. They mimic past debates in many ways: whether national history courses should take a triumphalist, pluralist, or critical stance; whether they should foreground multicultural education or antiracist education, or avoid uncomfortable histories altogether; whether they should feature political history or social history, great leaders and historic turning points, or the everyday life of rich and poor alike.[5] Today's most volatile curriculum debates center on teaching about the causes, effects, and persistence of the racial hierarchy that formed this nation. A passionate argument today centers on the question, *Does 1619 or 1776 best represent the story of the United States?* The approach taken in this book is to feature questions like this one and others that are similarly meaty, debatable, and central to the curriculum at hand, and to do so in order to build students' knowledge, voice, and powers of judgment. Teach them the inquiry skills and dispositions needed to apprehend the world and decide what changes should be made.[6] As William Stanley (1993) wrote, having himself walked the road from educator to ideologue and back again:

> No matter how strongly we as social educators have come to feel about particular social values, *it is our professional obligation to help enable the next generation to claim its own set of values*, even if we hope the values reflect those we presently hold. If education does not enable our students to embrace values via critical reflection, it is little more than a form of dogmatic cultural transmission. However noble the intent, this approach to instruction will serve to undermine the very basis for the democratic culture it seeks to impose. (pp. 298–990, emphasis added)

The mission of the social studies curriculum is a civic one. Students are not taught its disciplinary knowledge for its own sake but for the good of the liberal-democratic political community. For this reason, students' own judgment should be steadily developed and their knowledge and voice steadily encouraged and challenged along the way. Classroom discussion on provocative questions, I suggest, is a potent way forward—not a particularly easy one, which is why teaching itself is not easy, but certainly worth the effort and the reward.

CONCLUSION

In Lin-Manuel Miranda's musical *Hamilton*, our protagonist listens to Aaron Burr's advice: "Talk less, smile more. Don't let them know what you're against and what you're for." Astonished, Hamilton replies: "If you stand for nothing, Burr, what'll you fall for?"

I stand for civic education of the liberal-democratic kind. It is, by definition, a centrist or nonpartisan kind, which leaves it open to criticism that it stands for nothing. But that is not true. Liberal-democratic civic education stands for many things but, at its heart, for knowledge and voice. Knowledge—disciplinary knowledge, critical reflection on evidence—affords us a shared standard of truth. And voice—free speech—"is one of the most potent resources each of us has for achieving our own political empowerment" (Allen, 2014, p. 21). Voice, not violence, is the liberal-democratic mode of decision-making.

Alongside knowledge and voice, liberal-democratic civic education stands for pluralism, which allows for diversity and freedom together. Liberal-democratic civic education doesn't attempt to corral everyone into the same belief system, the same vision of justice, or the same definition of the purpose of life. In a diverse world, this matters fundamentally.

Liberal-democratic civic education stands *against* illiberal initiatives in the political sphere such as populist authoritarians who lie, attack the press, imprison opponents, suppress the vote, and stoke racial and religious resentments. And in the educational sphere it stands against illiberal initiatives such as book-banning or the partisan indoctrination of students. These violate liberal democracy's values. They stifle critical thinking, fact-finding, and voice, and they are fundamentally disrespectful.

So, liberal-democratic civic education is not neutral, and classroom discussion is its prime mode of instruction—not its only pedagogy, but the one by which students work their way toward deeper understanding, stronger writing, and a clearer voice. Classroom discussion teaches young people to talk to one another about academic and social questions and to form, intellectually and morally, their own interpretations and evaluations. The exceptional teacher "does not hand down wisdom but makes the other find it," Karl Jaspers (1962, p. 8) said of Socrates's method. The exceptional teacher creates courses in which students read deeply, express themselves, exchange reasons, and learn thereby to author their own claims.

Classroom discussion takes free speech seriously. John Stuart Mill (1978) argued in *On Liberty* that free speech affords two remarkable things. First, it provides access to other people's claims and arguments. When our own are false or ill-supported, discussion gives us access to better ones. Without the voices of others, we can only stare into the mirror, contemplating our own small universe. Second, even when true, our claims become solid and brittle when wrapped in agreement. Conformity bias (the implicit need to belong) prevails; dogma and groupthink replace inquiry. But subjected to the fresh air of plurality in a well-led discussion, our views are invigorated.

Liberal-democratic civic education is timely. It suits the civic crisis of our moment. May educators do what they can to help liberal democracy prevail in this nation.

Notes

Chapter 1

1. From Stephenson's endorsement of Jonathan Rauch's *The Constitution of Knowledge* (Brookings Institution, 2021, book jacket).

2. I invoke the moderate, middle-way traditions of Aristotelianism and Buddhism, as well as the American educational philosopher John Dewey.

3. Memorably put by Madison (2003a), the principal author of the U.S. Constitution: "In all very numerous assemblies, of whatever characters composed, passion never fails to wrest the scepter from reason. Had every Athenian citizen been a Socrates, every Athenian assembly would still have been a mob" (p. 339; also Kahan, 2007, who dubs this "cognitive illiberalism").

4. See also Southworth's (2022) insightful treatment of perspective-taking in relation to critical thinking.

5. On the meanings and uses of "voice," see Arendt (1958) in political theory, Moy (2020) in communication theory, and Kahne et al. (2022), Lundy (2007), and Mitra et al. (2014) in educational research and practice.

6. Chapter 2 presents a well-structured model for doing just this, and the question of indoctrination is addressed in Chapter 11, "Afterword: Cultivating Judgment."

Chapter 2

1. See Parker et al., 2013, 2018.

2. I am referring to Terry Beck, Afnan Boutrid, Steven Camicia, Mary Anne Christy, Carol Coe, Jenni Conrad, Patricia Espiritu Halagao, Wendy Ewbank, Sibyl Frankenburg, Tina Gourd, Diana Hess, Khodi Kaviani, Bruce Larson, Jane Lo, Janet McDaniel, Barbara McKean, Natasha Merchant, Jonathan Miller-Lane, Shane Pisani, Lisa Sibbett, and Brenda Weikel.

3. Most controversies have more than two "sides," of course. SAC simplifies the controversy to two, making it more accessible to more students. The controversy can always be complicated after the SAC lesson, at which point students, thanks to the SAC, will have enough background knowledge to make sense of the additional information.

4. Variation in the procedure is common and accepted. See Avery et al., 2013.

5. See Chapter 6, this volume, on the distinction between friends and kin, on the one hand, and acquaintances and strangers—the "public"—on the other.

6. Liberal democracies have elections and representative governments (this is democracy) that, by law, protect civil rights and liberties (this is liberalism).

7. See Article 12 of the United Nations Convention on the Rights of the Child.

8. This chapter draws, with permission, from two papers originally published in the journal *Democracy & Education*: "Feel Free to Change Your Mind," 2011, *19*(2), article 9; and "Reinventing the High School Government Course," 2016b, co-authored with Jane Lo, *24*(1), article 6.

Chapter 3

1. See Amy Gutmann's (1996) gloss on Churchill's statement.

2. Gary Orfield, "Schools More Separate: Consequences of a Decade of Resegregation," Harvard Civil Rights Project, 2001. Orfield found that "Whites on average attend schools where less than 20% of the students are from all of the other racial and ethnic groups combined. On average, Blacks and Latinos attend schools with 53% to 55% students of their own group. Latinos attend schools with far higher average Black populations than Whites do, and Blacks attend schools with much higher average Latino enrollments. American Indian students attend schools in which about a third (31%) of the students are from Indian backgrounds."

3. Information about the National Issues Forum is available at https://www.nifi.org/en/about and about Choices for the 21st Century at https://www.choices.edu/.

Chapter 5

1. This chapter was coauthored by my then–research assistant, Jane Lo. Thanks to Jane for terrific work as a multitalented collaborator throughout the Knowledge in Action project. We are grateful, in turn, to our teacher collaborators across the three school districts; Sheila Valencia of the University of Washington who directed the literacy research-and-development team; and anonymous reviewers at *Democracy & Education* for helpful comments on an earlier draft of this chapter. This work was funded by the Spencer Foundation and the George Lucas Educational Foundation. The former supported the final revision and implementation of the curriculum; the latter supported this research from its inception.

2. A critical assessment of the APGOV curriculum is beyond the scope of this chapter. Suffice it to say that other U.S. government curricula can be imagined and do exist, and they, too, are social constructs that reflect the power relations of the developers and the social structures in which they work (e.g., Bernstein, 1990). The APGOV curriculum has an important advantage over some alternatives: It results from a deliberative process—an argument—rather than a teacher deciding alone. Yet it has the disadvantages discussed in these pages.

3. We used (and continue to recommend) the online simulation LegSim (http://info.legsim.org/) in the first years of this DBIR because our teacher collaborators were already using it. But its technology requirements became untenable once we moved to underresourced, poverty-impacted urban schools.

Chapter 6

1. It follows that affluent White students may be at the greatest risk of miseducation because of the growth-stunting effect of their isolation.

2. In law, the "age of majority" is the age at which a citizen can vote and otherwise claim full legal rights as adult citizens in the polity.

3. See Leonard Waks's (2010) insightful work on listening.

Chapter 7

1. Both Marx and Kohlberg are children of the Enlightenment—"moderns" and "universalists." A range of postmodern critics will challenge them on this basis alone. See, for example, Walzer (1983) on Marx, and Gilligan (1982) on Kohlberg.

Chapter 9

1. The World Programme is just one example. It is a valuable initiative, and there are many others (e.g., Council of Europe, 1985). I would not claim otherwise.

2. See analyses by Osler (2016) and Panjwani et al. (2018).

3. See Tyack's (2003) account.

4. See also Keet (2015) and Zembylas et al. (2017).

5. See Foner (1998).

6. John Meyer's cross-national research is insightful, alongside that of Russell and Suárez (2017). For example, Meyer et al., (2010) show that HRE in textbooks has an implicit goal to construct a common humanity of rights-bearing individuals, each a sovereign actor on the public stage.

7. This section draws from Parker (2017).

8. Moore (2007) demonstrates the inadequacy of standpoint theory for explaining how knowledge is produced socially and, consequently, its inability to produce a school curriculum. By reducing knowledge to knowers and their contexts, standpoint theory inevitably must show that there is actually no knowledge, per se, of anything. See also Wexler (1987).

9. See the accounts of Moore and Muller (1999), Moore (2007), and Young (2008, 2013); see also Delpit (1988) and Gramsci (1971) for their critiques of progressive educators' abandonment of powerful subject matters for "progressive" child-centered pedagogies.

10. Studies of this phenomenon include Labaree (2010); McPhail and Rata (2018); and Morgan and Lambert (2018).

11. On the distinction between curriculum and instruction, see Deng and Luke (2008) and Young (2013).

12. See Eisner (2002) on the distinction between explicit, implicit, and null curricula.

13. Shulman's (1986) category "pedagogical content knowledge" points in a similar direction: educators' knowledge of how to "represent . . . the subject to make it comprehensible" to students (pp. 6–7). But in Bernstein's (2000) analysis, more than this is involved in the selection and transformation of knowledge into pedagogic communication.

14. In the field of human rights education, a short list of its specialist-interlocutors writing in English would include Bajaj (2011), Bowring (2012), Keet (2015), Osler (2015), Starkey (2012), Suárez (2007), and Tibbitts (2017). And the field's journals would include the journals in which these authors' articles were peer-reviewed and published and others, such as *Human Rights Education Review*. (Of course, an argument will ensue over the "short list" proffered here, which exemplifies the point I am trying to make.)

15. See Bernstein, 1999.

16. This core-periphery strategy is not to be confused with Hirsch's (1987) "core knowledge" project.

17. See Reid (2006) and Parker and Lo (2016a) on the theory and practice of deliberative content selection.

18. On this mediation, see also Barrett (2017) and Morais et al. (2001).

Chapter 10

1. A sample: Barton and Ho, 2022; Beck, 2013; Camicia, 2007; Conrad, 2019; Dabach et al., 2018 Garrett and Alvey, 2021; Hess, 2009; Journell, 2017; Larson, 2022; Lo, 2016; McAvoy, 2017; Pace, 2021; Parker, 2010; Reisman, 2022; Sibbett, 2018; Smith et al., 2021.

2. See Note 3, Chapter 2.

3. The same is true of this book.

Chapter 11

1. See Note 1, Chapter 1.

2. Section 1 draws on Parker, 2001; section 2 on Parker, 2019; and section 3 on Parker, 2015.

3. This is demonstrated famously by Socrates in the dialogue "Meno" (Plato, 1956).

4. Diane Ravitch (2010) derided these subjects as "tot sociology" in 1987 but later reversed course when she saw that the testing-and-accountability movement had backfired.

5. See Evans, 2004; Nash et al., 2000; Thornton, 2005; and Wineburg, 1999.

6. See the analyses by Johnson (2017) and Santiago and Dozono (2022), as well as the instructive debates not only between Counts and Dewey but, later, between Giroux and Penna (1979) and Cornbleth (1980).

References

Addams, J. (1913). Why women should vote. In F. Maule (Ed.), *Woman suffrage: History, arguments, and results*. National American Woman Suffrage Association.

Allen, D. (2004). *Talking to strangers: Anxieties of citizenship since Brown v. Board of Education*. University of Chicago Press.

Allen, D. (2014). *Our Declaration: A reading of the Declaration of Independence in defense of equality*. W. W. Norton.

Allen, D. (2020, October). The Constitution counted my great-great grandfather as three-fifths of a person: Here's why I love it anyway. *Atlantic Monthly*, 58–63.

Althusser, L. (1984). *Essays on ideology*. Verso.

Annenberg Public Policy Center. (2016). *Americans' knowledge of the branches of government is declining*. https://www.annenbergpublicpolicycenter.org/americans -knowledgeof-the-branches-of-government-is-declining/

Apple, M. W. (1979). *Ideology and curriculum*. Routledge-Falmer.

Arendt, H. (1958). *The human condition*. University of Chicago Press.

Arendt, H. (1968). *Men in dark times*. Harcourt, Brace & World.

Aristotle. (1958). *The politics of Aristotle* (E. Barker, Trans.). Oxford University Press.

Aronson, E., Blaney, N. T., Stephan, C., Sikes, J., & Snapp, M. (1978). *The jigsaw classroom*. Sage.

Asia Society. (2005). *Asia Society*. www.internationaled.org/statesinstitute

Avery, P. G., Levy, S. A., & Simmons, A.M.M. (2013). Deliberating controversial public issues as part of civic education. *Social Studies, 104*(3), 105–114.

Bajaj, M. (2011). Human rights education: Ideology, location, and approaches. *Human Rights Quarterly, 33*(2), 481–508.

Bajaj, M. (Ed.). (2017). *Human rights education: Theory, research, praxis*. University of Pennsylvania Press.

Ball, T., & Pocock, J.G.A. (1988). *Conceptual change and the Constitution*. University Press of Kansas.

Banks, A. M. (2021). *Civic education in the age of mass migration: Implications for theory and practice*. Teachers College Press.

Banks, J. A. (1993). The canon debate, knowledge construction, and multicultural education. *Educational Researcher, 22*(5), 4–14.

Banks, J. A. (Ed.). (2017). *Citizenship education and global migration: Implications for theory, research, and teaching*. American Educational Research Association.

Banfield, E. C. (1958). *The moral basis of a backward society*. Free Press.

Barrett, B. (2017). Bernstein in the urban classroom: A case study. *British Journal of Sociology of Education*. doi:10.1080/01425692.2016.1269632

Barrett, B., Hoadley, U., & Morgan, J. (Eds.). (2018). *Knowledge, curriculum, and equity: Social realist perspectives*. Routledge.

Barton, K. C. (2015). Young adolescents' positioning of human rights: Findings from Colombia, Northern Ireland, Republic of Ireland, and the United States. *Research in Comparative and International Education, 10*(1), 48–70.

Barton, K. C., & Ho, L. C. (2022). *Curriculum for justice and harmony: Deliberation, knowledge, and action in social and civic education*. Routledge.

Barton, K. C., & Levstik, L. S. (2015). Why don't more history teachers engage students in interpretation? In W. C. Parker (Ed.), *Social studies today: Research and practice* (2nd ed., pp. 35–42). Routledge.

Beadie, N., & Burkholder, Z. (2021). From the diffusion of knowledge to the cultivation of agency: A short history of civic education policy and practice in the U.S. In C. Lee, G. White, & D. Dong (Eds.), *Educating for civic reasoning and discourse: Recommendations for practice, policy, and research* (pp. 97–143). National Academies Press.

Beauvoir, S. de (1948). *The ethics of ambiguity*. Citadel.

Beck, T. A. (2013). Identity, discourse, and safety in a high school discussion of same-sex marriage. *Theory and Research in Social Education, 41*(1), 1–32. doi:10.10 80/00933104.2013.757759

Becker, J. M. (1969). *An examination of goals, needs, and priorities in international education in U.S. secondary and elementary schools*. U.S. Department of Health, Education and Welfare.

Bellah, R. N., Madsen, R., Sullivan, W. M., Swidler, A., & Tipton, S. M. (1985). *Habits of the heart: Individualism and commitment in American life*. University of California Press.

Berkowitz, M. (1981). A critical appraisal of the educational and psychological perspectives on moral discussion. *Journal of Educational Thought, 15*, 20–33.

Bernstein, B. (1971). *Class, codes and control* (Vol. 1). Routledge & Kegan Paul.

Bernstein, B. (1990). *The structuring of pedagogic discourse*. Routledge.

Bernstein, B. (1999). Vertical and horizontal discourse: An essay. *British Journal of Sociology of Education, 20*(2), 157–173.

Bernstein, B. (2000). *Pedagogy, symbolic control and identity: Theory, research, critique*. Roman & Littlefield.

Biesta, G. (2009). Good education in an age of measurement. *Educational Assessment, Evaluation and Accountability, 21*, 33–46.

Blatt, M., & Kohlberg, L. (1975). The effects of classroom moral discussion upon children's moral judgment. *Journal of Moral Education, 4*, 129–161.

Boler, M. (Ed.). (2004). *Democratic dialogue in education: Troubling speech, disturbing silence*. Peter Lang.

Bosniak, L. (2006). *The citizen and the alien: Dilemmas of contemporary membership*. Princeton University Press.

Boulding, K. E. (1968). Education for Spaceship Earth. *Social Education, 45*(7), 648–656, 669.

Bourdieu, P., & Passeron, J.-C. (1977). *Reproduction in education, society, and culture*. Cambridge University Press.

Bowles, S., & Gintis, H. (1976). *Schooling in capitalist America: Educational reform and the contradictions of economic life*. Basic Books.

Bowring, B. (2012). Human rights and public education. *Cambridge Journal of Education, 42*(1), 53–65.

Bozec, G. (2017). Citizenship and diversity in France: Controversies, local adaptations, and communities. In J. A. Banks (Ed.), *Citizenship education and global migration: Implications for theory, research, and teaching* (pp. 185–208). American Educational Research Association.

Bransford, J., Brown, A. L., & Cocking, R. R. (2000). *How people learn: Brain, mind, experience, and school.* National Academies Press.

Bransford, J. D., Vye, N. J., Stevens, R., Kuhl, P., Schwartz, D., Bell, P., Meltzoff, A., Barron, B., Pea, R., Reeves, B., Roschelle, J., & Sabelli, N. (2006). Learning theories and education: Toward a decade of synergy. In P. A. Alexander & P. H. Winne (Eds.), *Handbook of educational psychology* (2nd ed., pp. 209–244). Erlbaum.

Bridges, D. (1979). *Education, democracy and discussion.* Humanities Press.

Brown, A. (1992). Design experiments: Theoretical and methodological challenges in creating complex interventions in classroom settings. *Journal of the Learning Sciences, 2,* 141–178.

Bruner, J. (1960). *The process of education.* Harvard University Press.

Bruner, J. (1979). *On knowing.* Harvard University Press.

Caldwell, B. J. (2005). The new enterprise logic of schools. *Phi Delta Kappan, 87*(3), 223–225.

Camicia, S. P. (2007). Deliberating immigration policy: Locating instructional materials within global and multicultural perspectives. *Theory and Research in Social Education, 31*(1), 96–111. doi:10.1080/00933104.2007.10473327

Campaign for the Civic Mission of Schools and the Leonore Annenberg Institute for Civics. (2011). *Guardian of democracy.* Author.

Caporaso, J. A., & Mittelman, J. H. (1988). The assault on global education. *PS: Political Science and Politics, 21*(1), 36–44.

Center for International Understanding. (2005). *North Carolina in the world: Increasing student knowledge and skills about the world.* Author.

Christman, J. (2020). Autonomy in moral and political philosophy. In E. N. Zalta (Ed.), *The Stanford encyclopedia of philosophy* (Fall 2020 ed.). https://plato.stanford.edu/archives/fall2020/entries/autonomy-moral/

Code, L. (1991). *What can she know? Feminist theory and the construction of knowledge.* Cornell University Press.

Cohen, E. G. (1986). *Designing groupwork: Strategies for the heterogeneous classroom.* Teachers College Press.

College Entrance Examination Board. (2014). *10th annual AP report to the nation.* Author.

Collier, A. (1981). Scientific socialism and the question of socialist values. In K. Nielsen & S. C. Patten (Eds.), *Marx and morality* (pp. 121–154). Canadian Association for Publishing in Philosophy.

Conrad, J. (2019). Navigating identity as a controversial issue: One teacher's disclosure for critical empathic reasoning. *Theory and Research in Social Education, 48*(2), 211–243. doi:10.1080/00933104.2019.1679687

Cormack, M. J. (1992). *Ideology.* University of Michigan Press.

Cornbleth, C. (1980). A reaction to social education in the classroom: The dynamics of the hidden curriculum. *Theory and Research in Social Education, 8*(2), 57–60.

Council of Europe. (1985, May). *Recommendation R (85) 7 on teaching and learning about human rights in schools. The 385th Meeting of Ministers' Deputies.* Author. http://www.coe.int/t/dg4/education/historyteaching/Source/Results/Adop tedTexts/Rec(85)7_en.pdf

Counts, G. S. (1932). *Dare the school build a new social order?* John Day.

Cremin, L. A. (1990). *Popular education and its discontents.* HarperCollins.

Crick, B. (2008). Democracy. In J. Arthur, I. Davies, & C. Hahn (Eds.), *Sage handbook of education for citizenship and democracy* (pp. 13–19). Sage.

Cuban, L. (1990). Reforming again, again, and again. *Educational Researcher, 19*(1), 3–13.

Cunningham, G. L. (1986). *Blowing the whistle on global education.* Regional Office (Denver), United States Department of Education.

Dabach, D. B. (2015). My student was apprehended by immigration. *Harvard Educational Review, 85*(3), 383–412. doi:10.17763/0017-8055.85.3.383

Dabach, D. B., Fones, A., Merchant, N. H., & Adekile, A. (2018). Teachers navigating civic education when students are undocumented. *Theory and Research in Social Education, 46*(3), 331–373. doi:10.1080/00933104.2017.1 413470

Delpit, L. D. (1988). The silenced dialogue: Power and pedagogy in educating other people's children. *Harvard Educational Review, 58*(3), 280–298.

Deng, Z., & Luke, A. (2008). Subject matter: Defining and theorizing school subjects. In F. M. Connelly, M. F. He, & J. Phillion (Eds.), *Sage handbook of curriculum and instruction* (pp. 66–87). Sage.

Dewey, J. (1902). *The child and the curriculum.* University of Chicago Press.

Dewey, J. (1903). Democracy in education. *Elementary School Teacher, 4*(4), 193–204.

Dewey, J. (1935). The crucial role of intelligence. *Social Frontier, 1*(5), 9.

Dewey, J. (1956). *The school and society and The child and the curriculum* (combined edition). University of Chicago Press.

Dewey, J. (1985). Democracy and education. In *The middle works of John Dewey, 1899–1924* (Vol. 9, J. A. Boydston, Ed.). Southern Illinois University Press. (Original work published 1916).

Diamond, L. (2020). Breaking out of the democratic slump. *Journal of Democracy, 31*(1), 36–50.

Du Bois, W.E.B. (1962). *Black reconstruction in America, 1860–1880.* Atheneum.

Durkheim, E. (2001). *The elementary forms of religious life.* Free Press. (Original work published 1912)

Eisner, E. W. (2002). *The educational imagination* (3rd ed.). Merrill/Prentice Hall.

Evans, R. W. (2004). *The social studies wars.* Teachers College Press.

Fallace, T. D. (2016). The origins of classroom deliberation: Democratic education in the shadow of totalitarianism, 1938–1960. *Harvard Educational Review, 86*(4), 506–526.

Fast, H. (1961). *April morning.* Bantam.

Finn, C. E. (Ed.). (2003). *Terrorists, despots, and democracy: What our children need to know.* Thomas B. Fordham Foundation.

Flanagan, C. A. (2013). *Teenage citizens: The political theories of the young.* Harvard University Press.

Foner, E. (1998). *The story of American freedom*. W. W. Norton.

Foner, E. (2019). *The second founding: How the Civil War and Reconstruction re-made the Constitution*. W. W. Norton.

Frazer, E. (2007). Depoliticising citizenship. *British Journal of Educational Studies, 55*(3), 249–263.

Frederickson, G. (2015). *Racism: A short history*. Princeton University Press.

Freire, P. (1970). *Pedagogy of the oppressed*. Seabury.

Freedom House. (2022). *Freedom in the world*. https://freedomhouse.org/countries/freedom-world/scores

Fry, R. (2007). *The changing racial and ethnic composition of U.S. public schools*. Pew Hispanic Center, Pew Research Center.

Fukuyama, F. (2022). *Liberalism and its discontents*: Farrar, Straus and Giroux.

Fulton, B. (2008, February 23). Students say good things about IB. *Salt Lake Tribune*. www.sltrib.com

Galbraith, J. K. 1998). *The affluent society*. Houghton Mifflin.

Galston, W. A. (2001). Political knowledge, political engagement, and civic education. In N. W. Polsby (Ed.), *Annual Review of Political Science, 4*, 217–234.

Gamson, W. A., & Meyer, D. S. (1996). Framing political opportunity. In D. McAdam, J. D. McCarthy, & M. N. Zald (Eds.), *Comparative perspectives on social movements: Political opportunities, mobilizing structures, and cultural framings* (pp. 275–290). Cambridge University Press.

Garrett, H. J., & Alvey, E. (2021). Exploring the emotional dynamics of a political discussion. *Theory and Research in Social Education, 49*(1), 1–26. doi:10.1080/00933104.2020.1808550

Gastil, J., & Levine, P. (Eds.). (2005). *The deliberative democracy handbook*. Jossey-Bass.

Gay, G. (2018). *Culturally responsive teaching* (3rd ed.). Teachers College Press.

Gibbs, J. C. (1979). Kohlberg's moral stage theory: A Piagetian revision. *Human Development, 22*, 89–112.

Gibson, M. (2020). From deliberation to counter-narration: Toward a critical pedagogy for democratic citizenship. *Theory and Research in Social Education, 48*(3), 431–454.

Gilligan, C. (1982). *In a different voice: Psychological theory and women's development*. Harvard University Press.

Giroux, H. A. (1979). Toward a new sociology of curriculum. *Educational Leadership, 37*(3), 248–252.

Giroux, H. A., & Penna, A. N. (1979). Social education in the classroom: The dynamics of the hidden curriculum. *Theory and Research in Social Education, 7*(1), 21–42.

Goffman, E. (1974). *Frame analysis: An essay on the organization of experience*. Harvard University Press.

Gramsci, A. (1971). *Prison notebooks*. International Publishers.

Great Books Foundation. (2022). *Shared inquiry*. https://www.greatbooks.org/learning-center/training-courses/

Green, A. (1990). *Education and state formation*. Macmillan.

Greene, M. (1995). *Releasing the imagination: Essays on education, the arts, and social change*. Jossey-Bass.

Greene, T. (1954). The art of responsible conversation. *Journal of General Education, 8,* 34–50.

Greenleaf, C., & Valencia, S. W. (2017). Missing in action: Learning from texts in subject-matter classrooms. In K. A. Hinchman & D. Appleman (Eds.), *Adolescent literacies: A handbook of practice-based research* (pp. 235–256). Guilford.

Gutmann, A. (1996). Democracy, philosophy, and justification. In S. Benhabib (Ed.), *Democracy and difference* (pp. 340–347). Princeton University Press.

Gutmann, A. (1999). *Democratic education* (2nd ed.). Princeton University Press.

Habermas, J. (1971). *Knowledge and human interests* (J. J. Shapiro, Trans.). Beacon Press.

Habermas, J. (1984). *Theory of communicative action.* Beacon.

Habermas, J. (1995). Citizenship and national identity: Some reflections on the future of Europe. In R. Beiner (Ed.), *Theorizing citizenship* (pp. 255–281). State University of New York Press.

Habermas, J. (1996). Three normative models of democracy. In S. Benhabib (Ed.), *Democracy and difference: Contesting the boundaries of the political* (pp. 21–30). Princeton University Press.

Habermas, J. (2006). *Time of transitions.* Polity.

Hahn, C. L. (1998). *Becoming political.* State University of New York Press.

Hampshire, S. (1977). Epilogue. In S. Hampshire & L. Kolakowski (Eds.), *The socialist idea* (pp. 246–249). Quarter.

Hanh, T. N. (1988). *The heart of understanding.* Parallax.

Hanh, T. N. (2001, October). What I would say to Osama bin Laden. *Changemakers.Net Journal.* www.changemakers.net/journal/01october/hanh.cfm

Hanvey, R. G. (1978). *An attainable global perspective.* Center for Global Perspectives.

Hershberg, T. (2005). Value-added assessment and systemic reform: A response to the challenge of human capital development. *Phi Delta Kappan, 87*(4), 276–283.

Hess, D. E. (2009). *Controversy in the classroom: The democratic power of discussion.* Routledge.

Hess, D. E., & McAvoy, P. (2015). *The political classroom: Evidence and ethics in democratic education.* Routledge.

Hirsch, E. D., Jr. (1987). *Cultural literacy: What every American needs to know.* Vintage.

Hirschman, A. O. (1991). *The rhetoric of reaction: Perversity, futility, jeopardy.* Harvard University Press.

Ho, L.-C. (2017). Freedom can only exist in an ordered state: Harmony and civic education in Singapore. *Journal of Curriculum Studies, 49*(4), 476–496.

Hochschild, J. L., & Scovronick, N. (2002). Democratic education and the American Dream: One, some, and all. In W. C. Parker (Ed.), *Education for democracy: Contexts, curricula, and assessments* (pp. 3–26). Information Age.

Holmes, S. (1995). *Passion and constraint: On the theory of liberal democracy.* University of Chicago Press.

hooks, b. (2000). *Where we stand: Class matters.* Routledge.

Inman, M. (2006). Pluto not a planet, astronomers rule. *National Geographic News*. www.news.nationalgeographic.com

International Committee of the Red Cross. (2009). *Exploring humanitarian law*. Author.

Jacoby, R. (1975). *Social amnesia*. Beacon Press.

Jain, S. (2002). Urban errands: The means of mobility. *Journal of Consumer Culture, 2*(3), 419–438.

Jaspers, K. (1962). *Socrates, Buddha, Confucius, Jesus* (R. Manheim, Trans.). Harcourt, Brace and World.

Jefferson, T. (1954). *Notes on the State of Virginia*. Norton. (Original work published 1787)

Johnson, D. W., & Johnson, R. T. (1979). Conflict in the classroom: Controversy and learning. *Review of Educational Research, 49*, 51–61.

Johnson, D. W., & Johnson, R. (1985). Classroom conflict: Controversy vs. debate in learning groups. *American Educational Research Journal, 22*, 237–256.

Johnson, D. W., & Johnson, R. T. (1988). Critical thinking through structured controversy. *Educational Leadership, 45*(8), 58–64.

Johnson, D. W., & Johnson, R. T. (2009). Energizing learning: The instructional power of conflict. *Educational Researcher, 38*(1), 37–51.

Johnson, M. E. (2017). Emancipatory and pluralist perspectives on democracy and economic inequality in social studies and citizenship education. In C. Wright-Maley & T. Davis (Eds.), *Teaching for democracy in an age of economic disparity* (pp. 42–58). Routledge.

Journell, W. (2017). Framing controversial identity issues in schools. *Equity and Excellence in Education, 50*(4), 339–354. doi:10.1080/10665684.2017.1393640

Kahan, D. M. (2007). The cognitively illiberal state. *Stanford Law Review, 60*(1), 115–154.

Kahne, J., Bowyer, B., Marshall, J., & Hodgin, E. (2022). Is responsiveness to student voice related to academic outcomes? Strengthening the rationale for student voice in school reform. *American Journal of Education, 128*(3), 389–415. doi:10.1086/719121

Kahne, J., & Middaugh, E. (2008). *Democracy for some: The civic opportunity gap in high school*. Center for Information and Research on Learning.

Keet, A. (2015). It's time: Critical human rights education in an age of counter-hegemonic distrust. *Education as Change, 19*(3), 46–64.

Kegan, R. (1982). *The evolving self*. Harvard University Press.

Kemmis, D. (1995). *The good city and the good life*. Houghton Mifflin.

Khyentse, D. (1993). *Enlightened courage*. Snow Lion.

King, M. B., Newmann, F. M., & Carmichael, D. L. (2009). Authentic intellectual work: Common standards for teaching social studies. *Social Education, 73*(1), 43–49.

King, M. L. Jr. (1958). *Stride toward freedom*. Harper & Row.

King, M. L. Jr. (1963). Letter from Birmingham Jail. In *Why we can't wait* (pp. 76–95). Mentor.

King, M. L. Jr. (1967, August). *Where do we go from here?* (Address). Martin Luther King Jr. Papers Project at Stanford University. http://www.stanford.edu/group/King/speeches/

King, M. L. Jr. (2001). I have a dream (Address). In C. Carson & K. Shepard (Eds.), *A call to conscience* (pp. 81–87). Warner.

Kohlberg, L. (1971). From is to ought: How to commit the naturalistic fallacy and get away with it in the study of moral development. In T. Mischel (Ed.), *Cognitive development and epistemology* (pp. 151–235). Academic Press.

Kohlberg, L. (1979). Justice as reversibility. In P. Laslett & J. Fishkin (Eds.), *Philosophy, politics and society* (pp. 257–272). Yale University Press.

Kohlberg, L., Levine, C., & Hewer, A. (1984a). The current formulation of the theory. In L. Kohlberg (Ed.), *Essays on moral development, Vol. 11. The psychology of moral development: The nature and validity of moral stages* (pp. 212–319). Harper & Row.

Kohlberg, L., Levine, C., & Hewer, A. (1984b). Synopses and detailed replies to critics. In L. Kohlberg (Ed.), *Essays on moral development, Vol. 11. The psychology of moral development: The nature and validity of moral states* (pp. 320–386). Harper & Row.

Kohlberg, L., & Mayer, R. (1972). Development as the aim of education. *Harvard Educational Review, 42,* 451–496.

Kohlmeier, J. (2022). Socratic seminar: Learning with and from each other while interpreting complex text. In J. C. Lo (Ed.), *Making classroom discussions work* (pp. 63–72). Teachers College Press.

Korzybski, A. (1958). *Science and sanity.* Institute of General Semantics.

Kurtz, S. (2021, March 15). The greatest education battle of our lifetimes. *National Review.* https://www.nationalreview.com/corner/the-greatest-education-battle-of-our-lifetimes/

Kymlicka, W. (1999). Education for citizenship. *School Field, 20*(1/2), 9–35.

Labaree, D. F. (2010). *Someone has to fail: The zero-sum game of public schooling.* Harvard University Press.

Lacey, T. (2010). Access, rigor, and revenue in the history of the Advanced Placement program. In P. M. Sadler, G. Sonnert, R. H. Tai, & K. Klopfenstein (Eds.), *AP: A critical examination of the Advanced Placement program* (pp. 17–48). Harvard Education Press.

Laden, A. (2012). *Reasoning: A social picture.* Oxford University Press.

Ladson-Billings, G. (1995). Toward a theory of culturally relevant pedagogy. *American Educational Research Journal, 32*(3), 465–491.

Larmer, J., & Mergendoller, J. R. (2010). *Main course, not dessert.* Buck Institute for Education. http://www.bie.org/tools/freebies/main_course_not_dessert

Larson, B. E. (2022). Guiding principles for using classroom discussion. In J. C. Lo (Ed.), *Making classroom discussions work* (pp. 11–26). Teachers College Press.

Lewis, M. (2018). Has anyone seen the President? *Bloomberg.* https://www.bloomberg.com/opinion/articles/2018-02-09/has-anyone-seen-the-president

Lincoln, A. (1838). *The Lyceum address.* http://www.abrahamlincolnonline.org/lincoln/speeches/lyceum.htm

Lo, J. C. (2015). *Learning to participate through role-play: Understanding political simulations in the high school government course* (Doctoral dissertation, University of Washington). http://search.proquest.com/docview/1718414960/abstract

Lo, J. C. (2016). Adolescents developing civic identities: Sociocultural perspectives on simulations and role-play in a civics classroom. *Theory and Research in Social Education,* 1–29. doi:10.1080/00933104.2016.1220877

Lo, J. C., & Parker, W. C. (2016). Role-playing and role-dropping: Political simulations as portals to pluralism in a contentious era. In W. Journell (Ed.), *Reassessing the social studies curriculum: Promoting critical civic engagement in a politically polarized, post-9/11 world* (pp. 95–108). Rowman & Littlefield.

Lundy, L. (2007). Voice is not enough: Conceptualising Article 12 of the United Nations Convention on the Rights of the Child. *British Educational Research Journal, 33*(6), 927–942.

Madison, J. (2003a). Federalist No. 55. In A. Hamilton, J. Jay, & J. Madison (Eds.), *The Federalist Papers* (pp. 337–342). Bantam Classic. (Original work published 1788)

Madison, J. (2003b). Federalist No. 51. In A. Hamilton, J. Jay, & J. Madison (Eds.), *The Federalist Papers* (pp. 314–319). Bantam Classic. (Original work published 1788)

Marche, S. (2022). *The next civil war: Dispatches from the American future.* Avid Reader Press.

Marcuse, H. (1965). Repressive tolerance. In R. P. Wolff et al., *A critique of pure tolerance* (pp. 81–123). Beacon Press.

Marx, K. (1965). *Capital* (S. Moore and E. Aveling, Trans.). Progress Publishers.

Mason, L. (2018). *Uncivil agreement: How politics became our identity.* University of Chicago Press.

Mathews, J. (2009, August 28). Will Advanced Placement replace the SAT? *Washington Post.* http://voices.washingtonpost.com/class-struggle/2009/08/will_advanced_placement_replac.html

Maton, K. (2014). *Knowledge and knowers: Towards a realist sociology of education.* Routledge.

Matua, M. (2011). *Human rights: A political and cultural critique.* University of Pennsylvania Press.

McAvoy, P. (2017). Should teachers share their political views in the classroom? In B. R. Warnick (Ed.), *Philosophy: Education* (pp. 373–383). Macmillan Reference.

McAvoy, P., & Lowery, A. (2022). Structure matters: Comparing deliberation ad debate. In J. C. Lo (Ed.), *Making classroom discussions work* (pp. 90–105). Teachers College Press.

McEneaney, E. H., & Meyer, J. W. (2000). The content of the curriculum: An institutionalist perspective. In M. T. Hallinan (Ed.), *Handbook of the sociology of education* (pp. 189–211). Kluwer.

McPhail, G., & Rata, E. (2018). A theoretical model of curriculum design: "Powerful knowledge" and "21st century learning." In B. Barrett, U. Hoadley, & J. Morgan (Eds.), *Knowledge, curriculum, and equity: Social realist perspectives* (pp. 63–79). Routledge.

Meyer, J. W., Bromley, P., & Ramirez, F. O. (2010). Human rights in social science textbooks: Cross-national analyses, 1970–2008. *Sociology of Education, 83*(2), 111–134.

Mill, J. S. (1978). *On liberty.* Indianapolis: Hackett. (Original work published 1859)

Miller, B., & Singleton, L. (1997). *Preparing citizens: Linking authentic assessment and instruction in civic/law-related education* (book and video series). Social Science Education Consortium.

Miller-Lane, J. (2005). Constructive disagreement, the body, and education for democracy. *Social Studies, 97*(1), 16–21.

Mills, C. W. (1999). *The racial contract* (1st ed.). Cornell University Press.

Mitra, D., Serriere, S., & Kirshner, B. (2014). Youth participation in U.S. contexts: Student voice without a national mandate. *Children and Society, 28*(4), 292–304.

Moll, L. (Ed.). (1990). *Vygotsky and education.* Cambridge University Press.

Moll, L., Amanti, C., Neff, D., & Gonzales, N. (1992). Funds of knowledge for teaching: Using a qualitative approach to connect homes and classrooms. *Theory Into Practice, 31*(2), 131–141.

Montesquieu. (1758). *On the spirit of the laws* (T. Nugent, Trans.). https://en.wikisource.org/wiki/The_Spirit_of_Laws_(1758)/Book_XI

Moore, R. (2007). Going critical: The problem of problematizing knowledge in education studies. *Critical Studies in Education, 48*(1), 25–41.

Moore, R., & Muller, J. (1999). The discourse of "voice" and the problem of knowledge and identity in the sociology of education. *British Journal of Sociology of Education, 20*(2), 189–206.

Morais, A., Neves, I., Davies, B., & Daniels, H. (Eds.). (2001). *Toward a sociology of pedagogy: The contribution of Basil Bernstein to research.* Peter Lang.

Morgan, J., & Lambert, D. (2018). For knowledge—but what knowledge? Confronting social realism's curriculum problem. In B. Barrett, U. Hoadley, & J. Morgan (Eds.), *Knowledge, curriculum, and equity: Social realist perspectives* (pp. 33–44). Routledge.

Mosher, R., Kenny, R. A., Jr., & Garrod, A. (Eds.). (1994). *Preparing for citizenship: Teaching youth to live democratically.* Praeger.

Moy, P. (2020). The promise and perils of voice. *Journal of Communication, 70*(1), 1–12. doi:10.1093/joc/jqz049

Myers, D. (1999). Simulation as play: A semiotic analysis. *Simulation and Gaming, 30*(2), 147–162.

Narayan, U. (1988). Working together across difference: Some considerations on emotions and political practice. *Hypatia, 3*(2), 31–47.

Nash, G. B., Crabtree, C., & Dunn, R. E. (2000). *History on trial.* Vintage.

National Academies of Sciences, Engineering and Medicine. (2007). *Rising above the gathering storm: Energizing and employing America for a brighter economic future (executive summary).* National Academies Press.

National Academies of Sciences, Engineering and Medicine. (2018). *How people learn II: Learners, contexts, and cultures.* National Academies Press.

National Center for Education Statistics. (2009). *High school transcript study.* U.S. Department of Education.

National Commission on Excellence in Education. (1983). *A nation at risk: The imperative for educational reform.* Author.

National Education Association of the United States, Committee of Ten on Secondary School Studies. (1894). *Report of the Committee of Ten on Secondary School Studies.* American Book Co. https://books.google.com/books?id=PfcBAAAAYAAJ&pg=PA3#v=onepage&q&f=false

National Research Council. (2002). *Learning and understanding: Improving advanced study of mathematics and science in U.S. high schools, executive summary.* National Academy Press.

Newman, J. H. (1852). *Discourse 6.5,* "Knowledge viewed in relation to learning." https://www.newmanreader.org/works/idea/discourse6.html

Nie, N. H., Junn, J., & Stehlik-Barry, K. (1996). *Education and democratic citizenship in America*. University of Chicago Press.

Niemöller, M. (2022). United States Holocaust Museum and Memorial. https://encyclopedia.ushmm.org/

Nussbaum, M. C. (2002). Patriotism and cosmopolitanism. In J. Cohen (Ed.), *For love of country?* (pp. 4–17). Beacon.

Okihiro, G. Y. (1994). *Margins and mainstreams: Asians in American history and culture*. University of Washington Press.

Orfield, G. (2001). Schools more separate: Consequences of a decade of resegregation. http://www.civilrightsproject.harvard.edu/research/deseg/call_separateschools.php

Orwell, G. (1961). *1984*. Penguin.

Osler, A. (2015). Human rights education, postcolonial scholarship, and action for social justice. *Theory and Research in Social Education, 43*(2), 244–274.

Osler, A. (2016). *Human rights and schooling: An ethical framework for teaching for social justice*. Teachers College Press.

Oxford University Press. (1989). *Oxford English Dictionary online* (2nd ed.). http://dictionary.oed.com.offcampus.lib.washington.edu

Oyez. (1995). *United States v. Lopez, 514UW549*. www.oyez.org/cases/1994/93-1260

Pace, J. L. (2021). *Hard questions: Learning to teach controversial issues*. Rowman & Littlefield.

Paley, V. G. (1992). *You can't say you can't play*. Harvard University Press.

Panjwani, F., Gholami, R., & Diboll, M. (Eds.). (2018). *Education and extremisms: Re-thinking liberal pedagogies in the contemporary world*. Routledge.

Paris, D. (2012). Culturally sustaining pedagogy. *Educational Researcher, 41*(3), 93–97.

Parker, W. C. (2001). Classroom discussion: Models for leading seminars and deliberations. *Social Education, 65*(2), 111–115.

Parker, W. C. (2003). *Teaching democracy: Unity and diversity in public life*. Teachers College Press.

Parker, W. C. (2005). Teaching against idiocy. *Phi Delta Kappan, 86*(5), 344–351.

Parker, W. C. (2006). Public discourses in schools: Purposes, problems, possibilities. *Educational Researcher, 35*(8), 11–18.

Parker, W. C. (2008). Knowing and doing in democratic citizenship education. In L. Levstik & C. A. Tyson (Eds.), *Handbook of research in social studies education* (pp. 65–80). Routledge.

Parker, W. C. (2010). Listening to strangers: Classroom discussion in democratic education. *Teachers College Record, 112*(11), 2815–2832.

Parker, W. C. (2011). Constructing public schooling today: Derision, multiculturalism, nationalism. *Educational Theory, 61*(4), 413–432.

Parker, W. C. (Ed.). (2015). *Social studies today: Research and practice* (2nd ed.). Routledge.

Parker, W. C. (2017). Toward powerful human rights education in schools: Problems and possibilities. In J. A. Banks (Ed.), *Citizenship education and global migration: Implications for theory, research, and teaching* (pp. 457–481). American Educational Research Association.

Parker, W. C. (2019). Cultivating judgment. In M. Levinson & J. Fay (Eds.), *Democratic discord in schools: Cases and commentaries in educational ethics* (pp. 187–190). Harvard Education Press.

Parker, W. C. (2022). Structured Academic Controversy: What it can be. In J. C. Lo (Ed.), *Making discussions work* (pp. 73–89). Teachers College Press.

Parker, W. C., & Hess, D. (2001). Teaching with and for discussion. *Teaching and Teacher Education, 17*(3), 273–289.

Parker, W. C., & Lo, J. (2016a). Content selection in advanced courses. *Curriculum Inquiry, 46*(2), 196–219.

Parker, W. C., & Lo, J. C. (2016b). Reinventing the high school government course: Rigor, simulations, and learning from text. *Democracy and Education, 24*(1), Article 6. http://democracyeducationjournal.org/home/vol24/iss1/6

Parker, W., Lo, J., Yeo, A. J., Valencia, S. W., Nguyen, D., Abbott, R. D., Nolen, S. B., Bransford, J. D., & Vye, N. J. (2013). Beyond breadth-speed-test: Toward deeper knowing and engagement. *American Educational Research Journal, 50*(6), 1424–1459.

Parker, W. C., Mosborg, S., Bransford, J. D., Vye, N. J., Wilkerson, J., & Abbott, R. (2011). Rethinking advanced high school coursework: Tackling the depth/breadth tension in the AP US Government and Politics course. *Journal of Curriculum Studies, 43*(4), 533–559.

Parker, W. C., Valencia, S. W., & Lo, J. C. (2018). Teaching for deeper political learning: A design experiment. *Journal of Curriculum Studies, 50*(2), 252–277.

Parsons, T. (1951). *The social system.* Routledge.

Peirce, C. S. (2014). The fixation of belief. In J. Hoopes (Ed.), *Peirce on signs* (pp. 144–159). University of North Carolina Press. (Original work published 1877)

Penuel, W. R., Fishman, B. J., Cheng, B. H., & Sabelli, N. (2011). Organizing research and development at the intersection of learning, implementation, and design. *Educational Researcher, 40*(7), 331–337.

Pettigrew, T. F. (2004). Intergroup contact: Theory, research, and new perspectives. In J. A. Banks & C.A.M. Banks (Eds.), *Handbook of research on multicultural education* (2nd ed., pp. 770–781). Jossey-Bass.

Piaget, J. (1965). *The moral judgement of the child.* Free Press.

Pinar, W. (Ed.). (1975). *Curriculum theorizing: The reconceptualists.* McCutchan.

Plato. (1956). Meno. In *Protagoras and Meno.* (W.K.C. Guthrie, Trans.). Penguin Classics.

Plato. (1992a). Crito. In *The trial and death of Socrates: Four dialogues.* Dover.

Plato. (1992b). *The republic* (G.M.A. Grube, Trans.). Hackett.

Pocock, J.G.A. (1998). The ideal of citizenship since classical times. In G. Shafir (Ed.), *The citizenship debates* (pp. 31–41). University of Minnesota Press.

Postman, N. (1969). *Bullshit and the art of crap-detection.* Paper presented at the Annual meeting of the National Council of Teachers of English, Washington, DC.

Power, F. C., Higgins, A., & Kohlberg, L. (1989). *Lawrence Kohlberg's approach to moral education.* Columbia University Press.

Raskin, J. B. (2015). *We the students: Supreme Court cases for and about students* (4th ed.). Congressional Quarterly Inc.

Rata, E. (2016). A pedagogy of conceptual progression and the case for academic knowledge. *British Educational Research Journal, 42*(1), 168–184.

Rauch, J. (2021). *The constitution of knowledge*. Brookings Institution.

Ravitch, D. (1987). Tot sociology, or what happened to history in the grade schools. *American Scholar, 56*(3), 343–354.

Ravitch, D. (2010). *The death and life of the great American school system: How testing and choice are undermining education*. Basic Books.

Ravitz, J. (2009). Summarizing findings and looking ahead to a new generation of PBL research. *Interdisciplinary Journal of Problem-Based Learning, 3*(1), 4–11.

Rawls, J. (1971). *A theory of justice*. Harvard University Press.

Reid, W. A. (2006). *The pursuit of curriculum: Schooling and the public interest*. Information Age.

Reiman, J. H. (1981). The possibility of a Marxian theory of justice. In K. Nielsen & S. C. Patten (Eds.), *Marx and morality* (pp. 307–322). Canadian Association for Publishing in Philosophy.

Reisman, A. (2022). Document-based discussions in history. In J. C. Lo (Ed.), *Making discussions work* (pp. 106–123). Teachers College Press.

Rempel, G. (1989). *Hitler's children: The Hitler Youth and the SS*. University of North Carolina Press.

Resnick, L. B., & Klopfer, L. E. (1989). *Toward the thinking curriculum: Current cognitive research*. Association for Supervision and Curriculum Development.

Rickover, H. G. (1959). *Education and freedom*. Dutton.

Rochester, J. M. (2005). Unaddressed issues. *Phi Delta Kappan, 86*(9), 654, 657.

Rothstein, R. (2004). *Class and schools*. Economic Policy Institute

Rubin, B. C., El-Haj, T.R.A., & Bellino, M. J. (2021). Civic reasoning and discourse amid structural inequality, migration, and conflict. In C. Lee, G. White, & D. Dong (Eds.), *Educating for civic reasoning and discourse: Recommendations for practice, policy, and research* (pp. 245–272). National Academies Press.

Russell, S. G., & Suárez, D. F. (2017). Symbol and substance: Human rights education as an emergent global institution. In M. Bajaj (Ed.), *Human rights education: Theory, research, and praxis* (pp. 20–46). University of Pennsylvania Press.

Sanders, L. M. (1997). Against deliberation. *Political Theory, 25*(3), 347–376.

Santiago, M., & Dozono, T. (2022). History is critical: Addressing the false dichotomy between historical inquiry and criticality. *Theory and Research in Social Education, 50*(2), 173–195.

Sartre, J.-P. (1948). *The wall* (L. Alexander, Trans.). New Directions.

Schneider, J. (2011). *Excellence for all*. Vanderbilt University Press.

Schwab, J. J. (1964). Structure of the disciplines: Meanings and significances. In G. W. Ford & L. Pugno (Eds.), *The structure of knowledge and the curriculum* (pp. 6–30). Rand McNally.

Schwab, J. J. (1969). The practical: a language for curriculum. *School Review, 78*(1), 1–23.

Schwartz, D. L., & Bransford, J. D. (1998). A time for telling. *Cognition and instruction, 16*(4), 475–522.

Sennett, R. (1974). *The fall of public man*. Norton.

Sharan, S., & Sharan, Y. (1976). *Small group teaching*. Educational Technology Publications.

Shaw, G. B. (1985). *Caesar and Cleopatra*. Penguin.

Shklar, J. N. (1989). The liberalism of fear. In N. Rosenblum (Ed.), *Liberalism and the moral life* (pp. 21–38). Harvard University Press.

Shklar, J. N. (1991). *American citizenship: The quest for inclusion.* Harvard University Press.

Shulman, L. (1986). Those who understand: Knowledge growth in teaching. *Educational Researcher, 15*(2), 4–14.

Sibbett, L. (2018). Clarifying and challenging classroom controversy. *Theory and Research in Social Education, 46*(1), 155–163. doi:10.1080/00933104.2017.1380493

Siegel, L. (1977). Children and adolescents' reactions to the assassination of Martin Luther King: A study of political socialization. *Developmental Psychology 13*(3), 284–285.

Slavin, R. E. (1985). *Learning to cooperate, cooperating to learn.* Plenum Press.

Smith, W. L., Crowley, R. M., Demoiny, S. B., & Cushing-Leubner, J. (2021). Threshold concept pedagogy for antiracist social studies teaching. *Multicultural Perspectives, 23*(2), 87–94. doi:10.1080/15210960.2021.1914047

Southworth, J. (2022). Bridging critical thinking and transformative learning: The role of perspective-taking. *Theory and Research in Education, 20*(1), 44–63.

Spellings, M. (2005, November 9). *International Education Week 2005 announced.* http://usinfo.state.gov/scv/Archive/2005/Nov/09-19221.html

Stanford History Education Group. (2020). *Reading like a historian.* https://sheg.stanford.edu/history-lessons

Stanley, W. B. (1993). Curricular visions and social education: A response to Ronald Evans' review of *Curriculum for Utopia. Theory and Research in Social Education, 21*(3), 294–303.

Starkey, H. (2012). Human rights, cosmopolitanism and utopias: Implications for citizenship education. *Cambridge Journal of Education, 42*(1), 21–35.

Stitzlein, S. M. (2021). Defining and implementing civic reasoning and discourse: Philosophical and moral foundations for research and practice. In C. Lee, G. White, & D. Dong (Eds.), *Educating for civic reasoning and discourse: Recommendations for practice, policy, and research* (pp. 23–52). National Academies Press.

Suárez, D. F. (2007). Education professionals and the construction of human rights education. *Comparative Education Review, 51*(1), 48–70.

Sunstein, C. R. (2002). The law of group polarization. *Journal of Political Philosophy, 10*(2), 175–195.

Taba, H. (1945). General techniques of curriculum planning. In N. B. Henry (Ed.), *American education in the postwar period.* 45th yearbook, National Society for the Study of Education (Vol. 1, pp. 80–115). University of Chicago Press.

Taba, H. (1962). *Curriculum development: Theory and practice.* Harcourt, Brace & World.

Taba, H., Durkin, M. C., Fraenkel, J. R., & McNaughton, A. H. (1971). *A teacher's handbook to elementary social studies: An inductive approach.* Addison-Wesley.

Taber, C. S., & Lodge, M. (2016). The illusion of choice in democratic politics: The unconscious impact of motivated political reasoning. *Advances in Political Psychology, 37*(1), 61–85.

Talbott, W. J. (2006, March). *What's wrong with wishy-washy teaching of political philosophy?* (Special session on neutrality, objectivity, and viewpoint diversity in the teaching of political philosophy). Paper presented at the American Philosophy Association Pacific Division Meeting, Portland.

Tapp, J. L., & Kohlberg, L. (1971). Developing senses of law and legal justice. *Journal of Social Issues, 27*, 65–71.

Thornton, S. J. (2005). *Teaching social studies that matters.* Teachers College Press.

Tibbitts, F. L. (2017). Revisiting 'emerging models of human rights education.' *International Journal of Human Rights Education, 1*(1). http://repository.usfca.edu/ijhre/vol1/iss1/2

Tocqueville, A. de (1969). *Democracy in America* (G. Lawrence, Trans.). Doubleday.

Tucker, R. (1969). *The Marxian revolutionary idea.* W. W. Norton.

Tyack, D. B. (2003). *Seeking common ground: Public schools in a diverse society.* Harvard University Press.

United Nations. (1948). *Universal Declaration of Human Rights.* United Nations General Assembly.

United Nations. (1989). *Convention on the Rights of the Child.* United Nations General Assembly.

United Nations. (2011). *Declaration on human rights education and training.* United Nations General Assembly.

United Nations High Commissioner for Human Rights. (2005). *Revised draft plan of action for the first phase (2005–2007) of the World Programme for Human Rights Education.* United Nations General Assembly, Office of the High Commissioner for Human Rights. http://www.ohchr.org/EN/Issues/Education/Training/WPHRE/FirstPhase/Pages/planaction.aspx

Valencia, S., & Parker, W. C. (2016). Learning from text in an advanced government and politics course. *Citizenship Teaching and Learning, 11*(1), 87–103.

Valencia, S., Wixson, K. K., & Pearson, P. D. (2014). Putting text complexity in context: Refocusing on comprehension of complex text. *Elementary School Journal, 115*(2), 270–289.

Vygotsky, L. S. (1962). *Thought and language.* MIT Press.

Wakelyn, D. (2009). *Raising rigor, getting results: Lessons learned from AP expansion.* National Governors Association.

Waks, L. (2010). Two types of interpersonal listening. *Teachers College Record, 112*(11), 2743–2762.

Walberg, H. J., & Tsai, S.-L. (1983). Matthew effects in education. *Educational Research Quarterly, 20*(3), 359–373.

Walzer, M. (1983). *Spheres of justice.* Basic Books.

West, C. (1993). *Race matters.* Beacon.

Westbrook, R. B. (1991). *John Dewey and American democracy.* Cornell University Press.

Westbury, I. (2008). Curriculum in practice. In F. M. Connelly, M. F. He, & J. Phillion (Eds.), *Sage handbook of curriculum and instruction* (pp. 1–4). Sage.

Wexler, P. (1987). *Social analysis of education.* Routledge.

Wiebe, R. H. (1995). *Self rule: A cultural history of American democracy.* University of Chicago Press.

Willingham, D. T. (2017). *The reading mind: A cognitive approach to understanding how the mind reads.* Jossey-Bass.

Wineburg, S. (1999). Historical thinking and other unnatural acts. *Phi Delta Kappan, 80*(7), 488–499.

Wineburg, S., & Martin, D. (2009). Tampering with history: Adapting primary sources for struggling readers. *Social Education, 73*(5), 212.

Wood, A. (1972–73). The Marxian critique of justice. *Philosophy and Public Affairs, 1,* 244–282.

Wright-Maley, C. (2015). Beyond the "babel problem": Defining simulations for social studies. *Journal of Social Studies Research, 39*(2), 63–77.

Young, I. M. (1997). Difference as a resource for democratic communication. In J. Bohman & W. Rehg (Eds.), *Deliberative democracy: Essays on reason and politics* (pp. 383–406). MIT Press.

Young, M.F.D. (1971). *Knowledge and control: New directions for the sociology of education.* Collier-Macmillan.

Young, M.F.D. (2008). *Bringing knowledge back in: From social constructivism to social realism in the sociology of education.* Routledge.

Young, M.F.D. (2013). Overcoming the crisis in curriculum theory: A knowledge-based approach. *Journal of Curriculum Studies, 45*(2), 101–118.

Young, M., & Lambert, D. (2014). *Knowledge and the future school: Curriculum and social justice.* Bloomsbury.

Zakaria, F. (2003). *The future of freedom: Illiberal democracy at home and abroad.* W. W. Norton & Co.

Zembylas, M., Charalambous, P., Charalambous, C., & Lesta, S. (2017). Toward a critical hermeneutical approach of human rights education: Universal ideals, contextual realities and teachers' difficulties. *Journal of Curriculum Studies, 49*(4), 497–517.

Zimmerman, J. (2002). *Whose America? Culture wars in the public schools.* Harvard University Press.

Index

Academic curriculum, 50–51
Adaptive learning, 67–68
Addams, Jane, 43
Advanced Placement, 64
  U.S. Government course, 145–146
Albright, Madeleine, xi
Allen, Danielle S., ix, 9–10, 25, 36, 83, 85, 90–92, 94, 95, 96, 97, 171
Althusser, Louis, 116
Amoral familism, 43–44
Anderson, C., xi
Anna Christie (O'Neill), 89
Annenberg Public Policy Center, 168
Apple, M. W., 134, 138, 140
April Morning (Fast), 83
  seminar discussion, 85–87
Arango, T., ix
Arendt, Hannah, 90, 149
Aristotle, 8, 42, 90
Aronson, Elliot, 26, 48
Asia Society conference, 124
An Attainable Global Perspective (Hanvey), 127

Bajaj, M., 136, 146
Ball, T., 14
Banfield, Edward, 43
Banks, Angela M., 23, 136, 150–160
Banks, James A., x, xi, 13–14, 21, 160
Bannon, Steve, 4
Barrett, B., 135
Barton, Keith (K. C.), 136, 167–168
Beadie, N., 13
Beard, Charles, 165
Beauvoir, Simone de, 102, 116, 117
Becker, J. M., 127
Behaviorism, 104

Bellah, Robert, 44
Berkowitz, M., 108–109
Bernstein, Basil, 133, 135, 138, 143, 144
Biden, Joe, ix
Biesta, G., 139
Biological maturationist theory, 104
Blatt, M., 108
"Blowing the Whistle on Global Education" (Cunningham), 128
Bokat-Lindell, S., xi
Boler, M., 94
Bosniak, Linda, 152–153
Boss, Alan, 56
Boulding, Kenneth, 131
Bourdieu, P., 138
Bowles, S., 135, 138
Bozec, G., 137
Bransford, John D., 31, 66, 68, 69, 71–72, 78, 139
Bridges, D., 29, 87, 162
Bringing Knowledge Back In (Young), 141
Briscoe-Smith, A., x
Broadwater, L., ix
Brooks, David, xi
Brown, A., 65, 69, 72, 139
Browning, K., ix
Bruner, J., 30, 31, 68, 69, 145
Bubola, E., xi
Burkholder, Z., 13
Burr, Aaron, 170
Bush, George W., 126

Caesar and Cleopatra (Shaw), 122
Caldwell, B. J., 124
Campaign for the Civic Mission of Schools, 63, 80–81

Capital (Marx), 111
Caporaso, J. A., 135
Cave allegory (Plato), 112
Center for Civic Education, 80
Charity Hudley, A. H., x
Checking-challenge-review process, 13
The Child and the Curriculum (Dewey), 16–17, 146
Choices for the 21st Century, 51
Christman, J., 14
Churchill, Winston, 9, 10, 45
The Citizen and the Alien (Bosniak), 152–153
Citizenship
    active citizenship, 97
    cosmopolitanism and global citizenship, 128–129
    education for, 44–45
    idiocy/citizenship opposition, 42–43
    overview and definitions, 149–150
    and political friendship, 90–92
CityWorks curriculum, 80
Civic education
    centrist approach to, 1–2, 6–7
    and knowledge, 11–14
    and personal expression (voice), 14–15
    and regime types, 6
    role and importance of, 4
    in school setting, 4–5
    See also Curriculum for citizenship education, Angela Banks' proposal
Civic Education in the Age of Mass Migration (Banks), 150
Civil rights discourse, 136–137
Civil Rights Movement, 45
Classifying, 57–59
Classroom discussion
    deliberation, 87–89, 92–93
    and Kohlberg's model, 108
    listening to strangers, 93–96
    overview, 83–85, 162–164
    political friendship, 90–92
    school as public space, 89–90
    seminar, 85–87, 92–93
Close reading, 163

Cocking, R. R., 139
Code, Lorraine, 13
Cognitive developmentalism, 104
Cohen, Elizabeth, 26, 27, 37
College Entrance Examination Board, 64
Collier, Andrew, 113
Compromise and decision-making, 36
Concept development, 55–61
Conchas, G. Q., x
Consensus and decision-making, 36
Constitutional Rights Foundation, 80
The Constitution of Knowledge (Rauch), 13
Convention on the Rights of the Child (United Nations), 137
Cookson, P. W., Jr., x
Cooperative learning, 26–27; *See also* Structured Academic Controversy (SAC+)
Cormack, M. J., 112
Cosmopolitanism, 123, 128–129
Counts, George, 1, 165–166
Coups, 8
Cremin, Lawrence, 127
Crick, B., 8
Crito (Plato), 100–101
Cuban, L., 134
"Culturally responsive teaching," 17
Cunningham, G. L., 128
Curriculum, academic, 50–51
Curriculum and instruction, 15–19
Curriculum for citizenship education, Angela Banks' proposal, 150–160
    classroom activities, 153–156
    immigrant labor, 151–153
    instructional supports, 156–159
    objectives, 151
    rationale, 151

Dabach, Dafney, 151
Dayton, Margaret, 130
Decision-making, 36
    uncoerced, 165
Declaration on Human Rights Education and Training (United Nations), 142
Deep knowledge, 67–68

Deliberation, 31, 47–50, 87–89, 92–93, 156–157, 164
Delpit, Lisa, 17
Demagogues, 8
Democracy
    liberal contrasted with illiberal, 6–11
    popular sovereignty (democracy), 3, 14–15
Design-based implementation research (DBIR), 65–66
Dewey, John, 1, 16–17, 29, 39, 46–47, 90, 94, 135, 146, 165–166
Diamond, L., 8
Disciplinary knowledge, 12–13
Dowd, M., ix
Draper, R., ix
Du Bois, W.E.B., 13
Durkheim, Émile, 133, 135, 142

Edmondson, C., ix
Elections, ix, 7–8
Ellison, Ralph, 90
Encyclopedia of Diversity in Education (Banks), x
Engagement, enlightened political, 93, 97
"Engagement first" principle, 31, 71–73, 78–80
Enlightenment ideals, 6
Epistemic crisis, 3–4, 12–13
Erlanger, S., xi
Error-seeking, 12, 14, 15
The Ethics of Ambiguity (Beauvoir), 102
Exploring Humanitarian Law (curriculum), 129

Factual knowledge, 12–13, 16, 23
Falsification, 12, 15
Fascism: A Warning (Albright), xi
Fast, Howard, 83
Federalist 51, 8–9
Finn, C. E., 1
Fishman, B. J., 65
Flanagan, Connie, 29, 36, 71
Foner, E., 10
Framing, 152, 158
Frazer, E., 90

Frederickson, George, 10
Freedom House, 8, 10
Freire, P., 112
Fry, R., 89
Fukuyama, F., 8

Galbraith, John Kenneth, 44
Galston, William, 6
Gamson, W. A., 135
Gándara, P., x
Gastil, J., 157
Gay, Geneva, 17
Gibbs, J. C., 113
Gibson, M., 39
Gilligan, C., 113
Ginsburg, Ruth Bader, 157
Gintis, H., 135, 138
Giroux, H. A., 138
Globalization, 124–125; See also International education
Global studies. See International education
Goffman, E., 158
The Good City and the Good Life (Kemmis), 42
Gorski, P. C., x
Green, A., 131
Greene, Marjorie Taylor, ix
Greene, Maxine, 115–116
Greene, T., 162
Greenleaf, C., 159
Gutmann, A., 84

Habermas, Jurgen, 20, 29, 93, 97, 112
Hahn, C. L., 84
Hamilton (Miranda), 170
Hamilton, Alexander, 170
Hampshire, Stuart, 111
Handbook of Research on Multicultural Education (Banks), x
Hanh, Thich Nhat, 94, 106
Hanvey, Robert, 127
Heintz, Stephen, ix
Hershberg, T., 126
Hess, D. E., 28, 84
Hirschman, Albert, 168
Historical materialism, 111–113
Ho, L.-C., 137

Hochschild, J. L., 46
Holmes, Stephen, 9, 161
Holt, Rush, 125
hooks, bell, 111
Hopkins, M., x
How People Learn (Bransford et al.),
    139
Human rights, 7–8
Human rights education (HRE),
    133–147
    curriculum development, 133–135
    overview of in U.S. school curricula,
        135–140, 147
    strategies for future development,
        140–146

iCivics, 80
Idiocy, 41–46
"I Have A Dream" (King), 136–137
Illiberal democracy, 7–9
Immigrant labor paradox, 151–153,
    158–159
Implicit bias, 8
Individual rights (liberalism), 3, 7
Inman, M., 55, 56
International Astronomical Union
    (IAU), 55–56
International Baccalaureate (IB)
    programs, 123, 125, 130, 135–136
International education, 123–131
    cosmopolitanism, 128–129
    diversity of programs, 130–131
    and global perspectives, 127–128
    international student bodies,
        129–130
    and national security, 124–127
International Education Act (1965),
    127

Jacoby, Russell, 112, 119
Jain, S., 44
Jaspers, Karl, 171
Jefferson, Thomas, 9, 85
Johnson, David, 26, 28, 30, 36, 72, 156
Johnson, Roger, 26, 28, 30, 36, 72,
    156
Joseph, R. L., x
Jus nexi principle, 152–153

Just Community curriculum and
    schools, 49, 100
Justice
    in classroom environments, 118–119
    education for, 100–102
    new conceptual formulations,
        114–117
    psychological conceptions of,
        102–110
    sociological conceptions of, 110–114

Kahne, J., 63
Kegan, R., 104
Kemmis, Daniel, 42
King, Martin Luther, Jr., 45, 99,
        100–101, 102–103, 105–106, 110,
        114–115, 119–120, 136–137
King, M. B., 67
Klopfer, L. E., 54
Knowledge, 11–14
    deep knowledge, 67–68
    disciplinary knowledge, 12–13
    factual knowledge, 12–13, 16, 23
    "knowledge blindness," 137, 147
    knowledge-construction process,
        13, 15
    knowledge-correction process, 13
    types of knowledge, 141–142
Knowledge, Curriculum and Equity
    (Barrett et al.), 135
Knowledge and Control (Young), 140
Knowledge and the Future School
    (Young & Lambert), 135
Kohlberg, Lawrence, 49, 102, 103–104,
        105, 106–108, 110
Kohlmeier, J., 159
Korzybski, A., 80
Kristersson, Ulf, xi
Kurtz, S., 39
Kymlicka, Will, 100, 151

Labaree, D. F., 64, 147
Lacey, T., 64
Laden, A., 38
Ladson-Billings, G., 139
Lambert, D., 135
Landmark Cases, 80
Larmer, J., 67

"The Law of Group Polarization" (Sunstein), 162
Lee, C. D., x
Legitimacy crisis in U.S. political culture, 3–4
Leonhardt, D., ix
Leonore Annenberg Institute for Civics, 63
"Letter from Birmingham Jail" (King), 45, 100, 105–106, 110
Levine, P., 157
Levstik, Linda, 167–168
Lewis, M., 4
Liberal democracy, 6–7
    as aim of civic education, 10–11
    need for constitution, 9–10
    overview, 3
    use of term, ix–x
Liberal-democratic civic education, 171
Liberalism. *See* Individual rights (liberalism)
Lincoln, Abraham, 11
Listening
    agency in listening, 94–95
    listening to strangers, 89–90
    listening to strangers at school, 92–93
    strategies for listening to strangers, 95–96
Liu, Eric, ix
Lo, J. C., 69, 72, 78, 146
Locke, John, 109
Lodge, M., 8
Looping content, 31–32, 69–70, 77–78
Lowry, Arine, 18
Lundy, L., 146

Madison, James, 6, 8–9
Mahiri, J., x
Malcolm X, 137
Mallinson, C., x
Marche, S., 161
March on Washington address (King), 45
Marcuse, H., 1
Margins and Mainstreams (Okihiro), 20
Marx, Karl, 44, 102, 111–113, 115

Mason, L., 156
Master course questions (MCQs), 71
Mathews, J., 64
Maton, K., 137
Matthew Effect, 169
Matua, M., 136
Mayer, R., 104
Mayo, C., x
McAvoy, Paula, 18, 28
McEneaney, E. H., 139
McPhail, G., 142
"Meaningfulness bridges," 17–18
Meloni, Giorgia, xi
Meno (Plato), 146
Mergendoller, J. R., 67
Meyer, J. W., 135, 139
Middaugh, E., 63
Mill, John Stuart, 14, 171
Miller, B., 86, 87, 88
Miller-Lane, J., 85
Mills, C. W., 10, 156
Miranda, Lin-Manuel, 170
Mittelman, J. H., 135
Moll, L., 139, 146
Montesquieu, 7, 14
Moore, R., 138, 143
The Moral Judgement of the Child (Piaget), 103
Mosher, R., 49, 106
"Motivated reasoning," 8
Muller, J., 138
Myers, D., 67

Narayan, U., 96
National Academies of Science, Engineering, and Medicine (NASEM), 18, 125, 130
National Center for Education Statistics, 63
Nationalism, 123, 129, 131
National Issues Forum, 51
National Research Study, 67
National security and international education, 124–127
National Security Language Act (2003), 125
National Security Language Initiative (2006), 126

A Nation at Risk (National
    Commission on Excellence in
    Education), 126–127
Neoliberalism, 124–125
Newman, John Henry, 16
Nie, N. H., 93
Niemöller, Martin, 100
1984 (Orwell), 162
No Child Left Behind Act, 124
North Carolina in the World (Center
    for International Understanding),
    124
NSOE (new sociology of education),
    134–135, 140–141
Nussbaum, Martha, 128–129

O'Connor, Sandra Day, 80
Okihiro, Gary, 20
O'Neill, Eugene, 89
On Liberty (Mill), 171
Operation Public Education, 126
Orfield, G., 90
Orwell, George, 162
Osler, A., 137, 146
Our Common Purpose (Commission
    on the Practice of Democratic
    Citizenship), ix–x
Oxford English Dictionary, 89

Paley, Vivian Gussin, 29, 46, 48
Paris, D., 139
Parker, Walter C., ix–xii, 29, 37, 66,
    67, 69, 72, 78, 79, 84, 93, 96, 135,
    146
Parsons, T., 134
Passeron, J.-C., 138
Passion and Constraint (Holmes), 9
Peirce, Charles Sanders, 12
Pelosi, Nancy, ix
Pelosi, Paul, ix
Penuel, W. R., 65, 80
Personal expression (voice) in civic
    education, ix–x, 14–15
"Perspective consciousness," 121–122,
    127–128
Pettigrew, T. F., 48
Piaget, Jean, 103, 104, 105

Pinar, W., 134, 138
Plato, 100, 112, 146
Pocock, J. G. A., 5, 14, 149
Political autonomy, 14, 36–38
    political autonomy moments (PAMs),
    72
Political friendship, 90–92
Politics (Aristotle), 8
Popular sovereignty (democracy), 3,
    14–15
Postman, Neil, 14
Povoledo, E., xi
Power, F. C., 49, 100, 108
Project-based learning (PBL), 63
    rigorous PBL, 67–68, 77
Project Citizen, 80

Racial hierarchies, 9–10
Raskin, J. B., 15
Rata, E., 142, 144
Rauch, Jonathan, 4, 13, 15
Rawls, John, 109–110
Reading comprehension, 32–36
Reciprocity, 105
    ideal reciprocity, 110
Reiman, J. H., 117
Rempel, G., 6
Resnick, L. B., 54
Reversibility (ideal reciprocity),
    109–110, 118
Rickover, H. G., 1
Rising Above the Gathering Storm
    (NASEM), 125
Rochester, J. M., 53
Rothstein, R., 66
Rousseau, Jean-Jacques, 109
*The Routledge International
    Companion to Multicultural
    Education* (Banks), x
Rubin, B. C., 17
Russell, S. G., 133

SAC+ (Structured Academic
    Controversy). *See* Structured
    Academic Controversy (SAC+)
Sanders, L. M., 53
Sartre, Jean-Paul, 116

Schneider, J., 64
Schools
  democratic governance in, 49
  schools and idiocy, 44–46
  schools as public places, 46–48,
    89–90, 97
  as setting for civic education,
    4–5
Schwab, Joseph (J. J.), 50, 70, 140,
  141, 145
Schwartz, D. L., 71–72, 78
Scovronick, N., 46
Secon, H., ix
Segregation, 89–90
Self, "the evolving self," 104–105
Self-centeredness. *See* Idiocy
Seminar, as form of classroom
  discussion, 85–87, 92–93,
  164
Sennett, Richard, 101
Sharan, Shlomo, 26
Sharan, Yael, 26
"Shared reality," 11, 12–13
Shaw, George Bernard, 122
Shklar, Judith, 7, 14, 45
Siegel, L., 103
Singleton, L., 86, 87, 88
Slavin, Robert, 26
Social contract theory, 109–110
Social curriculum, 48–50
Social movement theory, 135
Social studies, 167–170
Socrates, 100–101
Socratic method, 100, 156, 159, 163,
  171
Spellings, Margaret, 124
Spiral curriculum, 31–32
Stahl, Lesley, 4
Stanley, William, 170
Starkey, H., 136
Stephenson, Neal, 4, 11, 161
Stitzlein, S. M., 6
Street Law, 80
Structured Academic Controversy
  (SAC+), 25–39, 72, 156–157
  content selection, 29–32
  and cooperative learning, 26–29

learning from text (reading
  comprehension), 32–36
overview, 25–26
revised model, 29–38, *37*
student voice and political autonomy,
  36–38
Student engagement, 37, 71–73, 78–80
Suárez, D. F., 133
Sunstein, Cass, 162

Taba, Hilda, 21, 56, 68, 69, 145
Taber, C. S., 8
Talbott, W. J., 167
Tapp, J. L., 107–108
Teaching Democracy (Parker), xii, 47
Teenage Citizens (Flanagan), 36
A Theory of Justice (Rawls), 109
Tocqueville, Alexis de, 42–43
Trump, Donald, ix, 3–4, 8, 136
Truth
  "objective truth," 13
  project-based learning and
    authenticity, 67
  standard of, 12–13
Tsai, S.-L., 169
Tucker, R., 113

United Nations, opposition to in U.S.
  culture, 133, 135, 137
United Nations High Commissioner for
  Human Rights, 133
Universal Declaration of Human Rights
  (United Nations), 121, 129, 137
U.S. Constitution, 9–10
U.S. government course, 63–81
  background and overview, 63–65
  curriculum, 73–76
  looping content, 69–70, 77–78
  method and design principles,
    65–73
  rigorous project-based learning
    (PBL), 67–68, 77
U.S. history and government courses,
  168

Valdés, G., x
Valencia, S., 79, 159

Verification, 15
Vigil, J. D., x
Voice (personal expression) in civic
     education, x, 14–15, 36–38
Vygotsky, Lev, 12, 146

Wakelyn, D., 64
Waks, L., 38
Walberg, H. J., 169
Westbrook, R. B., 166
Westbury, I., 134
"Where Do We Go from Here?"
     (King), 119–120
"Whole-ness" principle (Allen),
     92, 94

Wiebe, R. H., 8
Willingham, D. T., 168
Wood, A., 113
World Programme for Human Rights
     Education, 133
Wright-Maley, C., 67

You Can't Say You Can't Play (Paley),
     48
Young, Iris Marion, 116
Young, Michael (M. F. D.), 134, 135,
     138, 140–142

Zakaria, F., 8
Zimmerman, J., 15

About the Author

Walter C. Parker is professor emeritus of social studies and civic education and (by courtesy) political science at the University of Washington in Seattle. He is a member of the National Academy of Education, a fellow of the American Educational Research Association, and author of, among others, *Teaching Democracy: Unity and Diversity in Public Life* and *Social Studies in Elementary Education*. He has taught pedagogy to new and experienced teachers in Colorado, Texas, and Washington.